West Coast Plays

Out Comes Butch
David Schein

The AIDS Show
Artists Involved with Death and Survival

Coyote VI: The Sacred Dump

Coyote VII: He Brings the Waterfall
Murray Mednick

Family Portrait
Beverly A Smith

Vacuum
Chris Hardman

Twenty-Four Hours
Playwrights Lab, Back Alley Theatre

West Coast Plays is published two times a year (Spring/Summer, Fall/Winter) in Los Angeles, California, by the California Theatre Council. Subscriptions are available at $25 per year. Send checks or money order to West Coast Plays, California Theatre Council, 849 South Broadway, Suite 621, Los Angeles, CA 90014.

This project is supported by grants from Actors' Equity Association, Atlantic Richfield Foundation, the California Arts Council, the National Endowment for the Arts, the Yorkin Foundation, and the Zellerbach Family Fund.

West Coast Plays prints only plays which have premiered in a theater in the Western United States. Script submissions should be made to Robert Hurwitt, Editor, West Coast Plays, P.O. Box 7206, Berkeley, CA 94707.

ISBN: 0-934782-17-2

THE CALIFORNIA THEATRE COUNCIL

The California Theatre Council is the largest state theater council in the United States, serving over 300 theaters and theater-affiliated individuals throughout the west.

According to the most recent government census, California has more artists than any other state in the union and a large portion of those artists work in theater. The Council provides assistance in many forms to these professionals including:

- •• Publications
  - — West Coast Plays
  - — West Coast Theatre News
  - — West Coast Theatre Directory
- •• Annual State Theater Conference
  - — seminars in audience development, marketing, audition techniques, etc.
  - — workshops in new techniques in lighting, direction, and other areas
  - — social gatherings to meet the people who are creating theater in the west and other parts of the US
  - — receptions with national and international theater figures
- •• Information Services
  - — computerized on-line data base providing a theater message center, directory of job-listings, listing of what's playing in California, etc.
  - — set and costume resource bank
  - — grant guidelines and deadlines
  - — information about California theater to grant sources, arts councils, the press, and the travel industry
- •• 24-Hour Telephone Hot-Line with recorded audition information serving actors and theaters throughout the western region
- •• Western Regional Equity Actors' Auditions
- •• Performing Arts Management Institute

Membership in the California Theatre Council is open to theaters and individuals throughout the world. If you would like information sent to you, send your name, address, and request to: California Theatre Council, Member Services, 849 S. Broadway, Ste. 621, Los Angeles, CA 90014. (213) 622-6727

EDITOR

Robert Hurwitt

ASSOCIATE EDITORS

Shannon Edwards
Susan LaTempa

LAYOUT

Pam O'Connell

COVER DESIGN

Butler Advertising

TYPESETTING

The Illustrated Word

CALIFORNIA THEATRE COUNCIL STAFF

Brian Bennett,
Executive Director

Steven C. Helsel
Director of Programs and Services

Cynthia L. Pasion
Development Director

Contents

The Playwrights

PAUL ATTINELLO *(The AIDS Show)* was a singer and actor in the San Francisco Bay Area for five years before moving to Los Angeles to attend graduate school in music at UCLA. He has had leading roles in *Fifty Years of Broadway, Cabaret,* and *Fountain of Youth.*

BILL BARKSDALE *(The AIDS Show)* studied acting with Sanford Meisner in New York and began his solo performance career at the Hotel Utah Cabaret in San Francisco. With his lover, Joe Dowling, he produced his solo play, *Nightmare of the Son: My Shadow Land,* about the death of a close friend from AIDS.

SAM BOBRICK *(Twenty-Four Hours)* has written for stage, screen, and television. He is presently living in Los Angeles and doing his best.

DANIEL GREGORY BROWN *(Twenty-Four Hours),* born Kenneth Jeffrey Hartman on May 31, 1945, died on January 25, 1983. His professional credits began with *Peyton Place* in 1968, and he received an Emmy in 1976 as one of the original creators and writers of *Mary Hartman, Mary Hartman.* At his death he left numerous unpublished and unproduced works, including a novel which was his final effort.

KARL BROWN *(The AIDS Show)* studied electronic music and composition at UC Santa Cruz and under Gordon Mumma and David Cope. He was an active member of the San Francisco Gay Men's Chorus and SFGMC Chamber Singers from 1978 to 1982 and is the pianist and composer for the erotic jazz-wave ensemble Automatic Pilot.

PAMELA CHAIS *(Twenty-Four Hours)* has written two novels, *Split Ends* and *Final Cut,* in addition to writing for television and the stage.

DONA COOPER *(Twenty-Four Hours)* has had a career as a freelance director and producer and served as Artistic Director of the American Society of Theatre Arts in Washington DC for five years. She has since focused on writing for the stage and has had works performed in New York, Washington, Los Angeles, Minnesota, and Texas.

DAN CURZON *(The AIDS Show)* teaches creative writing at City College of San Francisco. He has had twelve plays produced, including the full-length *Cinderella II* which he wrote for the Angels of Light.

ELLEN BROOK DAVIS *(The AIDS Show)* worked in public broadcasting in her native Boston, attended the American Academy of Dramatic Arts in New York City, and has studied theater at San Francisco State and with Jean Shelton. She appeared in the national touring company of *Leftovers* and in *Hissy Fits*, which she co-wrote, and often performs stand-up comedy in San Francisco clubs.

OLIVER HAILEY *(Twenty-Four Hours)* not only provided the concept for and helped develop *Twenty-Four Hours*, he is the author of more than twelve produced plays. Among his other titles are *Father's Day, Who's Happy Now?* and *For the Use of the Hall.*

CHRIS HARDMAN *(Vacuum)* is a designer, sculptor, maskmaker, director, playwright, and former candidate for city council in Sausalito. He apprenticed with the Bread and Puppet Theater in Vermont, worked as an amusements designer at Coney Island, and in 1972 co-founded the theater company in Venice, California, that later became the Snake Theater after it moved to Sausalito. Hardman's plays with Snake Theater included *Auto, Somewhere in the Pacific,* and *Ride Hard/Die Fast.* In 1980 Hardman founded Antenna Theater, which debuted with *Vacuum.* With Antenna he has produced radio plays, scripts based on extensive interviews, and developed the concept of "Walkmanology." Antenna plays have toured to Europe, Mexico, New York, Washington, and the Spoleto USA Festival in Charleston. Hardman has also been an artist-in-residence at the Bay Area Playwrights Festival in 1981, 1982, and 1983.

BETH HENLEY *(Twenty-Four Hours)* has written four full-length plays: *Crimes of the Heart, The Miss Firecracker Contest, The Wake of Jamey Foster,* and *The Debutante Ball.* She has also written two one-act plays: *Am I Blue?* and *Sisters of the Winter Madrigal.* In 1981 she was awarded the Pulitzer Prize for *Crimes of the Heart. The Debutante Ball* received its world premiere in 1985 at South Coast Repertory in Costa Mesa.

DOUG HOLSCLAW *(The AIDS Show)* is the author of several children's plays currently touring the New York Public schools. He has performed on the East Coast in stock, dinner theater, and off Broadway, and has appeared in San Francisco as a standup comic and in *Hissy Fits* which he co-authored.

TERRY KINGSLEY-SMITH *(Twenty-Four Hours)*, a UCLA graduate, is an actor and author. His play *Breaking Up the Act*, with Betty Garrett, Jan Sterling, and Evelyn Keyes, was performed last year in New Orleans and Texas, and a new play, *Will Anyone Come Home With Me: A Night in the Life of Tallulah Bankhead*, is scheduled to open in Los Angeles. He has written a novel, *The Murder of an Old-Time Movie Star*, and is currently halfway through a Hollywood epic novel and a screenplay.

MICHAEL LEESON *(Twenty-Four Hours)* was born in southern Arizona and is now living in Southern California under an assumed name.

RICK LENZ *(Twenty-Four Hours)* has appeared as an actor in *Cactus Flower*, on Broadway and in the film, in TV series, and at the Mark Taper Forum, the Studio Arena Theatre in Buffalo, and at the McCarter. He is the author of *The Epic of Buster Friend*, produced at New York's Theatre De Lys and on PBS TV, and of *Every Other Baby*, which played at the Oxford Theatre in Los Angeles.

JEFF LEVY *(Twenty-Four Hours)* directs, writes, teaches, and runs three theaters at California State University, Northridge. He holds an MFA in playwriting from UC San Diego and was named an Outstanding Young Man of the Year in 1984.

MICHAEL LEWIS *(Twenty-Four Hours)* has had a number of his plays and musicals produced on both the East and West Coasts and was twice the recipient of Brandeis University's Franklin Giddon Memorial Playwriting Award. He lives with his wife and two small children in North Hollywood and is a practicing optimist.

DAVID LINK *(Twenty-Four Hours)* is a snappy dresser who has been with the Playwright's Lab of the L.A. Theatre Center (LAAT) for the past three years. His plays *Einstein's Dice* and *True Believers* have been produced in the Foundry Series of the Cast Theatre.

JACK MATCHA *(Twenty-Four Hours)* worked for many years as a journalist in the US and Europe and has written several plays and novels. He currently teaches journalism at Los Angeles Southwest College.

JERRY MAYER *(Twenty-Four Hours)* has written teleplays for *All in the Family*, *M.A.S.H.*, *The Mary Tyler Moore Show*, *The Bob Newhart Show*, and other television comedies. He is Executive Producer of *The Facts of Life* on NBC.

JIM MCGINN *(Twenty-Four Hours)* has written hundreds of television scripts and one film, *Nadia*. "Termination" is his first work for the stage.

MATTHEW MCQUEEN *(The AIDS Show)* has extensive musical training, danced for four years with Ed Mock Studios, and has toured with the SF Gay Men's Chorus. He founded the rock group Automatic Pilot.

MURRAY MEDNICK *(Coyote VI: The Sacred Dump* and *Coyote VII: He Brings the Waterfall)* is the founder and artistic director of the Padua Hills Playwrights' Workshop and Festival. His playwriting credits go back to the days of Theatre Genesis and he won an Obie in 1970 for *The Deer Kill.* Earlier episodes of Mednick's *Coyote Cycle* appeared in *West Coast Plays 7, 9,* and *13/14.* The full cycle is scheduled to be presented in Los Angeles by LA Theatre Works in the fall of 1985.

ALLAN MILLER *(Twenty-Four Hours)* has been a professional actor since 1949 and is Co-Producing Director of the Back Alley Theatre in Los Angeles. Miller is a professional teacher and coach and the award-winning director and author of *The Fox,* published in *West Coast Plays 13/14.*

MARKLEY MORRIS *(The AIDS Show)* has an MFA in Drama from the University of Texas and now lives in San Francisco where he works as a technical writer. He was for five years a member of the Bear Republic Theater in Santa Cruz where he served as a writer on three collectively created plays, *Wanderings, Wrinkles,* and *Santa Cruz Shuffle.*

LELAND MOSS *(The AIDS Show)* was a resident director at La Mama and Playwrights Horizons in New York where he also was major script reader for the New York Shakespeare Festival. Among his teachers he includes Lee Grant, Ellen Stewart, Tarthang Tulku, Andrei Serban, Ceil Smith, Thelma Moss, and Vit.

ADELE PRANDINI *(Twenty-Four Hours)* is a lesbian playwright whose *A Safe Light* was produced by Theatre Rhinoceros in San Francisco. She also wrote *Clown Olympics* for Make-A-Circus which toured throughout California in 1984.

ANN RAYMOND *(Twenty-Four Hours)* came from Warren, Michigan, to Los Angeles to pursue a professional acting career. During her marriage to TV writer William Wood, she discovered her own writing talents and is currently adapting her second novel into a full-length play.

PHILIP REAL *(The AIDS Show)* is the author of *Lunch, Dessert,* and *Breathing Room,* all produced by Theatre Rhinoceros in San Francisco. His *Moneytroubles* was presented at the Bay Area Playwrights Festival IV and he has had two plays, *Overload* and *The Desperation of the Belletoile Matron,* presented on KALW FM. He wrote *Showdown at the AIDS Ward* for the 1984 Castro Street Fair.

CHRISTINE RIMMER *(Twenty-Four Hours)* is a native of Northern California who has worked with several Los Angeles theaters since she moved south in 1976. Her one-act, *Obsidian,* premiered at the Group Repertory Theatre in 1984.

MARCIA RODD *(Twenty-Four Hours)* is a stage, screen, and television actress and a sometime director and TV writer. This is her first work for the stage.

DAVID SCHEIN *(Out Comes Butch)* is a member of the Blake Street Hawkeyes which he co-founded with John O'Keefe and Robert Ernst, and has performed ensemble and solo works in the United States, Canada, and Europe. Other solo works by Schein include *Chismo, Trucking in One Place, Life Is Not a Country-Western Song,* and *The Key of D.* He collaborated and acted with the Hawkeyes in *Hogstale, Kakos, Bite of the Rose,* and *Tantrums,* and wrote and performed *The Last Word* and *Reverence for the Dead* with Whoopi Goldberg. Other scripts include *The Bog People, Dick Jones,* and most recently *Tokens,* a massive piece on the Great Plague for which he also composed the music.

SUSAN SILVER *(Twenty-Four Hours)* has written television series and movies-of-the-week scripts for fourteen years. Her credits include *The Mary Tyler Moore Show, Maude,* and *The Bob Newhart Show.* She hopes someday to write a much longer play.

BEVERLY A SMITH *(Family Portrait),* a native of Phoenix, Arizona, moved to San Francisco in 1978. She has studied theater at San Francisco State University where she has appeared in numerous productions as well as working with the Black Repertory Group in Berkeley. *Family Portrait* is her second play to be produced.

ROBERT J. STONE *(The AIDS Show)* received his BA and MA in theater from the University of Michigan. He has appeared as an actor with San Francisco's Theatre Rhinoceros.

LEE THOMAS *(Twenty-Four Hours)* has received numerous awards for playwriting including a grant from the National Endowment for the Arts. Thomas also writes screenplays for movies and television.

FREDI TOWBIN *(Twenty-Four Hours)* studied at Bard College and received an MFA from Columbia University. She is a TV writer living in Los Angeles.

DAN TURNER *(The AIDS Show)* is an author, composer, and director in San Francisco. His play *Getting to Know the Natives* has been published by Samuel French.

RANDY WEIGAND *(The AIDS Show)* is a native of San Francisco, a graduate of San Francisco State, and attended the advanced acting program at ACT. He also teaches aerobics.

BONNIE ZINDEL *(Twenty-Four Hours)* was publicity director at the Cleveland Play House where she also hosted and produced a radio show. Her play *I Am a Zoo* was produced in New York and her most recent play, *The Latecomer,* adapted from the novel *The Star for the Latecomer,* which she co-authored with her husband, Paul Zindel, premiered at the Actors Studio Playwrights Unit in Los Angeles in 1985. She has also written another novel, *The Hollywood Dream Machine.*

PAUL ZINDEL *(Twenty-Four Hours),* a native of Staten Island, received the Pulitzer Prize and New York Drama Critics Circle Award for his play *The Effect of Gamma Rays on Man-in-the-Moon Marigolds.* Other popular plays by Zindel include *And Miss Reardon Drinks a Little* and *The Secret Affairs of Mildred Wild.* He wrote the screenplays for *Up the Sandbox* and *Mame,* as well as for the CBS mini-series production of *Alice in Wonderland.* His most recent novel is *When a Darkness Falls.*

Editor's Note

If one were to draw general conclusions about the state of drama as it is practiced in the western part of the United States, based on the contents of this volume, one would conclude that western playwrights are given to experimenting with non-traditional forms, have a penchant for taking on knotty social problems, and that our theaters are alive with full evenings composed of short playlets and monologues. That impression would only be incorrect in so far as it excludes a great deal of creative activity which doesn't conform to these criteria—since this volume ultimately reflects the idiosyncratic tastes of its editor. The full range of theater, even of new theater, produced in the west is too vast and diverse to sum up or characterize quite so patly.

Still, the characterization, if not exhaustive, is at least descriptive of much of the most exciting new work in California and the other western states. The amount of experimentation going on in the west, particularly but not exclusively in the San Francisco Bay Area, is one of the prime things that makes being a critic here so continuously rewarding, even if, as *San Francisco Chronicle* critic Bernard Weiner indicated in his essay "What is a Play Anyway?" (*West Coast Plays 15/16*), it also makes it pretty confusing at times. Two of the plays in this volume give some indication of the scope of Bay Area experimentation. David Schein's *Out Comes Butch* is a sample of the work of the seminal Blake Street Hawkeyes, especially in the demands it makes on the individual performer. A monologue in form, it is anything but a straightforward representative of the genre, calling on its actor to play a character in continuous and ultimately cyclical transition. It is also an unconventional and daring look at contemporary sex roles that ultimately affirms the common thread of humanity beneath the stereotypes of the surface, providing the viewer or reader with insights that remain hidden to the protagonist on his or her sexual odyssey.

Chris Hardman's *Vacuum*, on the other hand, represents an experimental tradition in which the performer is no longer central to the impact of the piece. As in the work of George Coates Performance Works, Soon 3, or Nightletter Theater, Hardman's Antenna pieces require a deceptively high degree of mimetic movement skill from actors, but use them almost mechanistically, more as puppets than as performers. In *Vacuum* the actors, their heads encased in large masks, never speak; their dialogue, mixed in with the dialogue, speeches, and commentary of others, is presented on a pre-recorded soundtrack. That device allows Hardman to give us not just the characters' words but their thoughts as well, perhaps their memories of what they've heard and been taught, and a running commentary on their thoughts and actions that combines both the comments of an omniscient viewer and those of others whose vision is just as limited as that of the characters. Thus Hardman is able to elevate what is essentially a very trite story into an archetype and to use that archetype as a commentary on an entire society, ours, in which personal relations are largely organized around the activities of buying and selling. Because Hardman achieves this effect with visual and aural presentations that weave in and out of each other, that generally reinforce each other but sometimes divide our attention, we have chosen to present *Vacuum* in a parallel text edition, with the visual story presented on the left-hand pages and the text of the soundtrack on the right.

Murray Mednick's *Coyote VI* and *VII*, which complete Mednick's epic *Coyote Cycle*, also fulfill the commitment we made to our readers when we started printing the *Coyote* plays in *West Coast Plays* 7. Robert Koehler's essay in this volume is a fine account of the full impact of the complete *Cycle*, as it was presented for the first time last summer, and provides a good analysis of Mednick's unique blend of styles and sources in creating an original American epic.

As originally presented, with each new play premiering at the Padua Hills Playwrights' Festival, the *Coyote* plays are also symptomatic of a West Coast wave of evenings made up of short pieces. The format is a particularly useful one as a showcase for the work of new writers and as a tool in the development of works in progress, and has been used annually in this manner by both the Padua Hills and Bay Area playwrights' festivals, as well as the Los Angeles Actors Theatre's Louis B. Mayer festival. Two of the most ambitious and most popular such evenings, each organized around a specific theme, have been the Back Alley Theatre's *Twenty-Four Hours* and Theatre Rhinoceros's *The AIDS Show*, both reprinted here in their entirety.

Twenty-Four Hours, consisting of twenty-four plays arranged in a chronological sequence, each treating a different hour of the day, was a grand experiment. Like *The AIDS Show* it is composed of playlets of many shapes and formats, and of varying effectiveness, where the whole has a greater impact than the sum of its parts. Both collections, too, provide a number of monologues useful for scene study or audition purposes as well as short plays good for production in a variety of formats. Beyond its immediate dramatic uses, *The AIDS Show* can serve as a model for other groups wishing to use a dramatic form to deal with a social crisis of great moment and complexity.

AIDS and child molestation, the topic dealt with in Beverly A Smith's *Family Portrait*, are social problems that benefit from dramatic treatment in that both are problems that need to be aired in public—for in both cases the lie of silence sanctions a cruel and dangerous neglect. But both are problems that are extremely difficult to deal with in dramatic form, as witness the numerous plays over the past few years that have made the attempt and failed. Both are problems that, however widespread their impact, ultimately strike one individual at a time and thereby suggest a particular form of dramatic treatment: naturalistic drama, the drama of individual suffering, in which vein most of the treatments of these topics that I have seen have been written. But naturalistic drama is the most inappropriate form for dealing with these or almost any other social problem. The form shifts our focus from the problem to the individual, from the general to the specific, and the very seriousness of the problem being treated overloads the drama and transforms it either to the stuff of melodrama or of soap opera.

Family Portrait avoids that problem by eschewing naturalism, a form more suitable now for television and movies than it is for the stage. One of the things that makes this, Smith's second play, so remarkable is her ability to see beyond the dominant forms of those media. Her characters are both individuals and archetypes; they step in and out of their story, now acting out the narrative, now confronting us directly, as storytellers. Smith has avoided being preachy in her use of confrontational theater by keeping her characters within the limits of their own knowledge. The result is a striking play that affects the viewer deeply while offering us enough distance so that our critical faculties are given room to work, to chew over the problem, to become as engaged in the problem as our emotions are with the particular situation.

The writers, musicians, and performers who came together to write and produce *The AIDS Show* achieved a similar success with a piece whose very fractured format stands as an embodiment for the disease's impact on society. Incorporating confrontational and presentational styles, scenes, monologues, and songs, emotional impact and appeals to reason, *The AIDS Show*'s cumulative impression is that of love and of finding strength through love. The collaborative format and the collaborative feel of the piece when staged is particularly appropriate for dealing with the impact of AIDS on the gay community. The piece is a group effort to deal with a group problem; it establishes and reaffirms a sense of community within the theater. It is particularly appropriate that this

18

piece originated in San Francisco, one of the cities hardest hit in the early stages of what is now a national problem. It is also particularly appropriate that the show originated at Theatre Rhinoceros where it serves as a fitting memorial to Allan Estes, the company's founder, who died of AIDS some six months before the piece went into production.

Robert Hurwitt

Out Comes Butch
David Schein

Out Comes Butch was first presented at 2019 Blake Street, Berkeley, CA, on February 28, 1981; written, directed, designed, and performed by David Schein.

THE COSTUME (from the inside out):

Macho leopard-skin bikini briefs;
Covered by froufrou nylon flesh-colored pantaloons, a black merry widow brassiere that comes down to the waist;
Cowboy boots;
Covered by a floral print dress, silk or synthetic;
Covered by a sequined jacket that can be worn with the dress;
Covered by a checkered flannel cowboy shirt that unsnaps, and a wide belt with a big belt buckle on a sharp-looking pair of dark designer jeans, into which the dress can be easily tucked; covered by a reversible synthetic jacket, black on one side, with pink stripes on the pocket slashes and an embroidered flamingo on the back, like a "letter jacket";
Covered by a very dirty mechanic's jumpsuit that zips all the way up and snaps at the top, concealing all the rest of the costume.
The actor also wears a carpenter's belt with a nail pouch, a tape holder, an angle holder containing a carpenter's angle, and a hammer loop from which a big framing hammer dangles.

The actor should be clean-shaven with a unisex fashionable haircut, covered by a longhaired shoulder-length wig. He/she wears a trim "gay" mustache that matches the wig, covered by a matching mustache-beard combination that is held on with ear-pieces, like spectacles.

Out Comes Butch
David Schein

The audience is kept in the lobby of the theater until the stated time of performance. The actor enters from behind them. If the theater hasn't a lobby big enough, and the audience has to wait in the theater, the actor should enter from behind them when the houselights are up, as inconspicuously as possible.

The actor enters from behind the audience muttering to him/herself, surprising them, looking like a red-neck hippie carpenter, who somehow wandered into a theater.

BUTCH (*coming through the audience, muttering, pissed off*): A bunch of strangers come and she didn't even come. Jesus Christ. Hello, good to see yuh. It's gonna start now. Oh gawd.

> BUTCH *adlibs with the audience, very angry, but trying to be bright:* "Lookin' good... foxy...." *etc. Beneath his forced good humor he is obviously furious.*

So let's have a really good time.... It's hard though...sometimes.... (*He trails off. By this time the actor has passed through the audience and gravitated to a chair in front of the audience. The house lights dim.*) to have a good time...when you got *such a fuckin' raw deal.* Sorry, huh. Hello. What the hell. So I got personal problems. Big deal. You got 'em too. I'm not the only one. Personal

problems meaning. . . sexual problems. Yeah, go ahead and laugh.
You don't know how hard it was for me to say that. It's not funny. . . it's sad. That bitch.

I mean I work all day long, eight hours a day, five days a week,
hammering nails, pound, pound, pound, to build the houses you
just lay around in. I gotta muscle under my right arm looks like a
growth. My wife seen me nekkid and said it looked like I'd grown a
polyp out of my ribs; I mean Jesus Fuckin Christ, when your own
wife sees you nekkid, she's supposed to get hot, she's not supposed to
call you a freak, say you got a polyp. I mean, no wonder I'm so
touchy. No wonder I feel, honestly, like sometimes I could just line
up every woman in the world and mash them with my truck. Oh
come on, I feel you girls out there getting all pissed off at me now for
telling you my most awful thoughts but you got 'em too. I'll give yuh
odds that most of you have felt the same way 'bout men. You've
wanted to run over every dick you ever had with a steam roller. I
mean, haven't yuh? Right. Well, that fuckin' bitch, man, got me so
pissed off, and then I got all pissed off for being pissed off. Hey, I
don't wanna be bitter all my life. I want to live in love and all that
jazz with a woman. I don't want to be pissed off.

It's just that I break my ass on the job eight hours a day, supporting
the bitch, an' I come home bone tired an' what the fuck do you
think I find? The house is a mess, she's been camped out on the
couch all day paralyzed by General Hospital, the kid has diaper
rash up to its nostrils. I support the bitch and she just lays around.
Sure, she's "over-qualified" and she's down about it, but she could
at least lift a finger to help out instead of sucking chocolate all day in
front of the box. I mean one time I came home from work, starving,
and I had peanut butter on the brain for some reason; I was hungry
and there was a dirty diaper on the toaster. Man it was just too
fuckin' much. But hey, I tried to do my part, be a good guy, you
know, the husband, the provider, I didn't bitch; I kept my feelings
in my heart and tried to help her through depressed periods. I'd
clean up the whole house, do the kid, rustle up some grub for supper, even though I was about dead on my feet. I'd worked all day to
support her ass and the bitch wouldn't even cook. And that's not all,
when the day was done and I'd got the dishes dried and the kid in
bed, I'd want to sit on the couch, pop a beer, and cuddle up with my
old lady, you think the bitch put out? No way, man. I'd say, "Come
here, come on fer Christ's sake," real tender, you know, and she'd
make me so mad. I'd put my finger right on the nerve that runs
down her throat, you know the nerve that's supposed to get the

blood supply going to their nipples yuh know. I mean, I read about that, I know about how to turn a woman on, but she'd say, "Your hands are too callussy." What the fuck am I supposed to do about it? I work. I mean, I *clean my nails.* And that's not all. Later on in the bed I'd try again, wait till she's almost asleep, and then I grab her, real soft and delicate but then the bitch would wake up; I mean she didn't have the energy to put a dirty fork in the sink, but she was sure full of juice when it came to fighting me off. She called me an "insensitive lover." Me! Christ on a crucified crutch, man, you ever been called an "insensitive lover?" You know it makes you feel like you got dogshit on your lips. She said, "You pound, pound, pound all day, and you just wanna pound, pound, pound all night too." All I could do was roll over and dream about knocking her teeth down her throat. But I didn't hit her, man. I wouldn't do that. I just wanted some affection.

But she beat me to the punch, man. One day I come home, been pouring concrete all day long dead on my feet, and what the fuck do you think I find? A note. The fuckin' bitch had split. Took the car, took the stereo, took the tapes, took the checkbook, even took the kid. Really broke my heart. Said she'd gone off with a fag dentist named Marty Arnold and that her lawyer'd be talking to me about the alimony. Maaaan. Right out of the blue. A sucker punch. I didn't know what to do.

He takes off the hard hat and sits.

I just sat on the couch with the note in my hand, and a hole in my heart deeper than the Grand Canyon. I was paralyzed. I sat there with that note. The sun went down, and I sat there, listening to the clocks tick through the night, my eyes brimming with tears too cold to fall. Didn't have a thought. Just empty, dark heartbreak with no way out. The sun came up. I sat there. I didn't go to work, I couldn't move, didn't eat. All day, sitting there; the sun went down again. Again I sat through the night, waiting for some feeling, some answer, some reason—why!? Sun came up and I'm still there, man, but something starts happening. I got a new feeling, something moving inside me in a place where nothing's moved for years; I get an idea! I see the light at the end of the tunnel but the tunnel is me and the light is saying, "The fucking bitch is right. You're an asshole."

She's right! No wonder she split. If she'd gotten some *understanding* she would have felt motivated to get off her lazy butt and do something. If I hadn't been so tired from work I could have taken the time with her that a woman needs, instead of just expecting her to pleasure me, like a whore, just cuz I was paying the bills. I would have satisfied her and she wouldn't have had to run off with Marty Arnold. I was kicking ass on the job, every day, and when I got home I couldn't stop forcing my way; I wanted to kick *her* ass, hell, I'd kick *your* ass right now if I still felt that way. But I don't anymore. I figured out that life is more than just a paper-stone-and-scissors game. You see, something happened to me. There, on the couch I realized that I hated myself even worse than she did. And I saw what was gonna happen to me unless I changed—living out my days on a barstool blubbering about what doublecrossing skunks women were and then going back to my lonely apartment full of beercans and TV dinners and jackoff pictures I couldn't even talk to. I *had* to change. And it was morning and I was thinking this, and the sun was up, but I didn't go to work. That was the first step, I didn't go back to that job.

He takes off his carpenter's belt.

I knew my job was here, with myself, turning myself into someone that I could stand being. But how to do it? I look over in the corner and I see these goddam sex manuals that she was always reading and I was always getting on her case about, and I figure, what-the-hell, let's see what they say about coming too fast and what a woman really needs. Hell, you gotta start somewhere. So I get this book off the shelf, open it up and you know, it's called "The Art of Loving," by Erich Fromm *(he pronounces the "ch" in "Erich")*. And the guy's not even a doctor. He's more than that, he's a great philosopher, Erich Fromm, and what he's saying, it's like some force greater than me told me to open that book, it's so right for where I'm at.

Fromm says that in order to get it, you've got to put it out, you can't grab for it, it has to come to you of its own accord. If you give love, it'll be returned to you, if you're open enough to accept it. Love's a gift and you can't demand a gift or else it's just a token, a hollow empty offering. Don't you know it? Didn't I know it? So I don't read the book, I gobble it up like it's medicine, and when I'm done I can actually feel the love beginning to ooze out of me into the atmosphere, and the anger beginning to fade *(spreads arms with a gesture of letting the love ooze out)*. It's an incredible feeling, it's not selfish, it's not just me, it's everything, and it's fantastic.

So I trot over to the shelf and pull down another one. And I'm into it. This one's called "Ee Ess Tee Training" by Werner Erhard.

Yeah, you laugh, but man, est has helped millions of people in many different countries get control of who they are. You know, "est," it's the French word for "is," and it's also a kinda training you go through when you hate yourself so bad that you're willing to go through like boot camp to learn how to be in command of your own will power. That Werner, man, what a hard-ass guy. He says that in order to change you've gotta concentrate on your trip, and in order to concentrate you've gotta learn how to put your appetites, your bodily functions and stuff, under control. For example, you don't have to go to the bathroom whenever you think you do; you know it can ruin your concentration. You're addicted to going to the bathroom as an escape from your problems, and it's your job to sharpen your will like a powerful sword, and cut through and not go to the bathroom. So I tried it out, sitting there on the couch, you know concentrating. I didn't go to the bathroom for ten hours and y'know—finally when I had to go...*I felt different!* It was working. I made myself up what they call a mantra *(he pronounces the first syllable as if it rhymes with "hand")*, when you repeat things over and over to drive them into your brain, you know. I'd sit there repeating, "I will change, I will change, I will change, I will change, I will change, I will change, I will change"—over and over, for hours, and I didn't go to the bathroom some more. You don't really *have* to go y'know. No, what's important, like Werner says, is to get the goals of your trip clear. "I will change, I will change, I will change, I will change, I will change, I will change, I will change,"—I did it for hours, and you know that made me feel very altered. I could feel my will inside me taking shape. I'd done something hard: I hadn't gone to the bathroom and that made me feel good about myself. So after my session I'm there in the bathroom taking a whiz, which feels *so* good, and I'm feeling good, and I'm washing my hands in the sink and I get a look at my face in the mirror, and Jesus Christ! Stop the bus! I can't believe it. What I look like is like I'm seeing it for the first time and it looks real strange to myself. Like an animal all covered with hair with little eyes looking out from a bush camouflaged behind the mask of a beard. And it came to me. That's my defense. I got cheeks soft as a woman and I've been afraid of my own softness, of my own vulnerableness. And "I will change, I will change, I will change, I will change," is running through my head like a roaring river of will, and before I know it I get the old razor off the shelf, soap her up, and...

He slowly peels the beard and mustache off his face, revealing a very hip little mustache underneath.

There I am! Underneath myself, is my real self.

He poses as if looking in a mirror, trying to get the right kind of grin for a photograph.

Not so bad, huh? Check it out. I looked kinda like a rock star or something. I had lips out to here. Good-looking enough, hell, even, pretty. Yes, I mean, what a trip, to let my own natural beauty come out, rather than trying to cover it up in shame. And that wasn't all. I looked at the clothes I was wearing. All hefty: overalls and lumbershirts covered with paint and sheetrock mud, and I said to myself, man you don't have to play Godzilla. It's time to let the peacock out. I mean, with birds, the male of the species, they really dress up, so why not me? So I threw out my work duds and tried out my face on a salesgirl and it worked like a charm. Hey, check it out. I got myself some threads. . . .

He unzips the jumpsuit, lets it fall to his ankles, and reveals his designer jeans and a tight synthetic jacket, under which is a cowboy shirt. He now has long hair and a mustache, and looks like a sort of groovy guy.

And how do yuh like this?

He turns around and on the back of the jacket is a big pink flamingo.

A pink flamingo! You see the pink flamingo sorta became my personal symbol, you know, a sensitive bird with a flexible neck—not a red neck, but a pink neck, which he can whip around to adjust to the breeze, delicately balanced on one leg. A pink flamingo doesn't force his way on the world, he takes his time, checks out which way the tide's flowing and stands real still before he flies.

And I was flying too, couldn't stop changin'. I got my threads together and then my wheels. Had an old '53 Ford F-100 pickup all covered with two-by-four shit, square-cornered, symbolizing rectangular thinking patterns that I was trying to break myself of. I sold it—I was never goin' back to that job again anyways—and I got myself a nifty little Karmen Ghia convertible; curves man, hyperboles, the shapes of the body reflected in the contours of a car. I felt a lot more open driving around in my convertible in my new clothes, good for the first time in years; so I figure what-the-fuck, might as well put some of this positive outlook into practice. And I bone up on my love vibrations, and do my mantra and don't go to the bathroom for *eleven hours,* before I go to this job interview. And I got so much power, personal power at this point, that I get the job, because *I lie!* It just proves that if you believe in yourself, really, and in what you're saying, if you got a positive outlook, people will believe you, even if it's a crock of horseshit. A job in a *record store!* No more pounding nails and splattering Fixall with a bunch of no-future, semi-alcoholic barbarians, not anymore. This was a place full of good vibes, where cultured people came to pick up on the mellow sounds of today. And they liked me, man; I could talk to them, because I knew I looked good, and taking care of my personal appearance made me feel good, so I believed I was good. And I *was* good.

And you should have seen the foxes come into this place, incredible class models and weathergirls, you know—like chicks you don't believe live anywhere but in an advertisement or on a centerfold. But they *are* real; they live in apartments and houses just like you and me. You wouldn't think it to look at 'em. . . . I used to hate their guts for being such fabulous pieces of ass that I couldn't have, but *they* got problems just like everybody else. *Worse.* I found out, you know, I'd chat 'em up on the job, and if their lips were pouting out and their makeup was smudged, I could tell they were upset, so I'd ask what was the matter. Half the time it'd be that their boyfriend was treating them like shit, so when I asked 'em out I knew I had a chance. But I wouldn't come on strong at all; I'd drive 'em around in my red car, and listen. It's amazing how many people just need someone to talk at. *I* was open. I'd got it from Fromm: if you don't impose yourself on a situation, and are open to what other people are saying, you know, it doesn't have to matter even *what* they're saying—you don't have to make a judgement on it, even if it's utter doo-dah, babytalk garbage—if you listen and are sensitive. . . you can get *laid* a lot more. I was getting *laid* two or three times a week, with *different* chicks man, *women* I mean. Cuz I listened to their crap. Cuz I was open. Try it out. You'll get laid too.

What a life, man: good looks, good threads, smooth wheels, mellow sounds, fine women. It was *fine!* I even got into my health and fitness, you know. My body-consciousness had been zero. I'd had a beer belly and a polyp, hands like dumptrucks and not much else, except for feeling bad from too many Coors and Camel Straights. But that was changing. I switched to Merit Lites and white wine, started working out, and getting other muscles to balance myself out. I felt good. I even took an aerobics dance class to learn some new steps. Hey don't laugh man, just try it, it's a work-out, it's just as good as karate anyday. I know what you mean. I mean if I'd caught myself going to a *dance* class six months previously, I probably would have punched myself in the nose, but hey, buddy, we've come a long way too, and some of those ballet dancers could make Mr. Universe look like Mr. Ed. And you can meet a lot of real interesting people at these classes, that's why a lot of people take 'em, you know. There was a guy named Steve there, what a monster! I mean that guy was fit, six two, neck like a fire hydrant, sixteen inch biceps. He was built. And he was smart. You know what he was into? It blew my mind. Classical music. That's right, you know Beethoven, Tchaikahovsky, Brahams, and Bock. Classical music! Anybody out there into classical music? Well I am! It's fantastic. Don't put it down. See, it wasn't always classical—what was top-forty in Brandenburg in 1792 is classical Johann Sebastian today and it's still got class. Like Steve, he had class—and after class sometimes we'd go out to these restaurants and eat *gourmet* food—raw fish and snails and stuff. It was different, you know, snails will fill you up as good as hot dogs do and they don't taste *too* bad—like boogers dipped in garlic sauce, you can't really taste the snail. It was pretty cultural hanging out with Steve. I was getting very refined. Well, he was my teacher.

One time I'm up there after class, stoned to the gills on this Nigerian pot that wasn't ceramic, get it? You ever smoke that stuff? It's really visual, like the light resolves into particles of color even if your eyes aren't shut, it just blasts you. And so Steve puts on this Mahler's Fifth Symphony so we can have a listen. Have you ever tuned into Mahler's amazing Fifth? Maaan *watch out!* It's the mother of the monster symphonies, got nearly two hundred pieces in it and what they create with this Kurt Fangler cat wielding the baton is like a tidal wave of sound, a sunami. I washed way up and back, hung from the trees for dear life as the earth became the water which became the fire which became the rock which became me. I saw the maidens with the mushrooms growing out of their breasts, I grooved with the Slavs in the Czechoslovakian groves, man I was *gone.* By the time I returned to the sphere and the dots resolved back into contours the record was over, but the music was still on. And right in front of my face were these big blue copcar lights. It took me a minute to realize that they were Steve's *eyes,* looking at me, looking through me, into my brain, periscoping right down my spine nailing my feet to the rug. And then I heard this voice, *his* voice. He said, "Do you want to turn into a bat?" A *bat?* I didn't know what the fuck he was talking about, but I was so stoned and gone, I said, "Yeah." And then he kissed me. Right on the lips, and he didn't stop there either. He kissed my chin and my neck and he undid my shirt and. . .

He upzips his jacket, unsnaps the top button of his shirt, and undoes his belt buckle.

And kissed my chest, and you know, I didn't have it together to tell him to stop. I mean I was his guest, and I was *loaded*, and well, it felt pretty good actually. So he undoes my belt buckle... and then my fly and he's kissing me, and he takes my cock out in his warm hands and he kisses me and he's kissing me and he's kissing me.... *(Pause as a smile bursts over his face.)*

PHOTO: CHUCK HUDINA

PHOTO: CHUCK HUDINA

It's fantastic!! It's like no other coming I've ever come. Surprise, surprise! You know why? Because it's a *man* with a *man*. A *man* knows what another man wants. There's none of this mysterious *gulf* to bridge. I mean why waste your time looking for the little button when there's a flagpole waving right in front of your face? He didn't need a map to find Myrtle Avenue or the Fertile Crescent, he just went right down Main Street and *got home*. And when I started driving it was like I'd been born on the same street as Steve, I just zoomed in the back door, no questions asked. I gave as good as I got and I didn't have to ask if he'd arrived. It was obvious!

Well, well, well... what a revelation. Although I'd never had it in me before, it turned out that I'd had it in me all along, if you get my drift. It had to come out. And it did. I was catalyzed out of my inert state in the crucible of Steve's love and I couldn't stop reacting to this wonderful world, the world of men loving men, men helping men. It was noncompetitive... no longer was I locking horns with every stud around over the few available cows. We were all studs, all cows. Liberating myself from the trappings of my former straight existence...

He throws off his wig. Now he has short hair and a little mustache.

I threw myself shamelessly at Steve's feet. It was like first love. It *was* first love. . . first *real* love. We went everywhere together, did everything as one. After a while it seemed silly for us to maintain two separate pads, so Steve asked me to move into his large well-furnished apartment. And that's not all. He was earning buckets of money managing the body-building salon and he suggested that I quit my straight job. He said that *he'd support me.* How long had I waited!! All I had to do was a little housekeeping, and the rest of the day was mine to do whatever I pleased.

Of course, there was more than I'd reckoned on, what with the shopping and the laundry and the cleaning. Steve needed a dust free environment for his records—you could just so much as sneeze and the wood floors would get sticky—but I didn't mind the work. Let me tell you it was a pleasure to make things comfortable for the person I loved. I read that book. . . about developing the left side of your brain? And I went crazy with it—whole new vistas of endeavor opened up to me. I started to decorate the house, buying pictures and hangings for the walls. I tried out ten coffee tables to find one to fit the room just so and I refinished it myself. And that's not all. As the flower of my visual sense blossomed, the first inklings of culinary skill began to bud. I'd never cooked before but it wasn't hard; with the books they have nowadays, if you have the right feel, you can make a radish seem like a dinner for five. It was ecstasy to see Steve's face light up when he'd get home from work and find something Tunisian hot on the table, with the wine and the crystal. But I didn't stop with haute cuisine. No, I figured that if I was spending so much time getting the externals to have a little style, I might as well turn *myself* into a work d'art as well. . . so. . . I started dressing up.

He unsnaps his shirt and there underneath is a shortsleeved rhinestone blouse that zips up the front. He tosses his shirt into the audience and giggles.

What d'you think, girls? How 'bout this?

He pulls his trousers down to below the knee, revealing a floor-length, tight, sheer dress that covers up all the other clothes now piled around his ankles. He puts on his wig and is now in high drag with a mustache.

Just a little something to make a boy's mouth water. And water it did. He'd come home and there I'd be—at the door looking fabulous. The house would be perfect, soft light, flowers, with a dinner that was elegant, yet ample enough for a hardworking red-blooded

PHOTO: CHUCK HUDINA

PHOTO: CHUCK HUDINA

stallion like Steve. And then after supper, we'd turn on the Mahler and sit back on the couch and maul each other as if the night would have no end. It was divine, a dream come true but. . . .

When your dream comes true your head is in the clouds, but the world keeps turning, gravity shifts, and you're left with your head up your ass. I mean, it always happens. You give your love, your body, and your soul to someone, and first they take it, and then they take it for granted. You become their fix; they develop a tolerance until they don't get off anymore. So they turn to someone else. I'm sure that's happened to you, those of you who've *really* loved. Steve would come home, and there I'd be at the door, having slaved all day over the food and the house, looking like Diana Ross or Tuesday Weld or someone—I switched around, I thought it would keep him more interested. But he'd just groan about how tired he was from working, clomp over to the table, and eat the lovely meal I'd prepared for him—grunting and slurping like a hog at a trough. And do you think I got a word of thanks for my offering? No. After supper, I'd flop down on the couch, turn up the music, and wait. . . for a tender look, a touch, a smile. And he'd tell me that he had to work late, and *leave*. Out the door, clomp, clomp, clomp. Well I wasn't born yesterday, you know. I could smell them on him when he'd crawl into bed late at night, trying not to wake me. Sometimes it smelled like a man, sometimes it smelled like a woman, and one time it smelled like something that was neither man nor woman. That dog! I was at my wit's end. I wanted to scream, I wanted to kill. One night I waited behind the door with a can opener, ready to

slice that two-timing cunt's nuts off.... But I couldn't do it. It
would have been like defacing a national monument. Finally I'd
had it. There I was in the bathroom, at three in the morning with
Steve not home, my face full of smudgy mascara...and I knew I
just couldn't go on. It wasn't him I hated so much as myself, for not
being enough. No matter what I did, I couldn't give him what he
really wanted. I looked in the mirror and then it came to me. For
the first time I saw the real being that was hiding there, under the
costume of a masquerade clown. It was a *me* that I'd never been
before, but that I could be—a *real* me that was closer to me than the
me that I was trying to be.... But could I do it?

I could. I found out the next morning. I called up Stanford University and talked to Dr. Eunice. He said that it cost a thousand
dollars and I made an appointment on the phone. But where to get
the money? I looked around the apartment and then it came to me
again. I sold the stereo, the tape recorder, the speakers, *and* his
Gentlemen's Quarterly collection—oh yes I did, and then I wrote
him the note, packed my bags, and split—bound for Palo Alto, soon
to be an alto.

They were so nice, such professionals. *(He removes his sequined
short-sleeved blouse.)* They laid me down on the cold white table,
Dr. Eunice and his staff, removed my clothes, shot me full of
morphine, and commenced. They cut in my scrotum a thin red line,
slitting the sack, and removed my testicles, discarding them like
broken eggs in the night. They folded back the scrotal skin, sculp-
ting therein lips, gentle petals, tender labia. Then, taking my penis
they cut with the scalpel yet another thin red line down its dorsal
side, removed the meat, and folded the skin back and down to make
external lips, a corrolla of flesh to guard the delicate envelope that
they then hollowed into my core. It was a deeper opening, a new
way into me, and when I awoke I knew...

> *He takes his mustache between his fingers and slowly peels it off
> his face, then lets it flutter and fall to the ground like a dying
> butterfly. She is now a woman, in a blonde wig and a dress.*

That I had indeed attained my peak experience. I had crossed over.
But into what? As the days of my recovery passed I thought long and
hard about what was to come. I had to go slowly, for I could no
longer pretend to define myself, because I didn't know what or who
I was. My feelings were different; the feeling of space inside, the
feeling of water, the feelings of empathy that pulled like a magnet
toward children and all living things—they were different, so dif-

ferent in fact that I knew I couldn't trust them entirely. I was scared of making some naive mistake. It was up to society to define *me* this time. I'd had it with propelling an identity out into the world only to have it turn shallow at a lover's whim. No, this time I would see where I fit in before I tried to fit in anywhere.

Well it didn't take me long to see where I *didn't* fit in. After I moved back to the city and began to search for work, it was obvious that, having made the change, I was being treated as if I was from a completely different planet, *and* a lower order of life. Walking proudly through the streets I was subject to more verbal abuse and random lechery in one afternoon than in my whole previous thirty-three years. It was both fearful and bitterly disappointing to realize that I couldn't go out of my house without being solicited for copulation and threatened with rape by the males of the species. And my horror was compounded when I found material rewards denied me *because of my sex*. The jobs that were offered were menial! I was expected to be thankful to acquire a waitressing or stenographic position at little above minimum wage. Oh yes, society defined me all right—it put me on my back, dependent on my looks and my acquiescence for my very survival.

I was becoming more and more despondent with the whole situation. One day, quite by accident, I went into a little bookstore close to where my last interview had been—this one with a stubby little man whose only criteria for hiring seemed to be how far he could look up my dress. I was attracted by the curious spelling of its name. It was spelled "Womynbrary" *(the syllable "myn" rhymes with "line")*. That was interesting. . . I understood the logic of it somehow. There was a sign by the register: "Wanted: Womyn to work and share with the Womynbrary Collective. Feminist outlook required. Smokers permitted." I talked to the womyn at the desk and for once I was getting straight answers. After I told her my history she became very enthusiastic, telling me that my unique perspective would be invaluable to their process of consensual collectivism and that I should come to their next meeting, if I wanted to become a womynbrarian.

Well I went and I was voted in, and after that I didn't look back. I'd made a near-fatal error you see in my analysis: I'd figured on integrating into a society that was built on a basic sexist duality. I hadn't known that it was possible to create a *new* society, based on an egalitarian feminist political outlook, a non-patriarchal, noncompetitive community of womyn working with womyn. What a fine feeling it was to work in a nurturing rather than a hostile environment, and to see the subtle politicization of every womyn who came into the store. Sure, the wages were low and the meetings boring, but the spiritual rewards superseded the pull of all of our ingrained, individualistic materialism. Our energy and belief and our love were our currency, not money. And didn't we have a goldmine? Of womyn?

At last I'd found a place. There was a young womyn named Caroline who joined the collective soon after I did, and, through working the same shift, we learned we had a lot in common and we became friends. Like me, she was very much a stranger; she'd come from another city after her husband had deserted her and her child. Like me, she was insecure with the new power she was feeling being part of the collective, and, like me, she needed somebody to like her. We would go out sometimes and often I would provide child-care with little Elizabeth on Wednesday nights when Caroline had her committee meeting. Gradually our friendship blossomed into a nonexclusive closeness. There was so much to share; we had political unity, economic unity through the collective, and a spiritual unity born out of our own individual suffering. It was as if there was a gap in each of us that only the other could fill. Soon the blossom budded into. . . I'm not going into the details of how and when we first discovered how much we had to give each other. But *let me tell you*. . .it was the slowest, most excruciatingly intense lovemaking I'd ever known. There was none of this shooting off at the gate to a finish line a quarter mile down the track. . . . No, this was a gradual mounting of sensation, from one plateau to another even higher plane, culminating in a langorous vivid explosion of feeling, and ending, as we melted together into each other. It had never felt so right before. I'd never had so much empathy with a lover. It was more a REALationship than a relationship.

We had economic unity, political unity, spiritual unity, and physical unity, and we decided to attempt a domestic unity as well. The other Womynbrarians were discouragingly dialectic about our coupling. They said that monogamy bred elitism and was dangerous to the spirit of true collectivism, and we on the other hand held out for our freedom to love as we chose. And we must have made a convincing case for our being able to put more hours in working, if we split the child care and worked separate shifts, because on the second ballot we achieved *consensus* and the collective let us attempt cohabitation on a six month probationary period. We started looking for a place large enough for the three of us, but the real estate inflation had put anything that looked feasible way out of range for our collective salaries. Even by putting in long hours at the store we couldn't seem to get enough for first and last month's rent. By this time I was becoming a little disenchanted with the scene at Womynbrary. It seemed that Caroline and I never got a moment to be with one another and, after some long and painful ruminating, I decided that I was going to go look for a job that paid me a living wage, work at the collective on a volunteer basis, and donate part of my salary each week to the store. But this time I wanted to be taken seriously—not made to look pretty for peanuts. So I cut my hair.

She takes off the wig. Now she has a unisex haircut.

And I changed my clothes into something more heavy, more me! And I went out to look for work.

She pulls off the dress, revealing a merry widow bra and a pair of leopard-skin bathing trunks.

PHOTO: CHUCK HUDINA

But where to find the job? As I was walking past a construction site trying to figure it out, some asshole in a hard hat yelled the usual obscene invitation. I was so mad! Here was this mindless idiot earning ten dollars an hour with some union while I was... of course! It came to me in a flash. There were no *womyn* working on the site. *And* there was a big sign about the company being an equal opportunity employer, so I went in there and told the super that he'd better hire me or there were going to be reports filed, pickets, the whole works. He didn't want to do it but he knew that I had him by the balls, so he told me to show up for work the next day and he'd try me out. But he said, "Most girls don't do good on these jobs. They're not cut out for it." "Most girls!" My ass, man. I got the gear for the job...

> *She pulls up the overalls and snaps back on the carpenter's belt, covering up all of the others costumes again. She swaggers with the hammer in her hand.*

And showed up there the next day at 7:30 a.m. raring to go. For ten dollars an hour. I was ready. All the men on the crew were snickering among themselves so I knew they had something planned. What it was, was they gave me the job of unloading hundred pound concrete bags from a truck and carrying them up a ramp. They figured that *that* would wear me out and I'd be in tears or something before the morning was over. Well I disappointed them. It wasn't so hard... I'd been there before. When they saw that I knew what I was doing, they left me alone—because it became obvious that I'd make them look slow if they worked next to me. Some of those old union farts had been leaning on their shovels for thirty years... and after a while they were asking me to take it easy. "It all pays the same," they'd say, and I'd just keep working as fast as I could. That drove them all crazy but I felt fine. Sure, I was tired at the end of the day, but it was a good feeling. I was getting strong again. I was even learning new skills. The super was watching me pick up stuff fast and outwork the other guys, and after a month he apologized to me for what he'd said that first day, and made me *boss* of the framing crew. And I even got to get along with the men working... sure they were ignorant, sexist, and hopelessly alcoholic, most of them, but a lot of them were just on the treadmill. It wasn't their fault; they'd been acculturated to be assholes.

Things were fuckin' great. We got a huge place with a washing machine and a dryer, the kid got her own room, I was happy, Caroline felt good. The collective appreciated my financial contributions. For the first time in my life I felt in *control*. I told Caroline, I said, "Hey, why don't you quit working those long hours at the collective and stay home and spend some time with your *kid* for once? They'll try to guilt-trip you and make you stay, but *they're* taking *my* money now—they can't bitch. You don't need to work. I'll support you."

And that's what she did. I didn't mind working, and the kid sure appreciated having her mother around but, you know, Caroline didn't seem to really like spending so much time with Elizabeth. I'd come home from work and she'd be wanting to go down to the bookstore, or go out to a demonstration—and she wanted me to baby-sit when all I wanted to do was cool out from work and talk to her. It became apparent that for all our similarities there was a basic class struggle going on between us. She was one of those people from Shaker Heights, Ohio—always had money, went to college, always had a desk job. She could talk an intellectual blue streak, but when it came down to understanding what it was like to *really* work, she didn't have any idea. What a fucking bitch. I was supporting her and after a while she hardly had the time of day for me. Things got terrible. Our economic unity wasn't real, our spiritual unity was gone, our political unity had never really existed, and as for our physical unity—I was lucky to get a piece of her cold ass once a week. How could this have happened? We'd had so much. I was depressed. I was pissed off. Well, one day I come home from work, all tired out, and what the fuck do you think I find? A goddamned note! The fucking bitch had split! The goddam cunt had split! *(She's beating the chair with the hammer.)* The fucking bitch had split!

Blackout.

The AIDS Show
(Artists Involved with Death and Survival)

Paul Attinello

Bill Barksdale

Karl Brown

Dan Curzon

Ellen Brook Davis

Doug Holsclaw

Matthew McQueen

Markley Morris

Leland Moss

Adele Prandini

Philip Real

Robert J. Stone

Dan Turner

Randy Weigand

The AIDS Show was first presented as *Artists Involved with Death and Survival* on September 6, 1984, at Theatre Rhinoceros in San Francisco. The following actors comprised the original company:

Paul Attinello, Bill Barksdale, Donna Davis, Ellen Brook Davis, Chuck Hilbert, Doug Holsclaw, Bruce Jones, Matthew McQueen, Markley Morris, Leland Moss, Sandy Schlechter, Robert J. Stone, Randy Weigand

Directed by Leland Moss
Assistant director: Chuck Solomon
Musical direction: Karl Brown

The show was revived at Theatre Rhinoceros on November 13, 1984, and subsequently toured, with the following cast:

Bill Barksdale, Robert Coffman, Stacey Cole, Donna Davis, Ellen Brook Davis, Mark Flora, Chuck Hilbert, Doug Holsclaw, Matthew McQueen, Thomas-Mark, Leland Moss, Keno Rider, Robert J. Stone, Randy Weigand

Stage manager and lighting design: Cayenne Woods

NOTES

The AIDS Show is a compilation of short pieces relating to the problems associated with Acquired Immune Deficiency Syndrome. Some of the pieces were pre-existing monologues, some were written expressly for this production, some were developed collaboratively with the cast. In some cases monologues have been adapted for more than one actor. The names of most of the "characters" in this script are simply the names of the actors who originally played those parts.

The character Murray is inspired by the offstage character with whom Arnold talks on the phone in Harvey Fierstein's *Torch Song Trilogy*.

Due to the topical nature of this piece, the script is undergoing a constant process of revision. Some skits contain current factual data about AIDS that need to be updated to the latest information for each performance (see, especially, "To Tell the Truth"). A completely revised version of *The AIDS Show* will be presented at Theatre Rhinoceros in the fall of 1985.

The AIDS Show
Invitation (Part One)
Dan Turner

Lights come up to reveal a number of stools or chairs arranged in a circle center stage. Hanging above the stage, center, is a sign that reads: 1984. MICHAEL *enters upstage and addresses the audience.*

MICHAEL: Let me tell you right now—my objective is to illuminate and not depress. I am here to tell you that there is a spirit which banishes all fear. *(As he speaks, men enter from three directions, silently acknowledging each other. They sit in the circle and hold a position.)* We had dinner together in Denver last year. Thirteen people with AIDS and me. There were men from New York, San Francisco, Houston, LA, and one guy from Colorado. I was asked to join because my lover was supposed to be at the health conference, too. He would have been the fourteenth person with AIDS at the table; as it was, I sat in his place. I couldn't take his place. I could only sit where he belonged. *(The men in the circle begin talking quietly with each other.)* We ate at the Top of the Rockies Restaurant. Have you heard of it? It's in the Security Life Building at 1616 Glenarm on the 30th floor. I'm a journalist; I have a memory for detail. The windows of the restaurant face the Continental Divide. You could see the sun beginning to set, and on one side of the mountains a large, white, neon cross began to glow.

DAN *(standing up from the circle)*: Michael?

MICHAEL *(walking to meet DAN)*: Hello, Dan. It was nice of you to include me with everyone.

DAN: You're welcome. I'm sorry that Mark couldn't be with us, but I feel he would have wanted you to sit in his place.

MICHAEL: Thanks. (MICHAEL *takes a seat. The other men look at him, unsure of who he is. An awkward moment.)*

BOBBI: Hello, Michael. Glad you're here.

MICHAEL: Hi, Bobbi. Good to see you.

BOBBI: Do you know Matthew? (MATTHEW *offers his hand.)*

MICHAEL: Hello, good to meet you. You're from New York?

MATTHEW: Yes.

ROGER: Hi, I'm Roger.

MICHAEL: Hi. *(He murmurs greetings to others; another awkward moment. To* BOBBI) Hey Bobbi, did you see the lightning flash?

BOBBI: Yeah, the visuals are pretty good up here. *(Some laughter. Then silence.)*

CAL: I wonder the last time they had a table full of faggots. *(Laughter.)* All right. So everyone can be involved in this conversation, I'd like to ask some questions. Let's go around the table and answer, one by one. *(General groans.)* Come on, it's a great way to break the ice. Question number one: where were you born— and when? *(He points to DAN.)*

DAN: Teeny Town, Illinois, 1947.

CAL: I've been there.

MATTHEW: Butte, Montana, 1952.

BOBBI: Detroit. *(The others look, waiting for the date.)* Well, after Lily Tomlin, but before the Corvette.

CAL: I was born on Oahu in 1952.

TOM: Oh, that made six islands!

RICHARD: Washington, DC. Sometime during Camelot.

TOM: Cleveland, but I'm not at liberty to discuss the details. You'll read about it in my book.

BOBBI: A book about Cleveland?

ROGER: LA, 1967. *(General disbelief.)*

ARTIE: Sacramento, 1957. . . . OK, '56.

OTHERS: '55. . . . '54. . . .

ARTIE: Stop!

ELBERT: San Marcos, Texas. Sometime in the twentieth century.

CAL *looks at* MICHAEL, *who has forgotten he is part of the group.*

MICHAEL: Oh! Uh—New York, Manhattan, 1948.

CAL: OK, next question: what was your occupation prior to diagnosis?

ROGER: I was a lesbian.

CAL: Your occupation, not your hobby.

DAN: I was a word processor in the Nuclear Fuels Department at Bechtel—typing proposals about waste disposal plants. Do you think I got KS from that?

MICHAEL: No.

DAN: I was going to leave if they started working on the MX missile proposal.

MATTHEW: I was a choirmaster.

TOM: Vienna Boys, no doubt.

MATTHEW: I never touched them!

BOBBI: I worked for customer service at Pacific Gas and Electric.

CAL: I worked in advertising—and what did you do, Richard?

RICHARD: That's not funny.

CAL: Go on, tell him. *(Others encourage* RICHARD *to tell; he hesitates.)*

MICHAEL: What did you do?

RICHARD: I was a hustler.

BOBBI: Now that's customer service.

CAL: OK, next question: what was your feminine name, and how was it given to you?

BOBBI: Mine was Bobby Sue—and given by Darryl Ann—but I don't recall why.

CAL: On gin.

BOBBI: What's a little Tanqueray between friends?

TOM: I was Crystal Dawn.

ARTIE: And you still are!

TOM: I was working in a drag bar in Toledo, Ohio.

BOBBI: For that you need crystal.

DAN: I worked as a cupbearer at Olympus—that was a place in North Beach billed as the first bisexual nightclub.

MATTHEW: How do you bisexual? With a Macy's card? *(Everyone groans.)*

DAN: We were all dressed as Greek boys serving Greek food. They called the uniform a toga, but it was *very* skimpy. One night, between pinches, we gave each other names. There was Blanche and Bette. I was Rita—for Hayworth.

BOBBI: Oh God remember those days—when sex was easy and you didn't have to worry about it. . .

ARTIE: So carefree. . .

ROGER: Gay was good.

MICHAEL: Gay was good. *(He stands and addresses the audience).* And isn't it still good? But how can we tell ourselves? How can we believe it unless we come to each other's aid and face the pain as we faced the pleasure? I'd like to write about it, but it's been so difficult—so much has happened. Do I really want to relive those frightening moments so soon? Can't I just wait a few years to get some distance? Or is the point that to be meaningful it must be said now—right now? *(The sound of a clock ticking: a metronome.)* Where would I begin? How would I begin?

The entire cast starts a countdown ("5-4-3-2-1") as the men move the chairs aside. CAL *reaches up and pulls the 4 off the year sign to reveal a 1. The sign now reads: 1981.*

Party 1981
Paul Attinello

Metronome sound continues throughout. Guests congregate in the center. Party ball starts revolving, scattering colored light all over. Streamers are tossed and horns tooted. As the scene progresses, people leave party debris scattered around.

ALL: HAPPY 1981!

> *Hubbub, loud for a few beats, then softer. All of this is ad lib, based on what follows.* DOUG *and* MATTHEW *fall into a passionate embrace upstage center.*

PAUL: Should I open another bottle, or are we going to. . .
CHUCK: So what have *you* resolved? You must be joking.
BRUCE: I wouldn't miss it for the world. Have you been yet?
BOB: Gives the greatest parties, except maybe the food.
ELLEN: Gee, it's so great to see you both again. . .
SANDY: Kiss me, you fool. Not on the cheek, stupid.

> *When the noise dies down,* DOUG *and* MATTHEW *are left alone on stage as the party has drifted into other rooms. They come up for air.*

DOUG: By the way, my name's Alan.
MATTHEW: Oh. Yeah. Greg. *(Grins, sticks out his hand.)*
DOUG: Greg? Why don't you come with me. I've got something I want to show you.

> MATTHEW *and* DOUG *leave,* MATTHEW's *arm on* DOUG's *shoulders.* PAUL *and* BRUCE *enter.*

PAUL: Don't waste your time, I don't know *how* long they've been together.
BRUCE: Thanks a lot, but when I need your advice, I'll ask for it.
PAUL: Oh, come *on*. . .

> BRUCE *exits.* BOB *and* CHUCK *enter.*

BOB: He said *that?* I think I'm gonna die. I've *gotta* tell Carl.
CHUCK: Not a word—remember, you promised.

> *They cross out.* SANDY *enters with tray and crosses to* PAUL.

SANDY: There you are! You just wanted a woman to co-host this thing so someone would stay sober long enough to serve dessert.
PAUL: Aw, come on, you really kill me sometimes. *(ELLEN enters, calls to PAUL.)*

ELLEN *(very meaningfully)*: Daniel, come into the kitchen, I need some help. *Now*, if you don't mind... *(SANDY, PAUL, ELLEN begin to exit.)*

BOB *(runs on)*: Oh, listen everybody, come in here quick! I love this song. *(They run out.)*

Rimmin' at the Baths
Karl Brown
Matthew McQueen

I went to the tubs
looking for a little love.
I wandered through the door
feeling like a whore.
The guy who took my money
smiled and called me "honey,"
stuck my wallet in a box,
threw me a towel, threw me a lock.

I wandered through the halls
peeking in all the stalls,
'till according to my plan,
I found the perfect man.
Eager to please,
I got down to my knees,
and when he turned around,
I didn't frown....

I really couldn't help myself,
It was such a gorgeous ass.
But now I've got amoebas
from rimmin' at the baths
          rimmin' at the baths.

I didn't know what I had done
'till the day I got the runs.
I felt like such a fool
always sitting on that stool.
My friend made a suggestion
there was life in my intestine.
I rejected the idea

but I still had diarrhea!

I went to the clinic.
The nurse gave me a plastic cup.
He sent me to the bathroom,
told me to fill it up.
I left it at the laboratory
still warm and smelling mighty bad.
The nurse called me in the morning
to tell me what I had, and he said:

"You really got to help yourself;
you are such a stupid ass.
And now you've got amoebas
from rimmin' at the baths
    rimmin' at the baths."

I went back to the clinic.
The nurse gave me a pack of pills:
Flagyl and Diodoquin,
then he stuck me with the bill.
I swallowed down a handful
then my stomach felt ill,
'cause if the disease don't get you,
the goddamn treatment will, so. . .

You really got to help yourself.
Be aware of what might come to pass.
My best friend he got hepatitis
from rimmin' at the baths.

No, don't be seduced by that sweet aroma;
think twice before you dive into that ass.
You might even get Kaposi's Sarcoma—AIDS!!—

from rimmin' at the baths
    rimmin' at the baths.

Murray 1981
Leland Moss

PHOTO: MARK I. CHESTER

*Murray appears, phone in hand, dressed in torn T-shirt and jeans.
He lounges on the sofa and dials. When the phone is answered, he
breathes heavily.*

MURRAY: Are you naked?.... What do you mean, who is this? It's
Murray! Arnold, who else calls you every Monday right after
"All My Children"? So how was your weekend?.... Uh huh...
uh huh...yeah...uh huh.... And that's it?? That's all? Oy oy
oy Arnold Beckoff, what are we going to do with you?.... Well,
I suppose you could say I had my hands full.... No, I didn't
meet Mr. Right. I did, however, meet Mr. Butch and Mr.
Smooth Buns and Mr. Big Dick.... Well, I didn't carry a ruler,
but it was at least nine and a half.... Because there's this certain
spot inside somewhere that kind of aches if it's over nine
inches.... I take care of myself!...I take CARE of myself.... I
don't make it with guys that look weird.... Well, there's good
weird and bad weird, you know what I mean?.... All right,
good weird is like, well, you know like when you're at the baths
and.... Oh yeah, right. Listen, Arnold, one of these nights you
ought to come with me!.... Don't be silly, there's something for
everybody there, Arnold, even you. There's this blackboard
down in the lobby, see, where you can advertise for what you're

into and. . . it is NOT disgusting, it's liberated! . . . . Yeah, like
the classifieds, they list fucking, sucking, fisting, wha. . . *(Shaking his finger at the phone)* Aah aah aah aah! I do not need to
hear another lecture from you on that particular subject! I enjoy
it, and that's that. . . . Arnold, do you realize how many men in
New York City get fisted every weekend? We're out to enjoy ourselves, remember, not kill each other. . . . All right, all right, you
told me so, will you forget about this and listen to what I'm telling
you? On this blackboard they have a section for vanilla sex! . . .
Well, of course, I thought of you. . . . Well, it *is* blank most of
the time, but you'd be surprised. Really, some of the toughest-
looking men there, you know, after it's all over, all they really
want to do is cuddle. . . . Welll, once or twice. . . . Wellll, there
was—uh—well, let's see—hey! Remember I was telling you
about that guy last New Year's? . . . You know, from that party
at the Everard—the one with the hair. . . yeah, he was, real
sweet. . . . Well, there was him. . . . I dunno. Oh yes, I do. He
moved to San Francisco and got hepatitis. . . . It wasn't *that*,
Arnold, give me a break, will you? He just did too many drugs
or something. Look, honey, I've got to go. . . . Well, truth to
tell, I'm getting together with this incredibly hot man I met
there last night. *(Echoing)* Yes, I was still there Sunday night!
Give me a break, will you? I feel asleep about 5 a.m. on Saturday and when I woke up who the hell knew what time it was, so
I hung around the pool, kibbitzed with some friends, and I see
this guy—Arnold! He looks just like Charles Bronson on acid!
. . . No, we were both too zonked out to get into it, so he invites
me over to his place tonight, get this—JUST THE TWO OF US!
. . . I know it's only three o'clock, it takes me a while to get
ready, you know, nails, all that. . . . Thank you. I hope so, too.
And Arnold, listen, do me a favor, will you? Get your ass out of
the house and into the streets before you turn into your mother.
Good-byyyye!

Party 1982
Paul Attinello

From offstage, the countdown: "5-4-3-2-1—HAPPY 1982!" *Horns
and shrieks. On 2,* MURRAY *removes the 1 from the date sign to
reveal the 2 and runs off.* BOB *enters, drunk. Throughout this scene,*

the stage becomes littered with party debris—streamers, horns, hats, etc.

BOB: Are we having the first orgy of 1982, or is it just this awful sangria?

PAUL *(following him in)*: Pipe down. Sam and Ray are breaking up in the front room, and they need absolute silence to yell at each other.

PAUL *continues out.* BOB *sits or leans.* CHUCK *and* MATTHEW *come in, drift to a halt while talking.*

MATTHEW: You're kidding? Seven in one night?

CHUCK: Well, you can't really count the ones that went only halfway.

MATTHEW: You couldn't have done it without the crystal.

BOB: Oh, are we talking kitchens again?

CHUCK: What?

BOB: Oh, sorry. When you said crystal, I thought you meant, like, you know, glasses.

He laughs, stops, leaves in a huff. DOUG *and* BRUCE *enter, arguing.* CHUCK *and* MATTHEW *continue silently.*

BRUCE: Well, that's hardly a problem when you've already had all of the guests, is it?

DOUG: That's not fair, look at how long it's been since I've even looked at another. . .

BRUCE: How about last weekend at Earl's?

DOUG: Do you ever back off?

They continue out. SANDY *and* ELLEN *enter.*

SANDY: Goodness, it's drunk out tonight. It was like this last year, too.

ELLEN: But why would he get so upset because there were mushrooms in the salad?

SANDY: Umm—that's kind of hard to explain. . .

ELLEN: Well, this is definitely the last time I give one of these parties. The neighbors won't put up with this even once a year. *(They continue out.* CHUCK *and* MATTHEW *become audible again.)*

CHUCK: Yeah, you should have *seen* that cat. But they *said* dust was an animal tranquilizer, so I thought. . .

MATTHEW: Oh, Jesus.

PAUL *enters alone; in the doorway.*

PAUL: I would have said aging hippie, but then your type is your business *(Coming in, to* MATTHEW) Greg—excuse me, you two— do you have any—you know?

CHUCK: Sorry, I'll be in the kitchen. (CHUCK *exits.*)

MATTHEW: You had to do that now?

PAUL: Hey, business is business, mister.

They leave as BOB, DOUG, *and* SANDY *enter.*

BOB: I just wish someone would ask me to go home.

DOUG *(placing a television center stage):* Will you go home?

SANDY *(to* DOUG): Oh, come on, it is *so* tacky to turn on the TV at a party.

DOUG: I just wanna see this one thing. This guy is such a hoot!

Reverend What's His Name
Dan Curzon

Organ music plays "Jesus Loves Me." *A toy truck rolls across the stage.* DOUG *and* SANDY *join other cast members trooping on as children in a Sunday School Bible class, sitting around the edges of the stage. Shortly,* REVEREND *enters, Bible in hand, and stands behind the TV.*

REVEREND: Welcome! Welcome to Bible study! How nice to see that you're already in your places. How you little children today?

CHILDREN: Fine, thank you. *(Etc.)*

REVEREND: That's *good!* Now what do you say we start! Today we're going to talk about A-I-D-S. Everyone? *(He always spells out the letters.)*

CHILDREN: A-I-D-S.

REVEREND: That's right! That nasty new disease the homosexuals are trying to give to us normal folks. Even you little children! Isn't that awful! Even little babies. Little precious babies! And why?

SALLY: Why?

REVEREND: Because they can't have any little babies of their own, and so they're jealous! Jealous. Now I want you to know that I don't have anything against those people. They've got a right to live! But if they're going to have sex outside of marriage, then what can they expect? That's the way God ordained it. You have to have sex with the same person for your whole life—or you die.

Read your Bible! (JIMMY *raises his hand.*) Yes, Jimm.

JIMMY: Is A-I-D-S God's punishment?

REVEREND: I'm glad you asked that! It most certainly is! All ɩ
is God's punishment. If you are without sin, you are withɩ
disease.

JIMMY: Well, what about sickle cell anemia? Is that God's punishment too?

REVEREND: Of course! It's the mark of Cain. Read your Bible! You
start interfering with natural institutions like marriage and
slavery, and you see what happens! (MARY LOUISE *raises her
hand.*) Yes, Mary Louise?

MARY LOUISE: If homosexuals deserve A-I-D-S, then do children
who disobey their parents deserve polio?

REVEREND: I'm glad you asked that, Mary Louise! It's a proven fact
that most of the children who got that horrible scourge of infan-
tile paralysis did so because they disobeyed their parents or legal
guardians and went swimming! They were told and told, and
still they went swimming, and that's why they were punished
with crippled limbs for the rest of their natural lives! Read your
Bible! (THEODORE *raises a hand.*) Yes, you in the back there.

THEODORE: Why do we have venereal diseases? Is it because we
don't yet know enough science?

REVEREND (*angry*): What's your name?

THEODORE: Theodore.

REVEREND: Well, Theodore, we have venereal diseases—and that's
what A-I-D-S is—because that's God's way of making people behave themselves! I don't have any truck with all this interfering
with God's will—sulfa drugs and heart bypasses, and I don't
know what all! It's all this science that's leading people astray!
Faith! Faith is the answer! Read your Bible! (BILLY *raises his
hand.*) Yes, Billy?

BILLY: Was bubonic plague a punishment for wickedness?

REVEREND: I'm glad you asked that, son. Not only bubonic plague,
but also tuberculosis, scarlet fever, and Alzheimer's disease! To
say nothing of earthquakes, droughts, and tornadoes! His eye is
on the sparrow! It's all this wishy-washy tolerance of other
religions. They all catch diseases and get covered with spots!
READ YOUR BIBLE! (SALLY *raises her hand.*) Yes, Sally?

SALLY: What would happen if they discovered a cure for A-I-D-S?

REVEREND: Why, we'd have to destroy it, of course. You can't inter-
fere with God's will! Is that what you want to do? Huh?

SALLY: Uh—no, no . . .

REVEREND: You bet your britches you don't! Because God doesn't like folks interfering with His will. It makes Him real mad! And you know what He does when He's real mad? He brings plagues. Plagues and plagues and more plagues! Hallelujah! Praise Jesus! He is a merciful God, but He brings *plagues* on those who challenge His laws! Read your Bible! Read your holy Bible! (JOHNNY *raises his hand.*) I guess we have time for one more question. Yes, Johnny?

JOHNNY: How did A-I-D-S get started?

REVEREND: Well, that's easy! God saw what was happening—those people having sex with each other, going to those discos, and so He took a great big test tube of Christian viruses—right in His mighty hand—and God put those viruses into the heating system of those baths and then just let nature take its course! And He'll do it again—or have somebody do it for Him—I'm not mentioning any names—if they keep on trying to cure this A-I-D-S. Because God Almighty just wants people to be good and He loves them, just like I do, and that's why He gives them diseases. Let us pray.

Organ chord. The children start to sing "Jesus Loves Me" *as they stand and file out in a line, followed by the* REVEREND, *wearing his most pious expression, and clutching his Bible.*

The Nurse
Ellen Brook Davis

A woman enters carrying a toy box, finds the floor littered with toys, streamers, party residue, etc. She is dressed in casual clothes. She puts the box down and starts to address the audience while picking up toys and storing them in the box.

NURSE: You know, I was always a good nurse. I never shirked responsibilities to my profession. I was always willing to work an extra shift, sometimes at the expense of my personal life. I took duties no one else wanted. I worked in the emergency room before it became glamorous and they started calling it the "trauma unit." Remember that staffing crisis out at the VA Hospital? I don't know, maybe you don't, it was a long time ago. They were bringing back boys from Vietnam—actually, they were bringing back pieces, right from the field hospitals. We called them the "basket boys." And we sort of joked how it was mix-and-match, leftovers; how it would take five or six of those poor guys to make one whole person. It was an awful mess. I also worked in the cancer wards—and we are talking no-hope cancer here.

That's where they were putting them back then, with the rest of the "no-hopes." Oh, we had in-service trainings and workshops, and they would tell us to "Wear the masks, wear the gloves, wear gowns," but basically we were on our own because nobody really knew anything. Every week it was something different, a major breakthrough, a new link, but all that did was add to the confusion. Parasites were the villains for a while, then it was protein-binding carbohydrates from the parasites and there was the thymus gland and T-cells. But "exchange of bodily fluids" is the one that got to me. You could sort of see it got to everyone. But nobody ever talked about it. Work was always a place where we shared an affection for each other, a hug, a taste of a new recipe, birthdays, but now everyone was walking around in their own invisible masks and gowns. And it wasn't fair, it just wasn't fair being put in that position. I mean, the staff was as much a victim as the patients were because no one knew who was immune and who might be next and no one was dealing with it. . . . Oh, except the media! Every day they'd report some earthshaking information. How no health worker has died—and then two lines down they would tell us that the incubation period was two years. Five years. It got to the point where I didn't know what was fact and what they wanted us to believe. But you know it isn't just me. I have a little boy, seven, and a girl, nine, and what about their immune systems? I'm raising them on my own, I have a responsibility to them, too.

At first it wasn't really clear who was your garden variety cancer patient and who actually had it. But let me tell you, whenever one of them looked a little too effeminate or talked that way, well, you know what I mean—God, would I wash my hands. I'd practically scrub the top layer of skin off. I would go through this whole cleansing ritual after a shift. But I never knew what I was bringing home. What I couldn't see, I could feel crawling all over me. It got so bad that I was afraid to touch my own kids. I became such a nervous wreck that I broke out into a rash.

Within six months the ward was half of them. And it seemed like I was spending more time with them than I was the regular cancer patients. Frankly, I began to resent having that time taken away from patients who had no choice. But these people know, because these people have created their own illness, and it could have been prevented—maybe—but that doesn't stop them from going out to parks or those bars and dressing up like you see them in the newspapers and on TV. I'm not saying that they deserve to die, no one should die like that. But they know and it doesn't stop them, they just keep right on going out there for more. I don't understand, I just don't.

There was this one, a Mexican fella, he was only on the floor for two weeks. He was very sweet, he'd share his candy and cookies with us. He worked for the city in Golden Gate Park, and his hands were cracked and stained from planting flowers and taking care of trees. And you could almost read the number of seasons he had worked there from the lines etched into his hands. And you couldn't tell, I mean, I couldn't tell, except that his friend would come and sit with him and all through visiting hours he would hold his hand. He had been with this same man for fifteen years. That's longer than my husband and I stayed married. And he would just sit there holding this big strong hand that had lost all relation to what its life had been.

Even after he died, his friend just sat there holding his hand. I watched him crying and wanted to go to him. I couldn't. I just wouldn't.

I've been a nurse for thirteen years, and I've never seen anything like this. We've always been able to cure or at least fight everything. Look, I'm not a bad person, really I'm not. I'm just scared. I don't know why I didn't do it a long time ago. Maybe when the kids started school? That would have been a good time. You know, because a mom should be there when the kids come home, standing at the door with cookies and milk when they get off the bus. I like being a normal person, and this new job lets me be normal. It's not as exciting, but it's Monday through Friday, regular hours, holidays off, and I can be there for the kids. I don't know why I didn't do it years ago.

She picks up the toy box, now full, and walks offstage.

Murray 1982
Leland Moss

MURRAY *enters, excited and speedy, wearing a new T-shirt. He sits on the couch and dials a number—now ten digits—on his push-*

button phone. Waits for Arnold to answer.

MURRAY: Hi there, sweetie, it's the travelin' boy! *(Sings a la Jeanette McDonald*—San Francisco!!—*laughs; the first time they've talked since* MURRAY *has moved.)* Oh it's great, just great, it's everything I thought it would be. Arnold, I still can't get over it. Two weeks ago everyone on Christopher Street looked like Nanook of the North, right? And here the boys are just busting out of their britches and chaps and shorts and oy oy oy, girleen! Oh and hey you'll never guess who I ran into. Remember that sweetheart from New Year's a few years ago?.... No, no, not that one—-Jesus!—you know which one, that guy I met at the Everard...with the hair.... Oh yeah, that's right, he called himself Sunrise then.... Joe.... He's into reality now. *(Laughs.)* Yeah, I ran into him at the Caldron.... The Caldron? Oh, it's sort of like the Mineshaft only—ummm—cleaner.... Arnold, when you've been around these places as much as I have, you don't need light to tell. You don't *slide* as much.... Anyway, there I was a few nights ago ripped to the tits and who should wander into my field of vision but this incredible hunk: marine-style haircut, smooth, gorgeous chest, leather vest—and nothing else! *(Shriek.)* I just grabbed hold and told him I was never gonna let go.... What do you mean, grabbed hold of what?... Ha ha ha, well we're not really at that stage yet. Besides, he has a roommate.... I don't know if they're lovers, it's hard to tell. Everything is so *vague* here. Anyway, he's sick.... No, not Joe, his roommate. *(Stands up, starts to walk aimlessly.)* I don't know, some kind of cancer. But it's nothing serious, he's walkin' around healthy.... Yeah, on his leg. How'd you know?... Oh yeah? You're kidding. What a coincidence.... Of course it must be a coincidence, you can't catch cancer like you catch the flu.... The gay what?? Where did you read that?...Oh, that rag. I wouldn't believe anything I read in that.... Arnold, you know me. You know I take care of myself. *(Sits; forcefully)* Arnold, I have told you a million times, I can tell if someone's got something, it's an intuition I have.... This is getting tired! Can we change the subject, please?.... You had to ask? The unemployment is still holding out. Besides, Arnold, it isn't easy finding a job that will give you time off every day for "All My Children." ...Oooh, listen to him! I find LOTS to do with my time, thank you very much. I'm still a tourist here, remember.... Oh, grow up, Arnold, this is the '80s! Nobody does tearooms anymore. I go to Buena Vista Park.... Just a joke! Listen, love, I'd love to talk forever, but funds are low, you know? But wait, before you go, I have to know—who are you doing for Halloween?...Martina who?...Navatilova? What is she, a Polish movie star?

Music for Ricky *blasts on as* MURRAY *runs off.*

Ricky
Randy Weigand

RICKY, *the aerobics teacher, dressed in the latest chic aerobics get-up, leads his class of four panting students center stage. Music is loud.*

RICKY: ALL RIGHT! Let's go! (*Ad-libs encouraging remarks. Students start with hip bumps.* RICKY *walks downstage left. Music fades.*) Oh, get over it, girl! You've got to admit that next to Miss America being a dyke, it's got to be the most tired subject. You know why scientists can't find a cure for it, don't you? 'Cause they can't get the mice to butt-fuck! (*Music up; turns to students.*) All right! Kick it to the front! All right! (*Walks down right; music down.*) You know, I don't even read the papers anymore. It's like every page is AIDS, AIDS, AIDS. I mean, whatever happened to the good old days when they had Porn Corner and pictures of the Dog Show? Now all you see are those goddamn obituaries. "In memory of Hank, who was only 47 and was so well-loved by all the guys at the Polk Street Saloon. We'll miss you at the Corn Holes." You'll notice it's never "In memory of Lance Matlock who just turned 21 and taught gymnastics. We'll miss you at the juice bar." (*Music up; turns to students.*) OK! Keep it going! Take it knee and kick! All right! (*Music down; walks center stage.*) And what's worse is that it's all you hear about in the bars. I mean, you're standing there cruising some cute guy and you hear him say something like, "Sixteen of my best friends and eight of my ex-lovers and seven of my roommates have died since March." I mean, that is soooo gross! What kind of crowd do you hang around with, sister? (*Bounces down left.*) Not to brag or anything, but I don't know anyone who's got it. And do you know why? 'Cause I hang out at the right places. Really. I mean, just look at the guys who get it. It's always like the older South of Market crowd with all their whips and stuff. If they would just stop all that grossness it would probably go away. (*Music up; to students*) All right! Kick it front! (*Walks center.*) But do you know what the worst thing is about AIDS? Having to hear about safe sex. Oh please! Just cause some guys get it don't tell me what I can't do in the sack! I mean, like every week there's some new chart telling what you can and can't do. What are you supposed to do, tape it to your pillow? "Stop that, Michael, it's not on the list!" Anyway, I'm not gonna let it get me down. I mean, do I look like a sick person? Be serious!

Music up; he leads his class back offstage.

Nobody's Fool
Markley Morris

PEACHES *strolls on, decked out in his finest summer clothes. He is an elderly gentleman of indeterminate age, although the amount of makeup he wears indicates he wishes to look younger than he is. He sits on a bench and leans back, soaking up the sun. After a few moments,* RICKY *hurries on, gym bag in hand, eager for a bus that is obviously late. Catching sight of* PEACHES, RICKY *stares—a bit too long, for* PEACHES *returns his glance.* RICKY, *embarrassed, looks away. After a moment, he stares at* PEACHES *again. This time* PEACHES *won't let him off so easily.*

PEACHES: You don't stop staring, you'll wear your eyes out. Is my mascara smeared? I'll tell you something. I've even got makeup on the backs of my hands. If you think I look odd wearing makeup, you should see me without. No, no, you shouldn't! You should have seen me a hundred years ago, when the glow in my cheeks was natural and I didn't give it a thought. Now when I walk down Polk Street on a sunny afternoon, nobody speaks to me. That's OK. I don't need to talk to those old queens. They know who I am. They know I'm Peaches, Queen of Larkin Street. Heads turn as I pass by. All those old girls who haven't gotten it up in fifteen years and who don't speak to me stare and whisper. Because they're jealous. You know what about? (*Leaning forward and whispering.*) I got AIDS. I am a person with AIDS.

RICKY, *disbelieving, walks away, looks for bus.*

PEACHES: I know what you're thinking. You're thinking, Peaches don't have AIDS, Peaches is too old to have AIDS. Well, it's true I'm no spring chicken. I'm not ashamed of it. I'm 77 years old. I'm the oldest person with AIDS, living or dead. And everybody

on Polk Street knows it. And they're jealous! Those lonely old
queens have visions of me catching AIDS: me surrounded by
cocks... (RICKY, *embarrassed, moves away.*) dozens of hard
cocks—and me sucking on these cocks—and these cocks cum-
ming inside me. Because I got AIDS. Don't that beat all?

Pause; RICKY, *hoping the worst is over, sneaks a glance at*
PEACHES, *who starts in immediately.*

PEACHES: They tell us we catch AIDS when we have sex. Because
queer sex is a sin. Isn't that what they say? Well, Peaches is here
to tell you that's a crock! Peaches ain't nobody's fool. Look at the
statistics: six percent of the men with AIDS are over 50. Two
percent are over 60. And I'm 77! Where you think us old geezers
are getting AIDS? Making out at the baths? Tricking at Buzz-
by's? Please, Louise! Let me tell you something. I got AIDS and I
haven't had sex in thirty years. You might not believe me but
cross my heart, that's the truth. Peaches, Queen of Larkin Street,
hasn't had sex with man, woman, or dog in thirty years. Here I
am before you, living proof that AIDS is not caused by queer sex.
And I'm no junkie and not a Haitian and I never had a blood
transfusion. *(Rises; crosses to* RICKY.*)* Blood transfusions, now
there's a thing! Easy to understand why they want to kill us
queers and junkies and Haitians—but how come nice middle
class people needing blood? I got a theory. What's the word for
these people needing blood? Homophiliacs! Sounds dirty, don't
it? We better kill them too. So the poor bleeders are getting AIDS
right along with the rest of us.

RICKY, *thoughtful, sits on the bench;* PEACHES *follows.*

PEACHES: You know the worst thing about having AIDS? It's the
doctors! One doctor didn't believe I hadn't had sex in thirty
years—he thought I was in the closet. *(Laughs.)* Listen, honey,
Peaches has never been in the closet—not since they kicked me
out of the Navy—and that was 1938. Conduct unbecoming. I
came right away to San Francisco, got me a sunny little apartment on Larkin Street, and I've been here ever since, happy as a
clam. Peaches ain't nobody's fool. Oh, those were the days. The
big war. The whole country turned upside down. San Francisco
full of uniforms—gorgeous. I was in heaven. Peaches wanted to
do her part for the war effort, so I sucked two military cocks a
day till the war was over. How come I gave sex up? I didn't. Sex
gave me up. I reached the age when I became sexually invisible.
That doctor, though, he just wouldn't believe me. "You must

have had some sexual contact!" he said. I said, "Honey, you making me an offer?" And he backed off pretty quick. But finally he pried it out of me. The one thing I didn't want to tell. My birthday treat. *(Pause.)* Each year on my birthday I give myself a present. I set aside fifty dollars and I hire a model from the ads in the back of the B.A.R. Over the phone I make clear exactly what I want. He comes to my place on Larkin Street in the late afternoon. I'm all dressed up for my birthday and wearing my purple scarf. I give him the fifty dollars when he comes in the door, so we don't have to worry about money. Then I go lie on my bed and cover myself with the afghan my grandmother made. We don't talk. I watch him take off his shirt. That's all he takes off, his shirt. Late afternoon sun pours through my window. I watch him standing in the sunlight, turning slowly, running his hands up and down his chest while I lie there, remembering. Finally I come. I lie there panting under the afghan and wipe myself off with a hand towel. I ask him to come over to the bed. When he comes over to me, I rub my fingers lightly over his chest. If his nipples are erect, I know he enjoyed it, and I invite him to share a birthday dinner with me at the P.S. But that's as far as it goes. I swear that's all that ever happens. It only happens once a year on my birthday and never with the same boy twice. That doctor, though, he just wouldn't believe me. He said these sores on the back of my hands are liver spots! Liver spots! I ask you, do these look like liver spots to you?

He holds out his hands to RICKY, *who looks at them, then at* PEACHES. *They* do *look like liver spots.* PEACHES *blushes.*

PEACHES: Well.... Got you to listen to me, didn't it? Now you keep on listening, because I've got more to say: it's clear as sunshine, AIDS is being forced on us by our enemies. *(Pulls out clippings and waves them around.)* I saw it on "60 Minutes"! The Army secretly gave LSD to soldiers in a VA hospital, remember? Also back in the '50s the CIA experimented with germ warfare—they released a flu virus right here in San Francisco. Hundreds got sick, a few people died. Is it any more far-fetched to suggest that AIDS might be yet another experiment, larger and more lethal? Was the AIDS virus secretly mixed into poppers? Or sprayed through the air conditioning of a particular bar? Or put into Lite beer? Lots of questions. Peaches don't have answers, but Peaches ain't nobody's fool. Peaches just sits here in the sun, with AIDS all around. And wonders. The next time a gay man gets sick, think about it.

PEACHES *blows* RICKY *a kiss, smiles, and exits.* RICKY *sits, thinking, alone.*

Party 1983
Paul Attinello

The metronome begins as soon as PEACHES *has walked off, then the countdown: 5-4-3-2-1. Horns and shouts of "HAPPY 1983!"* DOUG *runs on and pulls off the 2 on the sign as he shouts, to reveal the 3 beneath it.*

DOUG: One more year till Big Brother time! *(*DOUG *continues off;* PAUL *and* MATTHEW *enter.)*

PAUL: I don't see what the fuss is all about. I never gave blood, I'm sure.

MATTHEW: Yeah, well, they refused mine.

PAUL: What for? *(*SANDY *enters.)*

SANDY *(to* MATTHEW*)*: Greg, someone's looking for you on the deck.

   *(*MATTHEW *exits.* SANDY *speaks to* PAUL.*)* Of course he's cute, but —well, if you don't know what I mean by careless, I'm sure I can't tell you.

PAUL: That's easy for you to say, it's not your problem, is it?

   They exit. BOB *and* DOUG *pass through.*

BOB: No, it was silly of me, they just *looked* like needle tracks.

DOUG: Well, next time, think before you say something like that.

BOB: Why does it always have to be my fault?

   They continue out. ELLEN, CHUCK, *and* BRUCE *enter and sit on the couch.*

ELLEN: Well, actually, it's the tourist trade that worries me. People overreact to the slightest thing.

CHUCK: Oh God, what a capitalist thing to say.

ELLEN: No, I'm serious.

BRUCE: But what's so great about it is the opportunity to stabilize personal relationships. I was talking to my ex about it the other day...

CHUCK: Actually I think it's mental, you know? No guilt, no spots. *(*BOB *comes to the door and signals* ELLEN.*)*

ELLEN: I think that's for me. *(She exits.* MATTHEW *drifts in during the following speech.)*

CHUCK *(to* BRUCE*)*: See, if I thought there was a real risk, I'd probably slow down, but you know, they say you could catch it anywhere and, I mean, why bother? If I've got it, I've got it.

BRUCE: I think it's terrible when people like you are so careless as to. . .

MATTHEW: Hey, hey, calm down.

BRUCE: Well, it needs to be said.

DOUG *and* SANDY *enter.*

DOUG: Well, my shrink says it's this sort of neurotic fear of intimacy, you know what I mean? *(Sees* BRUCE, MATTHEW, CHUCK; *to* MATTHEW, *ignoring* BRUCE *)* Oh, hi, how have *you* been? *(Back to* SANDY *as they exit)* Anyway, his theory is that we all really need to. . .

BRUCE *stomps out.* MATTHEW, CHUCK *follow him out as* PAUL *and* BOB *enter.*

PAUL: Nosebleeds aren't one of the warning signs, you twit.

BOB: Well, I don't know. Anyway, it's all vitamins, really. My chiropractor has this book, and it. . .

PAUL: Hey, thanks, but I *have* a doctor.

They continue out.

Murray 1983
Leland Moss

MURRAY *enters, obviously upset and distracted. He pauses a moment, deciding what to do. Then he reaches for the phone and sits on the back of the couch, dialing Arnold. He speaks softly.*

MURRAY: Arnold, it's Murray. Are you busy? I've got to talk. . .I'm *not* good. . . .No, I mean I'm OK but—Arnold, you remember my friend Joe? *(Frustrated)* You know, you know the one from New Year's. . . .yes. . . . and you know I told you about his roommate Fred. . . .Well, Arnold, he's dead. Fred's dead. . . . It was that cancer, that Karposi's, you know, A-I-D-S that they're writing about. Arnold, it happened so fast I can't get over it. All these—they call them lesions?—they started popping up all over his body. Arnold, he used to be so cute, sort of like Sal Mineo, you know? And then this thing started spreading, and his face—my God, you wouldn't believe it—all puffy and it just didn't look like the same person. . . . Well, finally, Joe couldn't handle it anymore and he asked him to move out. . . . I know, but Arnold you didn't see what he looked like. *(He stands up.)* Wait a minute. . . . Arnold, will you WAIT A MINUTE? . . . . He moved in here. . . . Yes. . . . Yes, I put him up! *(Pacing.)* It *wasn't* easy, but my God what was he going to do? He was in no condition, and most of his friends—Arnold, I'm telling you it was shocking what some of those bastards did. . . . No, I talked to some doctors and they said as long as we didn't eat out of the same dish, you know, like that, that they thought it would be OK. . . . Well, I did sterilize a lot. But Arnold he was only here a few days. It got so bad I *had* to take him to the hospital. Arnold, that cancer had gotten inside him and on his throat and everywhere, the poor kid couldn't even swallow. Then he came down with some weird kind of pneumonia—and something I couldn't even pro- nounce. . . . Arnold he was 27 years old, he was a baby! *(He cries.)* Last Thursday. . . . Arnold, you're the first person I've talked to about this. . . . BECAUSE NOBODY WANTS TO HEAR, THAT'S WHY. *(He takes a deep breath; another.)* Well, I. . .*(Starts another deep breath; then, abruptly)* All right, enough with the deep breaths. *(Pacing again.)* Nothing. . . . What do you mean, what do I mean, nothing? Nothing is nothing! I don't know what to do with myself. Ar- nold, I have cleaned the apartment half a dozen times in the past three days. No, I will not go outside. No! Arnold, don't you know what is out there?? I have sworn off sex completely. I am terrified to kiss anyone, let alone do anything else. *(Sitting; slamming down the phone.)* Arnold, don't you realize it's people just like me who are getting it? The same people I have been screwing night and day for the last hundred years?. . . What?. . . You're kidding. Eddie? Our little Eddie Jampolis? But Arnold, he was practically a monk, he never. . . I don't get it, I just don't get it. What is happening to us? *(Pacing again.)* Oh yeah, you can talk, you sit home with your husband and your cute little boychick and play "I Love Lucy". . . . Come again?. . . . Wait a minute. Let me get this straight—Arnold Beckoff, also known as Kitty Litter, also known as Bertha Venation, is going to nursing school. Tell me another!. . . No, no, it sounds just fine, honey. MAMA IS PAYING? *(Shrieks with laughter.)* Well it figures, if she can't have a doctor, she'll settle for a nurse. . . . *(Laughs.)* Yeah, well, actually I'm waiting to hear. . . . Yes. Yes, a real job, it'll keep me occupied. . . . So I'll miss it, my whole life is a soap opera now anyway. . . . You're right, I should have call- ed sooner. . . . I don't know, Arnold, it's hard to meet people

here, everybody's kinda scared, you know? And I guess—I guess
I never really knew HOW to meet people—in the daylight...

Lights fade.

To Tell the Truth
Robert J. Stone

*The stage is black. Sound of the panelists' laughter. Lights up. Two
stagehands cross the stage and arrange the seats in the proper order.
As they do, the panelists appear, laughing and joking with each
other, very sophisticated and silly:* CONSTANCE GOODRICH,*elegant,
bejewelled, a fixture on the show;* CONGRESSMAN JIM SPENCER, *a
smooth-talking probable Reaganite;* TONI THYME, *a New Wave
songstress, dippy but bright; and* ANGEL BOCABLANCA, *a Puerto
Rican actor. When the set is ready, one technician calls out.*

TECHNICIAN: We're ready for you, Mr. Goodwin! (MODERATOR
bursts on to the scene, talking directly to the invisible camera.)
MODERATOR: Hi! Welcome to "To Tell the Truth." I'm Bob Goodwin, your host, and before I bring out today's mystery guest, I'd
like to introduce our celebrity panel. First, we have Constance
Goodrich. (TECHNICIAN *holds up* APPLAUSE *sign. Other
panelists, and audience, applaud* CONSTANCE.) A former Miss
America from the state of Idaho, Constance is a successful actress
and international spokesperson for Porcelana Skin Cream. On
her left is Congressman Jim Spencer of Missouri. (APPLAUSE
sign again.) A member of the House Ways and Means Committee, Jim and his brother Felix are co-founders of the Bowling Ball
Hall of Fame located in St. Louis. To Jim's left, we have Miss
Toni Thyme! (APPLAUSE.) An international recording artist,
Toni's new wave rendition of the Helen O'Connell song
"Tangerine" is now at the top of the pop charts. And last, but
certainly not least, is Angel Bocablanca! (APPLAUSE.) A former
model and break-dancer, Angel's new TV show starts this fall.
Entitled "Somoza Doesn't Live Here Anymore," it's a light-
hearted look at nuns in El Salvador. And now, panel, it's time for
our mystery guest. (*Theme music up; enter three contestants—
two men, one woman. They stand in front of their chairs as the
narrator reads.)* Before the questioning begins, I will read from
the signed affidavit our mystery guest has submitted: "I am a
person with AIDS. I am appearing here today without giving my
name because of potential repercussions for my family. I was

first diagnosed six months ago. Since that time my life has been turned upside down. I was forced to move from my apartment when my landlord learned of my health problem. I was fired from my job for the same reason and have no health insurance as a result. I have been refused service in restaurants when waiters have noticed the purplish spots on my arm from Kaposi's Sarcoma. Hoping to save other people with AIDS from the same indignities, I have initiated legal action against my former employer and my landlord. It is not likely that I will live long enough to see the cases go to trial. Hopefully, my appearance on this show will produce more immediately positive results for other people with AIDS. Signed, Mystery Guest." Well, if our guests will be seated, we'll begin the questioning with Constance Goodrich.

CONSTANCE: Thank you, Bob. Mystery Guest Number One, the Kaposi's lesions on your arms, have you had any treatments to get them to go away?

NUMBER 1: Yes, my doctor and I have tried chemotherapy, interferon, and megadoses of vitamin C, but they weren't successful. With KS, once a lesion appears, there's just no proven way to get it to disappear. But if you'll ship me a case, I'll give Porcelana a try.

CONSTANCE (flustered): Well, I . . . .

NUMBER 1: Don't worry, honey. I may be dying, but I haven't lost my sense of humor. I even saw a holistic healer who recommended coffee enemas, but they didn't agree with me. I think I was using too much Sweet 'N' Lo.

CONSTANCE: Uh . . . Number Two, did you frequent gay bathhouses?

NUMBER 2: No, never.

CONSTANCE: Number One, same question.

NUMBER 1: Yes, I used to go once a month. Twice, tops.

CONSTANCE: Tops? Hmm . . . Number Three, I thought women didn't get AIDS. How did you acquire the disease?

NUMBER 3: My doctors aren't sure. It may have been from a blood transfusion or possibly from a sexual contact. Over 7600 people have been diagnosed with AIDS in this country, and 500 of them have been women.

CONSTANCE: Thank you, dear. Number One, considering all the terrible things you have gone through due to AIDS, don't you think that we should all return to the exclusive practice of heterosexual behavior?

NUMBER 1: Oh, Connie, Connie, Connie—they've been practicing that for two thousand years and they *still* haven't got it right.

Anyway, the world needs exclusive heterosexuality about as much as it needs an all-white production of "Porgy and Bess."

MODERATOR: Time's up. Now we move the questioning to Congressman Spencer.

SPENCER: Thank you, Bob. Number Three, if you could ask Americans to do something to alleviate this crisis, what would it be?

NUMBER 3: Put pressure on people like yourself to provide funding for AIDS research. I feel that the government has been too slow in responding to the crisis. They also haven't demonstrated a genuine concern for saving human life.

SPENCER: Well, I feel that I must mention what our government has done. The Center for Disease Control in Atlanta, a federally funded agency, is committed to finding a cure. Also, the Reagan administration plans to spend $85 million in the 1985 fiscal year to fight AIDS.

NUMBER 3 *(interrupting* SPENCER): Excuse me, Congressman, but, first of all, the Reagan administration has refused to release those funds. And, second of all, how does $85 million compare to the defense budget?

SPENCER: National defense is a completely different issue, but I don't want to argue. Number Two, how do you feel about appearing in public as an AIDS victim?

NUMBER 2: Congressman, I'd like to correct your terminology. People with AIDS prefer to be called just that—"people with AIDS." The word "victim" carries too many negative connotations. As for how I feel, I guess I'm a little nervous about being on TV, but not because I have AIDS. I've just never been on TV before.

SPENCER: Don't worry. You look marvelous! Number One, what advice would you give to gays now?

NUMBER 1: I'd ask them to practice safe sex. There's been an old expression in the gay community about someone having the "dick of death"—well, it's not a metaphor anymore.

MODERATOR: Number One, I have to remind you that this is being taped for television. The last part of that response will have to be edited out of the show. PLEASE be more careful.

NUMBER 1: Where were you when I needed you?

MODERATOR: Congressman, please continue.

SPENCER: Guest Number One, has there been any creed or motto that has governed your life up to this point?

NUMBER 1: Yes: Always look your best for first dates and ex-lovers. Thank you.

MODERATOR: Time. Toni?

TONI: No, it's Toni Thyme.

MODERATOR: Yes, Toni. I meant that the Congressman's time was up and now it's your turn.

TONI: Oh, yeah, right. Like, I don't want to make anyone up tight or anything, but I'm totally freaked out by this. Uh, well, like if we have to meet you after the show and shake hands or something, am I gonna get AIDS—or what?? *(Pause.)*

MODERATOR: Toni, to whom are you addressing that question?

TONI: Oh, sorry, Number One—no, Number Thr—no, Number Two!

NUMBER 2: There's no evidence that casual contact of that nature can spread AIDS. *(A long pause;* TONI *has gotten lost in her thoughts.)*

MODERATOR: Toni, do you have another question?

TONI: Yes. Number Two again. How fast is it spreading?

NUMBER 2: There are about 150 new cases diagnosed each week in this country. In San Francisco, where I live, there are two new cases diagnosed every day. And although New York City has the highest number of AIDS cases, San Francisco has the highest per capita incidence of the disease.

TONI: How many people have died?

NUMBER 2: Over 3600.

TONI: Wow. Umm . . . Mystery Guest Number One, what is your occupation?

NUMBER 1: A welder . . . Just kidding! I'm a hairdresser.

TONI: I thought so. Number Two, same question.

NUMBER 2: I'm an attorney.

TONI: Number Three, same question.

NUMBER 3: I was a buyer for a major department store.

TONI *(screams with laughter):* Forgive me. Number One, if you're a beautician, you can tell me what coloring most ladies like my mom put on gray hair.

NUMBER 1: Piece o' cake! Clairol's White Minx. But most of them leave it on too long and end up with pale blue.

TONI: Do you think if I mixed a little black in with it, I could get purple? I've been trying to get a color to match this new dress I bought . . .

MODERATOR: Time.

TONI: What?

MODERATOR: No, Toni, I mean it's time to move to Angel.

TONI: I knew that.

MODERATOR: Angel, before you begin, why don't you tell us something about your next picture.

ANGEL OK, Bob. I'd be glad to. It's gonna be called "Unfinished

Melody." This one's a tragedy. It's about this female impersonator who tries to lip-synch the Hallelujah Chorus. He gets
murdered after his first attempt. I play the vocal coach.

MODERATOR: And who's going to play the female impersonator?

ANGEL: They've signed Michael Jackson, but the studio thinks he
talks funny. To give him an idea of how a man's supposed to
sound, they're having him listen to tapes of Lauren Bacall.

MODERATOR: Uh-huh. And how does Michael Jackson die?

ANGEL: Well, I don't exactly remember. But it has something to do
with a crucifix, Howdy Doody, the Mormon Tabernacle Choir,
and...uh....

MODERATOR: Well, it certainly sounds interesting. I can't wait to
see it. But for now, why don't you continue the questioning.

ANGEL: Sure thing, Bob. Number Three, do you feel that gay people
are responsible for this horrible disease because of their lifestyle?

NUMBER 3: First of all, I think you should know that I'm not gay,
I'm bisexual. But in any case, I don't think gay people are any
more responsible for AIDS than the American Legion was
responsible for Legionnaire's Disease. It just happened to them.
And now it's happening to me.

ANGEL: Number Two, isn't it true that this is really a white man's
disease?

NUMBER 2: Actually, no. Blacks make up twenty-five percent of all
reported AIDS cases, and Hispanics represent fourteen percent
of the total.

ANGEL: Madre de Dios! Of course, everyone knows I don't have
anything to worry about. Isn't that right, Toni? *(He touches a
part of her anatomy.)*

TONI: Oh, for sure. *(Covering herself up.)*

ANGEL: Number Two, when do they think a cure will be found?

NUMBER 2: No one can say. Scientists hope to have a blood test soon
to detect the presence of AIDS even before symptoms appear.
But a cure still seems to be several years away.

ANGEL: Number One, are safe sex practices the only sexual activity
we can advise for gay men at this time?

NUMBER 1: Yeah, I guess so. For the time being, gay men are pretty
much left holding their own, so to speak.

MODERATOR: Well, I'm sorry to have to interrupt, but we've exhausted our time for today. All right, panel, it's time to make
your choice. Is the real person with AIDS mystery guest Number
One, mystery guest Number Two, or mystery guest Number
Three? All ready? Constance, we'll begin with you. Tell us who
you selected and why.

CONSTANCE: Well, Bob, they were all just wonderful, and so convincing. But I voted for mystery guest Number One. I think it was his answer to Toni's hair coloring question that convinced me.

MODERATOR: Thank you, Constance. Congressman Spencer?

SPENCER: I cast my vote for mystery guest Number Two. He seemed so well informed that I feel he must be the real AIDS vic... uh, person with AIDS.

MODERATOR: Toni, who did you cast your vote for?

TONI: I voted for mystery guest Number One, too—three, four. *(Singing loudly)* Tangerine...

MODERATOR: Toni!

TONI *(laughs)*: Sorry, Bob. That's Number One—my vote AND my song. Got it?

MODERATOR: Yes, Toni, we got it. Angel, who did you vote for?

ANGEL: I voted for mystery guest Number Two, but I sincerely hope they are all imposters.

MODERATOR: Well, all the votes are cast. Now, will the real person with AIDS please stand up?

The three contestants look at each other, pause, then all three stand up sequentially.

Stronger and Stronger
Philip Real

Note: the original piece was written as a monologue for one man. In the production, however, the piece was staged using six men and two (silent) women, who moved between three different areas at intervals whenever the sound of a hospital bell was repeated three times. The areas represented a doctor's waiting room, a diagnostic room, and a hospital room. The women alternated between appearing as a receptionist in the waiting room and a nurse or doctor in the hospital room. The men who did not speak during a particular segment appeared as other waiting patients in the waiting room or the doctor or nurse checking the patient in the diagnostic or hospital room.

Sound of hospital bell rings three times, in group of four notes. After each sequence of four notes, the actors appear and freeze in position at each of the playing areas as follows: Waiting Room: PAUL, BRUCE, DONNA; Diagnostic Room: BILL, CHUCK; Hospital Room: BOB, RANDY.

PAUL: When they told me I had AIDS, I read every medical fact I could find about it. Five minutes later I was still confused. It's as though my body's gone ahead without me. I don't mind so much.

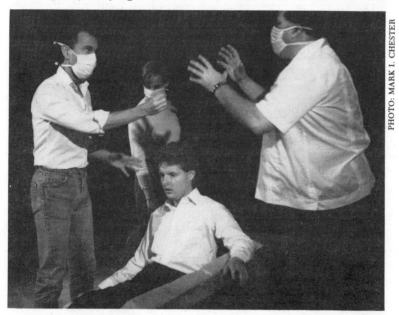

It can do whatever it wants. But I wish it would ask me first, at least as a formality.

BRUCE: I'm defenseless against infection. I try to clean it out, but nothing works. It was controlled for a while, but now I have lesions.

BOB: I've been taking interferon. The doctors are guarded. They're careful not to be overly optimistic. I feel that even though my immune system's shot, that somewhere in me, I'll find the resistance I need. Even if it's a tiny bit, that I can stretch it so it'll be enough to fight with. At least I've got one thing on my side. I never believed in statistics.

Waiting Room: SANDY, RANDY, CHUCK; *Diagnostic Room:* BOB, BRUCE; *Hospital Room:* BILL, DONNA, PAUL.

RANDY: I had health insurance from my job, but it stopped when they laid me off for being sick. I'd saved some money. That ran out the first time I went into the hospital. Now I have Medi-Cal. I have no financial worries. I have no money, so there's nothing to worry about.

CHUCK: I guess I mistreated myself sometimes. I pushed too hard.

But don't tell me I did it to myself because I didn't. I was healthy. It came out of the blue. Who ever heard of the immune system breaking down for no reason?

BILL: There's no cure. That fact has burned itself into my brain. They're working on it, looking for clues. The doctors don't know what to do. It must be hard on their egos. They're taught to be God, but they can't stop this.

RANDY: There seem to be precautions you can try, such as living in a controlled environment, like a shopping mall. I don't think I could take it.

BILL: Did I do something to deserve this? Did I go one step too far? Tell me what it was. I'll undo it. A touch, a kiss, a thought? Nobody knows. Another mystery.

Waiting Room: DONNA, BOB, RANDY; *Diagnostic Room:* PAUL, BILL; *Hospital Room:* BRUCE, CHUCK, SANDY.

BRUCE: I never had sex until I was 23. All the straight kids in my high school were running around fucking like bunnies, and I was saving myself for the right man, so I say straight people have a lot of nerve calling me promiscuous.

BOB: I guess I've kept at arm's length from respectability. I was afraid it would cramp my style. I had a cat once that was respectable. She got run over by a Buick. She limped away, and we didn't know where she'd gone until a week later, our neighbors' basement started to stink. They went down to look and found she'd gone there to die. I just hope I don't stink up anybody's basement when I die.

PAUL: I've scaled down a lot. There are things I know I can't have now, but that doesn't bother me. I have a lot already. I have my lover, Joe, who makes me laugh, and friends to spend time with. I'd like to live to be eighty, but we'll see. If nobody knows anything about this, why can't I show them you can survive?

Waiting Room: BRUCE, RANDY, SANDY; *Diagnostic Room:* CHUCK, BILL; *Hospital Room:* BOB, PAUL, DONNA.

CHUCK: I don't have a lot of will power. But this makes you change fast, whether you want to or not. I get tired easily. I have these pains. I fought them at first, but it didn't work, so now I try to go with them, hoping they'll ease off. They do, eventually.

BRUCE: A friend of mine was in intensive care. He had pneumocystis pneumonia. They put him on a respirator. I went to see him. It upset me a lot. I went out and got drunk afterwards. I never do that anymore, but I did it, anyway, that night. He died.

BOB: I feel like a cockroach somebody wants to squash.

RANDY: My friend's lover planted a tree in the park for him. If people would plant trees for me, I wish they'd plant them on ugly concrete streets that don't have them. But I don't want die to get that done.

BILL: Fortunately, Joe doesn't think of me as an invalid. He's too hypochondriac for that. When I found out I had AIDS, I thought he'd hate me. He moved in when I told him. I was depressed. I didn't accept getting sick gracefully. Joe reinforces me. I thought I'd shelter him from the storm. But he ended up sheltering me. He taught me a language that didn't exist. I love him in ways he doesn't understand. But then, I don't, either.

RANDY: I wish it was a political plot. I wish I could blame somebody specific, even myself. I wonder sometimes why one person gets sick, and somebody else stays healthy. I think there must have been some payoffs somewhere.

Waiting Room: BOB, PAUL, SANDY; *Diagnostic Room:* BRUCE, RANDY; *Hospital Room:* CHUCK, DONNA. BILL *exits.*

PAUL: It'd be so much easier to have something uncontroversial, like leukemia. I'm not a political person, so I shouldn't get a political disease. Sometimes I think I'll tell people I have measles and let it go at that. Somehow people aren't held morally responsible for having measles.

CHUCK: I don't mind staying in bed as long as I have attractive sheets. I hate the dizziness. I'm ashamed of it. I fight it, and that makes it worse. I wonder sometimes if I'm stretching farther than I can. (SANDY *exits.*)

BOB: Joe says my name—"Aaron"—*(Each man echoes the name.)* as though he's trying to ward off evil spirits. I love the texture of Joe's voice, the way he slides over words, how cynical he is, his harshness and his wildness. It'll keep death away. I know it will. I hear his voice in my head even when he's not there. He doesn't have to tell me it's all right because I know with him there, it is. (BOB *exits.*)

BRUCE: Sometimes I feel as though all the gay men I like are my lovers. I know their secrets. I hear their voices in my head when I'm sick and scared, and I feel like we can wrap ourselves in our voices and be safe because we care about each other. We can be at peace. I believe that. (BRUCE *exits.*)

CHUCK: I suppose I should be afraid of dying. It's the usual approach. But it takes too much energy. I thought if I had to die, I'd rather fade away from exhaustion. But I have no exhaustion left. It takes too much energy to be exhausted. I've left it behind. I just want to dissolve lightly in the air. (CHUCK *exits.*)

RANDY: I wrote a will, although it doesn't matter much because I don't have anything to leave. My main reason for wanting one was to keep people I can't stand from going to the funeral. But I didn't have the nerve to include that. (RANDY *exits.*)

PAUL: I want to go in a burst of light, a flash, and then disappear. I'd like to be reincarnated as a pair of blue jeans. A tight pair. At least I biodegrade.

Note: at this point in the original production, the following piece was inserted.

Hospital
Paul Attinello

PAUL *starts to exit, but at the sound of the hospital bells first* CHUCK, *then* SANDY, *then* DONNA *appear at the three exits, blocking his path. They all wear surgical masks and become, variously, doctors, nurses, visitors, relatives, swirling around* PAUL *who is the unwilling patient.*

PAUL: Wait, this isn't right. . .

DONNA: Darling, being right has nothing to do with it. We accept what happens and try to continue in spite of everything.

PAUL: You don't understand, it's not my turn to. . .

CHUCK: It's your turn, then it's my turn, it's everybody's turn. We all deal with it in our own way, at our own speed.

PAUL: I was just up here, I'm not supposed to. . .

SANDY: None of us supposes anything. I guess it just had your name on it.

BOB *(enters, masked):* I only wish it could have been me instead. Thank God it's not.

PAUL: Wait, I didn't agree to this, turn it off. . .

SANDY: Doctor, his temperature is hovering between a hundred and two and a hundred and three. . .

CHUCK: Respiration is—shallow and somewhat spastic; pulse is a little strange.

PAUL: I said turn it off! Stop it, I won't go through with this!

BOB: Facial expression is that of a hunted animal. . .

DONNA: I'm sorry, dear, but they're doing all they can.

CHUCK: Hey, is that dial really supposed to register two-twenty?

SANDY: Maybe we should leave?

BOB: Only if you feel you have to.

PAUL: How about me?

SANDY: Oh no, you can't leave, dear. Not now.
CHUCK: We'd better do it now and get it over.
DONNA: Please do *not* disturb the patient.
BOB: Well, look, one's collapsed already—I don't think it's good to. . .
CHUCK: Well, it worked once.
SANDY: I think he can hear you. . .
BOB: A prognosis? Well, at this point. . .
CHUCK: This won't work, get me another one.
DONNA: Please do *not* touch the patient.
BOB: I haven't ever used it this way, but if you say so. . .
CHUCK: Not worth a damn like that, turn it here. . .
SANDY: Can't he hear you?
CHUCK: Well, it worked once.
BOB: If we had more time. . .
CHUCK: Well, nothing ventured. . .
DONNA: Please do *not* think about the patient.
CHUCK: Not capable of much, but maybe still alive. . .
BOB: Watch it, there are malpractice suits for that.
CHUCK: I'm trying, dammit!
SANDY: He *can* hear you!

ALL FOUR (*start rather slowly and build speed and volume; go to chaos at the end, fragments of words.*)

Don't do that.
It wasn't my fault, I can only...
If we could just talk to him.
Get them out of here.
I have a gurney.
Perhaps you'd better wait outside.
Pull back there.
It's already too late.
Come back, please come back.
Gone yet?
We'll try, but don't really know.
Don't.
If I could just. . .
Stop. . .
Not yet, but. . .
Don't let him. . .

PAUL: Wait—
It'll be all right
I'll wait for you,
if they let me.
I want to...I saw the
world end,
it's bright, you can't see it,
but I see it at night—
so don't worry, but don't leave
me.
This can't be the last,
I'll get through this one too,
wake with another machine in
my arm,
my leg.
Why me?
Don't leave.
When?
Not now, not when I—
no *time*. . . STOP!

When PAUL *yells the last word, all four echo:* STOP!

PAUL: BUT I'M STILL ALIVE.

Note: The next speech is the last speech of Stronger and Stronger *and in the original production was delivered by* PAUL *as he lay in bed. The four other actors walk off during the last line of* Hospital.

PAUL: I feel like I'm being shoved against a wall. But the wall is soft. It folds me up like a goosedown quilt. I sink as though I'm on a featherbed, and bounce back out into the air. I feel like I'm being held by everyone I care about. The air is dangling around me. I'm *new*. I'm physical in the easiest way. No more pain. No more body pulling me back. I don't want to make a spectacle of myself, but no one seems to notice, so I might as well go ahead. I'm electrical. I have no resistance. I don't want to resist. This is a moment of transition. All I have are transitions, but I've never gone this far before. The words are pouring out of my brain, but the air is eating them up. I'm not dying, I'm changing. I'm changing the elements of my body into other elements. The muscles and the bones and the skin are changing to air. I've never been so human. Joe's squeezing my hand, and the hand is turning into bone, and the bone is spitting itself into the air. It's rushing out so fast nobody can see it. I don't mind. I keep changing all the time. I'm changing again. Just keep holding my hand. Keep me safe. Keep me.

Fade out.

Party 1984
Paul Attinello

Metronome starts, perceptibly slower. Mirror ball starts turning. Offstage countdown: 5-4-3-2-1—HAPPY 1984! BOB *runs on, followed by* DOUG *and* CHUCK, *and pulls off the 3 of the year sign.*

BOB *(calling offstage):* Just a Calistoga, thanks. You can't be too careful these days, if you know what I mean. *(He continues through;* CHUCK *stops* DOUG.)

CHUCK: Were you just talking to Hank's parents? His father looks like he's going to have a stroke if he hears one more word about...

DOUG: Well, if I did say anything, I didn't mean it like that. He's so touchy. Everybody's so touchy these days.

They exit. MATTHEW *crosses rapidly, angry. He speaks over his shoulder.*

MATTHEW: You didn't see me there. I don't go anymore. *(*SANDY *and* BRUCE *enter.)*

SANDY: I don't even know what to wear. I mean, black jeans, or what?

BRUCE: Don't ask me, the only funeral I remember is grandfather's, and we all wore dark suits.

SANDY: Well, I guess he only had himself to blame.

BRUCE: Hey, what is that supposed to mean?

SANDY: Oh, you know. Okay, okay, sorry, don't be that way. I mean, face it. . .

They exit. PAUL *enters, talking to a bored* CHUCK.

PAUL: Because somehow it doesn't click, you have a sort of—day personality, with precautions and things you don't do. You read brochures, and you notice articles, even the ones your mother sends you; and then, at night, it all washes away and you forget everything. . . and then in the morning, as you find your way through the streets to your own bed, sort of resolving something or other, not really about anything you did or didn't do, you see this space, like a fault line, a sort of. . .

CHUCK: Hey, that's really interesting. Listen, I'll see you in a minute, okay? I want to get another drink.

PAUL: Oh—well—I'll be here. *(*CHUCK *exits.* PAUL *sits, staring into space.* DOUG *and* BOB *enter.)*

DOUG: Guess we're rid of *him.* Anyway, this guy last night said, you can't catch anything from the end of a whip. So I left.

BOB: You think you have problems. This thing Ken's using, it's like a Hefty bag, I swear. Don't tell him this, since I said it was all right, but I've "had a headache" every night since. . .

DOUG: Well, you know, safety's not everything, is it?

They exit. ELLEN *enters, approaches* PAUL.

ELLEN *(gently):* Hey, what's wrong? You've been so strange all night.

PAUL: I don't know. . . . This morning, I woke up and noticed this purplish mark on my arm, right about here—I just sat on the bed and—thought about nothing for maybe five minutes. Of course, it was just a bruise.

ELLEN: I remember a time when everything seemed curable, one way or another. (CHUCK *dashes through, talking into the next room; as he crosses.*)

CHUCK: Hey, everybody, I have a joke: How does Anita Bryant spell relief?

ELLEN *(to PAUL, angry now):* I don't know why we can't have a simple, fun party without constantly harping on this. . . this. . .

PAUL *(after a beat):* Go on, say it. *Say it.*

Two beats; then blackout.

Alice
Markley Morris

ALICE *enters, walks nervously up and down. Clearly she's upset. She picks up the telephone, dials, waits while it rings.*

ALICE: Hello, Jimmy, it's your sister. How are you? Dying—yes, I know. Well, I'm glad you can still make little jokes. You're so brave. Look, Jimmy, how'd you sleep? Really? Not till 9:00? Gosh, that's fabulous, Jimmy.

Me? I did have trouble sleeping. Oh, thinking. My mind wouldn't stop. Oh, just things. Thinking about you. Hoping you'll be OK. Hoping you were having a good night. Watching the shadows move on the ceiling as the wind blew through the trees. Listening to the night noises. Listening to Norman breathing there beside me. Norman sleeps like a log. He really does. Doesn't roll over all night long. When he's asleep his breathing gets slow. I snuggle up to him, carefully so I won't wake him up, and listen to his breathing and I feel safe. That man makes me so happy it's hard to put into words. He's a rock. I don't know what I'd do without Norman. I try to slow my breathing down to match his and I can't breathe that slow and I end up gasping for air, so I try again. It made me remember when we were kids. Remember, Jimmy? The time we went to Yosemite for a whole week? I must have been thirteen and you were fifteen. We had to argue so to get Mom to let us go. You and me and Danny Moffat. I loved it. It was one of the perfect times in my whole life. I had such a crush on you and I had you alone day and night for a whole week. Well, almost alone. And I always put my sleeping bag right next to yours and it was like last night, I'd lie there and listen to you breathing, you instead of Norman. And when you were deep asleep, I'd inch my sleeping bag over and snuggle up to you. I swear I could feel your heart beating through the sleeping bags. I'd have been so embarrassed if you woke up, I'd have died. Did you know what a crush I had on you?

What? You? You had a crush on Danny Moffat? No, I had no idea! I swear, at that age I didn't even know men did it with each other.... Oh my God, it's gross. There I was snuggling up to you in the sleeping bag and dreaming dreams about you and all the time you were lying there dreaming about Danny Moffat. I can't believe it. Danny was so, so straight arrow. Did you and Danny ever.... Did you ever get it on?

What? Come on. He was one of the great loves of your life and nothing ever happened? Nothing? You must be kidding. Come on, Jimmy, I suppose the next thing you're going to tell me is that's how you caught AIDS, having wet dreams. Oh, I didn't mean to say that. No, I'm not trying to pry. No. We certainly don't have to talk about it. I'm sure it's better if we don't.

Jimmy, I apologize. Let's start again. Here I am phoning to cheer you up and I end up being dreadful. Oh, God, I sounded like Mother. That's one of my worst fears, you know, that I'll end up being like her.... Let's start again. I've got some really big news. Maybe the biggest happiest news of my entire life. Yes. I am going to have a baby. Yes, I swear! The doctor said I'm doing fine. But the best part is this: you know what Norman and I decided, Jimmy? If it's a boy, we'll name him after you. Is that OK? Do you like the idea of a little Jimmy carrying on in your place? Good. I hope it's a boy. Of course I hope he takes after you.

But there is one thing, Jimmy. I don't know how to put it. I promised Norman. I hope you'll understand. Not to see you anymore. It's only sensible, don't you agree? I mean, I'm not just thinking of myself, I'm thinking of the baby. Nobody knows what might happen to a baby. Norman says it would be criminal to run a risk. It breaks my heart, but now that we're starting a family we've got to be responsible. *(Pause.)*

Thank you for saying that, Jimmy. I knew you'd understand. I love you too. *(She begins speaking rapidly, on the verge of tears.)* I was really looking forward to taking care of you, to being your nurse. I've been having Florence Nightingale fantasies for months. I thought I'd come to your apartment every day and cook and do your laundry and be with you. I know you don't want to go to the hospital and I wanted to help. I want to be there when you need me. I really do. But I promised Norman. You understand. Good. Look, I'll keep phoning every day, OK? I'll really be here for you, Jimmy, only over the phone. You'll be in my thoughts every minute, you and the new Jimmy. And I'll keep praying for you, Jimmy. I really will. I hope that doesn't embarrass you. I'll pray they find a cure. Pray you get better. I know you'll beat this thing and when little Jimmy's born you'll be well, and we'll all, all of us . . . be so happy and we'll . . . go camping in Yosemite.

She slams down the phone. Blackout.

It's My Party
Doug Holsclaw

Three men at a slumber party, dressed in pajamas, shorts, robes, etc., dance in carrying the "Trivial Pursuit" board and accoutrements, set it up on a table down center.

CRAIG, TIM, STEVE *(singing)*: "It's my party and I'll cry if I want to, cry if I want to, cry if I want to. You would cry too if it happened to you."

GEORGE *(the host; entering with tray of drinks)*: My neighbors aren't going to appreciate this.

TIM: Oh chill out and sing along.

GEORGE: I don't know the words. I couldn't possibly, I'm not old enough.

CRAIG: Oh, please!

GEORGE: I only vaguely remember the sixties. Teething, pre-school, that sort of thing.

TIM: Whose turn is it?

STEVE: Mine. Orange—oh no, sports and leisure. How come I never get the pink cards?

CRAIG: Do you think they did that on purpose? Making the movie questions pink?

GEORGE: "What game challenges you to double in and double out?"

STEVE: Double in and double out?

CRAIG: A four way?

GEORGE: Sex is not a sport.

TIM: Speak for yourself.

GEORGE: It's been so long I've forgotten.

CRAIG: Remember sex? Knock-down, drag-out sex. Four orgasms, one in each room.

TIM: You only have three rooms, dear.

CRAIG: I never brought them home, I always went to their place— and, of course, I never dated anyone who didn't have at least two bedrooms.

STEVE: Double in and double out?

GEORGE: What about the time with the cowboy in the Volkswagen?

TIM: Bucket seats? Kinky. Do tell.

STEVE: What was a cowboy doing driving a Volkswagen?

CRAIG: It was his son's car. (*General reaction.*) His truck was at the cleaner's.

STEVE: Stop.

TIM (*makes sound of game show music to suggest time passing*): Don't we have a time limit on these questions?

CRAIG: We should.

GEORGE: Buzzzz.

STEVE: I give up.

GEORGE: Darts.

STEVE: Darts? Like the things in a blouse?

CRAIG: Darts like you throw at your ex-lover.

GEORGE: My turn.

STEVE: I fooled around in a jeep last week. It was hot but rather cramped. I had to go to the chiropractor the next day.

TIM: Wait a minute, I thought you were Sally Safe-Sex. Safe sex in a jeep?

STEVE: We had the emergency brake on.

TIM: You and your safe sex. I figure if I don't have it by now, I'm not going to get it.

CRAIG, STEVE, *and* GEORGE (*in unison*): But there's a two-year

(CRAIG *says* ten-year; GEORGE *says* five-year) incubation period!

TIM: Oh fuck it. You can get hit by a truck crossing the street.

CRAIG: Darling, you get AIDS, you'll wish you had been.

GEORGE: Pink.

CRAIG: You always get the pinks.

GEORGE: Karma.

TIM: Ladies! *(Pulls card; reads.)* What substance did Fred MacMurray invent in "The Absent-Minded Professor"?

STEVE: Fred MacMurray of "My Three Sons"?

TIM: The same.

STEVE: Father of Chip and Ernie Douglas?

GEORGE: And Rob! Oh, I used to jerk off over Rob all the time, and I know the answer—Flubber!

TIM: Aaah! He's right!

CRAIG: You're kidding!

TIM: Flubber? Rob Douglas? For a person who was in preschool during the sixties, you sure know a lot.

GEORGE: Reruns, sweetheart.

CRAIG: Your surgeon did an excellent job.

STEVE: It's makeup.

GEORGE: I don't wear makeup. This is a tattoo. I just shower and blowdry my face. Perfect every time.

STEVE: When did you order that pizza?

GEORGE: While we were playing beauty parlor.

STEVE: Where did you order it from?

GEORGE: Alphonso's.

CRAIG: They're terrible.

GEORGE: I know, but the delivery boy looks like Matt Dillon.

TIM: So what are you going to do when he gets here, put on a wet suit and wrestle?

CRAIG: That doesn't sound too bad.

STEVE: Listen, you don't have to give up everything. You can still have a good time without exchanging body fluids.

CRAIG: Oh, body fluids! I love body fluids, I miss body fluids, I want body fluids!

GEORGE: I want pizza. It's blue—shoot.

TIM: But put on a rubber first. (TIM, CRAIG, *and* GEORGE *laugh.)*

STEVE: Don't make fun. I don't like this mess any better than you, but what choice do I have?

TIM: Well, I'm careful. I'm no slut.

CRAIG: Yes, you are.

STEVE: You are a slut.

GEORGE: He's a slut.

TIM: I'm not a slut! Fuck you!

STEVE: We're just concerned about the health of your heinie.

TIM: My heinie is just fine, thank you.

GEORGE: Blue please.

TIM (*pulls card*): In what country did Venetian blinds originate?

STEVE: Oh, that's easy.

TIM: Any moron could get that.

GEORGE: It's a trick question, it's too easy.

CRAIG: Well, what is it?

TIM (*throws card on board*): I'm not a slut! If I were a slut, would I be here with you when I could be out having a good time?

STEVE: Gee, thanks.

TIM: You're too paranoid. I don't think a virus causes it, I think it's all guilt.

CRAIG: And let me guess, you don't feel guilty.

GEORGE: I'm going to say Japan.

STEVE: Get real.

GEORGE: It's a wild guess, I'm losing anyway.

CRAIG (*picking up card*): You know it's Italy, it's got to be Italy. It's—Japan! You looked, you cheated!

GEORGE: I swear I never had that question before.

TIM: Well, what do you say to guys? Wanna come home and rub?

GEORGE: That's not bad.

CRAIG: I'll try that line.

STEVE: Don't tell them anything, just push them away when they start to do something unsafe.

TIM: Don't they get mad?

STEVE: Yes, it can be real hot.

CRAIG: Half of them say it's okay and then end up chasing you around the bed anyway.

STEVE: I used to be very civilized. "I hate to bring this up, but I'm sure you are aware of the health crisis and I've made certain decisions about how to conduct my life and I think we can still enjoy ourselves, etc., etc." And then they say, "Don't tell me you're one of those."

TIM: Terrific.

STEVE: Now I'm much more blunt: "You've heard of safe sex? Well, that's what I do."

TIM: What about kissing?

CRAIG: You can't even kiss?

GEORGE: Is spit body fluid?

STEVE: They used to say wet kissing was okay as long as there was no blood.

TIM: Blood?!

STEVE: Yeah, like from flossing.

TIM: That's too much.

STEVE: Now they have a pamphlet out that says June 1984 Safe Sex Practices, and they have wet kissing listed as possibly safe.

CRAIG: So if you kissed before June you're okay?

GEORGE: Pink again

CRAIG (*pulls card*): What weapon is tattooed on Glen Campbell's arm?

STEVE: You're making that up!

CRAIG: Glen Campbell has a tattoo? Oh baby!

GEORGE: You like Glen Campbell?

CRAIG: Well, he's better than Robby Douglas.

TIM: And guys go along with it?

STEVE: Most. Some get belligerent. When I'm finished, I say, "You're lucky you met me tonight and not someone else. We both came and it felt just as good and now you've got nothing to worry about. Everybody gets a good night's sleep."

TIM: Do you ever use a rubber?

GEORGE: A gun.

TIM: You use a gun?

GEORGE: On Glen Campbell's arm.

STEVE: Glen Campbell has a rubber tattooed on his arm?

CRAIG: No, a gun, but that's wrong. It's a dagger.

GEORGE: That's ridiculous. Who would know that?

CRAIG: Tanya Tucker. (*Replaces card; throws die.*)

TIM: I guess I should be more careful, but rubbers, gloves, to kiss or not to kiss—I just can't deal.

GEORGE: Can't women still get pregnant using a rubber?

STEVE: That's how I got here.

CRAIG: Green, please. What's that?

GEORGE: Science.

CRAIG: Shit.

STEVE: Believe it or not, it forces me to be more creative. I've had men tell me it's the best sex they've ever had.

GEORGE (*pulls card*): What's the strongest muscle in the body?

CRAIG: Whose body, mine or the normal person's? Never mind, I'll say the heart.

GEORGE: Wrong. The tongue.

CRAIG: That ain't my strongest muscle.

GEORGE: Honey, that muscle was stretched out years ago.

CRAIG: I'll have you know I can still break the lead on a number two pencil.

TIM: But I like sex. I like to get drunk and smoke grass and use poppers and fuck with strangers. Call me old-fashioned, but that's what I like.

CRAIG: Me too.

GEORGE: I can't take this. I'm getting depressed.

TIM: I'm getting horny.

STEVE: Well, let's have a circle jerk.

GEORGE: You wanna?

TIM: Is that safe?

CRAIG: Are you kidding?

STEVE: What do you think?

TIM: God, it's been years.

CRAIG: Wouldn't that be like—you know—incest?

STEVE: Dry incest, it's on the list.

GEORGE: Well. . .

TIM: Well. . . *(The doorbell rings, they all scream, startled.)*

GEORGE: Shit, it's the pizza.

Safe Livin' in Dangerous Times
Karl Brown
Matthew McQueen

So many ways that people die—
    (Safe livin' in dangerous times)
A car on the street, a bomb from the sky—
    (Safe livin')
But livin' with fear is no damn fun
Watching my friends die one by one

I'm no fool, I want to survive.
I think it's time we opened our eyes
To the possibility something's wrong
The nurse is scared—her gloves are on.

Safe livin' in dangerous times,
Safe livin' in dangerous times,
Safe livin'—in desperate times.

I don't want to preach or sound like a fool
I don't like jokes, don't want to be cruel—
Morality plays are not what we need,
Just find a cure for this damn disease!

Don't be flip, it could happen to you—
Doctors, lawyers, housewives too—
Help your lovers, help your friends,
Now's the time to lend a hand!

Safe livin' in dangerous times,
Safe livin' in dangerous times,
Safe livin'—in desperate times!

Land's End
William Barksdale

BILL *enters, dressed in a windbreaker and jeans. Sits center stage.*

BILL: Hi honey. . . . I don't know if you can hear me. . . but I just
really need to talk to you right now. . . so I will, and maybe
you're listening. . . . I come to this spot a lot now. . . to watch the
bay, the Golden Gate. . . some ships sailing out to sea. . . I think
of you as being here. A lot's happened since you died. . . nearly a
year has passed. . . Earth time. *(Chuckles.)* Sometimes at work or
when I'm sitting in your old room, I glance at a picture of you
and suddenly I find myself at another time. . . two of us standing
next to that icy creek on Mt. Hood, you walking up the beach by
Syreeta's house. . . . I remember you didn't want me to take that
picture because you weighed 185 pounds. . . . I don't have any
pictures of you when you only weighed a hundred. I felt helpless
then to provide you with whatever it was you really needed. . . .
I guess you needed something I couldn't give you. *(Pause.)* I miss
you so much. . . I want to hold you tight and close. . . sometimes
my whole body aches from the hollow feeling—there's nothing I
can do except sit back. . . . It hurts. . . for a while. *(Pause. He col-
lects himself.)* I was really shaken when you died. . . . Guess I'd
always assumed we'd grow old together. . . somewhere in the
country. . . houses we built ourselves. . . Joe. . . Markie. . . sunny
days. . . carrying wood. . . maybe we are old. *(Pause.)* Anyway
. . . I called your mother on Mother's Day. . . . We stay in
touch. . . . She's OK. . . she misses you a lot. . . . She said she
followed a guy all through a shopping center the other day be-

cause, she swears, he looked just like you. . . same hair, everything. . . he even had on five pair of pierced earrings. . . . She's
going to stop by on her way to LA for Christmas. When we were
hanging up I said "I love you." She said, "What?". . . . I said, "I
love you." "Just wanted to make sure I heard you right," she
said. . . "I love you too." *(Pause.)* I did not have an "estate sale"
just as you requested. . . gave many things away to friends. . . I
kept your dance costumes. Your old closet still smells like you. . .
ten years of familiar smells. I stick my head in there sometimes
. . . take a big whiff. . . . Someday it will just smell like a regular
closet. *(Pause.)* I feel you around me. . . especially at this spot
where you used to sit. . . watch the sun set. . . listen to the waves
. . . think. . . . Not much else to say I guess except that I love
you. . . I always will.

Party 1985
Paul Attinello

Mirror ball starts spinning. Metronome is perceptibly slower.
BRUCE *and* DOUG *cross through.*

BRUCE: No, the family is handling the estate. I was lucky to get to
keep his letters.

DOUG: I know. Lance and I were going to buy the house, but now
what's the point?

They exit. BOB *and* ELLEN *enter; stop, looking into next room.*

BOB: Sorry, you know me and names, who was that woman?

ELLEN: Which—the brunette or the red dress?

BOB: I guess the brunette. . .

ELLEN: Oh, she's here with the big guy. In the polo shirt. Hey,
there's Sally, I thought she was out of town.

BOB: You mean that one? I thought he was here with the guy in the
green sweater. . .

ELLEN: No, no, they just met, I think. He's with the two guys by the
couch.

BOB: But they came in later. . .

ELLEN: No, they went out for more ice or something. Jesus, Nan
sure looks weird in that green thing. Anyway, the first time, they
came in together.

BOB: But what about the big blond guy?

ELLEN: What about him, Bob?

BOB: Haven't I met him with someone else—dark hair, moustache? Tall?

ELLEN: Oh, him. I know who you mean. He's dead.

> BOB *stares at* ELLEN *for a moment, then follows her out.* SANDY *and* CHUCK *enter.*

SANDY: He still *smokes*? You'd think he'd change some habits by now.

CHUCK: What good would that do?

SANDY: Anyway, I think it's really tacky that he would be trying to have all those places closed down. I mean, what business is it of. . .

CHUCK: I don't think we should close them; I think we should burn them.

SANDY: Oh, well, suit yourself.

CHUCK: It's his own fault, after all.

SANDY *(heated)*: That's not fair! I'm sure he never did anything to deserve. . . (CHUCK *exits.* PAUL *enters and fixes his attention on* SANDY)

PAUL: The air, the water, don't touch the. . . You know this city is really small. I mean, really, small. So what if it got everywhere, you know, because they don't know how it's spread, and it might be real easy to catch; and then, the incubation period, two years, ten years? What would they do, if suddenly everybody had it—and I mean everybody; they would seal us off, maybe bomb Daly City; you can see them destroying the bridges, the skyline burning. . . . It's not much land, really. Airlifts, maybe some helicopters—or *would* they drop us food? Can you see the six hundred thousand of us trying to survive? What would we do? (MATTHEW *runs on, shouting.*)

MATTHEW: Hey, everybody. It's almost time!

ALL (offstage): 5-4-3-2-1! HAPPY 1985!

> *All party guests enter. Hubbub ad-lib as at beginning, but muted; little laughter.*

BRUCE: I'm sorry, how clumsy, let me buy you a new one.

CHUCK: Thanks, but we've got to be going. No, really.

ELLEN: Don't you know when you've had enough?

SANDY: Are you all right? Well, you look so pale. . .

> *All exit except* DOUG *and* MATTHEW. BOB *crosses, alone.*

BOB: Somebody please take me home, please. . . (BOB *continues out.* DOUG *and* MATTHEW *smile uncertainly at each other.* MAT-

THEW *moves in for a kiss.*)

MATTHEW: Where have you been all night? (DOUG *offers him his hand.*)

DOUG: Happy 1985.

MATTHEW (*disappointed*): Oh. Thanks.

They part, embarrassed. Lights dim; metronome trails off.

Mama's Boy
Adele Prandini

DONNA *enters, carrying load of laundry in basket. Sets basket on couch and starts to fold laundry. Stops, smiles, remembering.*

DONNA: Somewhere in the cellar there's a box. In that box are two thousand, seven hundred and twenty-four baseball cards. Seven hundred and fifty-three bear the likeness of a Mr. Willie Mc-Covey. My son loved baseball. One of the happiest days of his childhood was when he finally got his first uniform. Anderson's Feed and Grain, in red letterin' 'cross the back of it. For two weeks he wore it every day. While all the other mothers managed clean bright white pants, his affection for sliding into second left his with a permanent gray patch on the back of the left thigh. Ask any mother, they don't stay young for long.

It broke my heart when he left home to live out in California. "I love you, Mama, but I can never be what you want me to be." At the time I didn't understand; what was so terrible about growing up, getting married, and becoming the mayor, or least the coach at the high school? I didn't have much imagination then. But he did. He was going to California and was gonna get himself on the radio.... Well, he didn't. He almost did, but he didn't. He wound up as a camera man for one of those educational stations out there. Well, I was real proud of him. That's when I started watching educational TV. One day I was doing my ironing, watching one of them San Francisco stations, cuz that's where he lived. Do you know what? There he was, sittin' on some kind of panel or something. I picked up the phone and started to call my friend Muriel. Then they announced what the show was about. I hung up on Muriel without even saying hello. My boy was sitting there with another boy talking about being family. . . in the same house. You know what I mean? Well, I burnt a hole clean through the shirt I was workin' on. That house could of come down around me, but I wouldn't of moved. To this day Muriel wonders who interrupted her facial.

I loved my boy, even if I didn't understand him. And I knew he was raised right. I saw to that. For months and months I asked myself one question. Why? Why my boy? The next summer he came out to visit. I watched him like a hawk, to see if he was any different, see if he'd changed. I couldn't find a thing. I never told him about the TV show. For some reason I felt like I was spying on him. Like readin' his diary or openin' his mail. I never told his father, neither. If I didn't understand this thing, I knew he would never understand it. I just kept asking myself why.

About a year later something happened here in town. Frank Jenkins worked for the druggist here. Frank never hurt nobody. Everyone said he was that way, but he stayed to himself pretty much. One night as he was walking home from work, he ran into Bobby Carter, Big Joe Hale, and some other men. These men from the bar been drinkin' pretty heavy. At the trial they said Frank was talkin' dirty to one of them. Now everybody knew Frank was queer, but he wasn't crazy. He sure wouldn't say nothin' to a bunch of drunken farm hands. They say that his talkin' dirty made 'em so mad they lost control. Frank died in the alley next to the bar. . . . I knew why my son moved to California.

When my son got sick, I asked myself the same question again. Why? Big Joe's wife been to the hospital more than once with a broken nose. From walkin' into the door, she said. But Joe's walkin' around healthy and free. Why? By the time I got myself out to California, my son was in the hospital. I couldn't hold my boy cuz there were so many machines hooked up to him. After some hours the doctor came in to talk to me. He said it was time to make a decision. He said it was my decision. I looked at my son's friend. "No, Doctor, it's our decision." We turned off them machines. . . . My son, my boy, died twenty-four minutes later.

I took a cab to my son's home to be with his family. I gave the driver the address and he said something about being careful not to catch a disease in that neighborhood. I asked that young man if he'd ever seen anybody die. . . . "Sure lady, I was in Nam. Did my share of the killin', too." Inside I asked myself that question, that same damned question.

Murray Now
Leland Moss

The phone on stage rings. MURRAY *runs on to answer it, well-dressed and getting ready for company. He is staring intently at an imaginary TV in the corner of the room, annoyed by the phone.*

MURRAY: Hello?... Arnold! Hi, hon, how ya doin'? Good....
Yeah. Wait, hold on one sec, will you, I've just got to put it on
hold. *(He pushes a button under the imaginary TV.)* OK....
The Betamax.... Oh, didn't I? Oh honey it's changed my life!
..."All My Children," what else? Every day right after work!
...Yeah, it's not so bad. Half the queens in town work at the
phone company!... Yeah, I have, actually. Very nice people.
We went on a picnic last week out to Mt. Tam....Tamalpais
...I don't know, it's somewhere west of here—no, no, that
couldn't be—east, uh, no, uh—well, anyway, honey it's gorgeous. I never knew outdoors could be so much fun!... Well, the
hiking got a little strenuous for my taste. I didn't know what kind
of shoes to wear, but Robert seemed to take it in stride....
Robert.... Honey, how long has it been since we talked??...
Well, I don't know, you can't say "boy friend." Not yet anyway,
we've only been out a couple of times.... And the weird thing
is, Arnold, we haven't even had sex yet. Just kissed.... Very
romantic, yeah, and frustrating as hell. I tell you, I do not know
how those straight people did it.... Yeah, I guess we are. But
Arnold it's weird, the better I get to know him the less I want to
carry on like I used to.... No I still carry on, but mostly it's on
the phone.... Yeah, you know, you call up people and you talk
dirty to each other.... It is not disgusting, it's liberated!
(Laughs with Arnold.) Well, it was a little weird at first. I mean,
who knew from electronic glory holes? But after a while you get
used to it, and now it is amazing, I mean I am actually in awe.
Gay men are the most adaptable species on the face of this earth.
Who needs the baths? Nowadays you can pick up a phone and
get exactly what you used to get there.... Lust, lies, and attitude!... Well, it is strange, I'll tell you. Problem is, I just don't
know what turns me on anymore. I do know I like to be touched.
But—not anymore by strangers.... Yeah.... Speaking of
whom, I can't talk!... Well, Robert's coming for dinner
and...I am!... Give me a break, will you? I learned. I took a
course.... All right. We're having carrot soup, zucchini
quiche—shaddup....He's bringing the salad, and I made my

Aunt Tillie's coffee cake for dessert.... Listen, it worked for her four times, it should work for me once! *(Laughs with Arnold.)* OK. Yeah. Soon, OK. *(About to hang up; remembers something.)* Wait, wait, Arnold? Hey. How long have we known each other?... Isn't that incredible?... No, no, I just wanted to say —in all that time, I don't know if I ever told you—you mean a lot to me.... Thanks. I love you too.

He hangs up and smiles; fade out.

The Bar
Robert J. Stone

Music up. BOB *dances out, soon followed by the rest of the cast. All use whistles, tambourines, the latest dance paraphernalia. Song continues, till cast forms semi-circle. Music stops and* BOB *speaks.*

BOB: There have been a lot of dance bars in my life in San Francisco.

Once a week I light up a joint, get out my boogie shoes, and drive over to this year's favorite dance bar.

Music; dancers gradually form check pattern. Music stops, they freeze.

BOB: In the late seventies, you could go dancing everywhere. But since John Travolta *(Dancers pose in Travolta "Saturday Night Fever" fashion.)* and NIK-NIK shirts killed disco, it's gotten harder to find the right music, the right place, and the right crowd.

Music; at climax, dancers all jump in unison and crouch in circle around BOB.*)*

BOB: Some of my friends are pretty worried. They're so afraid of AIDS that they're talking about giving up sex. Well, I can tell you this: you don't get AIDS from dancing or I'd be dead by now.

Music; BOB *dances with* RANDY. *Music stops, freeze.*

BOB: And as far as sex goes, well—maybe I should settle down with someone and be monogamous. For years people have said that's the right thing to do. But every time I try it, I end up sitting at home while he's out screwing around.

RANDY *back to circle. Music;* BOB *dances with* DOUG; *freeze.*

BOB: Sometimes I'm not sure how to handle sex. I know there's no knight in shining armor on the horizon. And if there were, I'd probably be safer dating his horse.

Music; general dancing till freeze when all dancers face upstage.

BOB: But, I haven't stopped loving or touching the people I'm close to. Only now I don't have to go home with a man to appreciate his beauty. And I don't have to have sex with someone in order to love them. If there *is* a positive side to AIDS, I guess that's it. But listen, I didn't mean to preach or lecture, I just want to have a good time. So if you see me on the dance floor some night, say hello—and ask me to dance. I'd love to.

SANDY *asks* BOB *to dance; all dance off.*

Spice Queen
Doug Holsclaw

DOUG: I never really thought of myself as a hustler until that day. I mean, the kindness of strangers and all, but consciously hustling —never. I left Reno when I was eighteen. I mean, what was I going to do? Become a Keno girl? It was hard at first. I was living in this sleazy hotel in the Tenderloin, and you're damn straight I could be had for the price of a dinner.

But that day I was sitting on the stoop in front of the hotel and this mailman comes by. And he says, "You look like you could use a little help," and I was so stupid, I was so naive, I said, "You have a job for me? You have kids? I'll babysit, I'm great with kids." And then he offers me twenty bucks for a hand job. And I said, "Thank you. Thank you! Because if I look so bad that a pig like you thinks he can say that to me, then it's a good thing I found out now." The next day I got dressed up in the only decent clothes I owned and I got that job at the Ben Her Bookstore, and I kept it for a year and a half.

That's where I met Jeffrey, and we hit it off immediately—girl-friends, sisters—nothing more. We did everything together, and fight! Vicious! That girl could be Cruella DeVille sometimes. Once, on Memorial Day, we went on a picnic to Land's End and I made potato salad. The recipe said to garnish with paprika, right? So I went out and bought paprika and sprinkled it over the top. Well, you should have heard that one with the paprika jokes. He kept calling me Donna Reed like I'm bourgeois—because I garnish my salads? Please. It became a big joke between us. He called me a paprika queen for days.

But together we clawed our way off Polk Street. I think we did very well for ourselves. I got into catering, and Jeffrey worked his way up to assistant manager at Waldenbooks. I mean, I think the fact that he even had health insurance when all this started says a lot.

The day he found out he was pissed off! He sent a telegram to the CIA: "I'm dying. Do you have an antidote?" We laughed about it later and he would always tell visitors to speak into the flowers. He said he wanted his ashes sprinkled over the dance floor at Trocadero at midnight on New Year's Eve. Talk about fairy dust! *(Looking up.)* Just kidding—I didn't mean it—I'm sorry!

The bartender is giving me dirty looks. He doesn't like me to talk about it, he says it's a social downer. *(To bartender)* Well, if Eartha Kitt could stand up and speak her mind at the White House, I can sure as hell speak mine in a dive like this! *(To audience)* You see, in this land of free speech, the dying are supposed to go quietly for the sake of the living. Well, Jeffrey shattered the myth of the dignified death. He was pissed off, and he didn't care who knew it. He said fuck "Death Be Not Proud" and "Marcus Welby" and "Love Story" and "Brian's Song" and "Bang the Drum Slowly." He had this voracious kind of self-pity that is usually reserved for homeowners who have lost their belongings in mud slides.

It was a strain being around him, it wasn't easy. But I admired him for it. And I think some of the nurses did too. Sometimes, behind their clenched jaws and pinched little smiles you could see them thinking, "Good for you. I don't blame you, I'd be mad too. Why do you have to be on my floor? But good for you."

Towards the end it got really bad, he got some kind of fungus and his toenails started falling out. I just couldn't take it anymore. One day I just lost it. I said, "Take me, honest to God, if I could trade places with you I would. Don't take him, take me!" And Jeffrey tried to comfort me. He said, "Oh, come on now, you know you don't really mean that." And I said, "You're right, take Nancy Reagan!"

Well, he laughed so hard he tore the tube out of his nose and we had to ring for the nurse. It wasn't pretty. I don't know. Sometimes it all seems like a dream. I look around and nothing's changed, it's business as usual. Of course, some men would have sex in a burning building. But I don't know, I think if I were eighteen and in Reno today, I wouldn't leave. Talk about depressing.

It's harder on holidays. Easter, the Fourth, his birthday, my birthday. Halloween! Oh, Halloween is going to be a bitch this year. We had such a wonderful idea, we were going to go as Olivia de Havilland and Joan Fontaine. Memorial Day was hard. I didn't go to Land's End this year, I went to the cemetery. But I didn't put flowers on his grave, I just sprinkled a little paprika.

Invitation (Part Two)
Dan Turner

With CAL's *first line delivered as he walks on, the other men appear and arrange the seats into the original configuration.*

CAL: All right, let's talk about sex. *(Chorus of groans, laughter.)* Come on, come on, it's time to heat up this party. I have a few questions here, why don't you take your pick: What was your most poignant love affair? What was your favorite sex act before diagnosis? And after diagnosis? *(Hesitation.)* Well, come on, let's hear some dirt.

DAN: That reminds me about the time I told the people at the Health Department about my diaries—the fact that they list every sexual contact since 1974.

BOBBI: Sort of like a Book of Lists?

DAN: With a few exceptions. I wanted to do a book of poems dedicated to each one of them entitled, "You Thought I Forgot You."

ELBERT: My most poignant love affair is the same one I've had for the last sixteen years.

MICHAEL: Sixteen years! I wonder if I could love someone for sixteen years.

BOBBI: Maybe now. AIDS has the effect of acting like a matchmaker, you know.

DAN: I'm lucky I met my lover after I was diagnosed. He's the first man who used that word—*lover*—to introduce me as "my lover." Who would have thought that could happen after living single in San Francisco for ten years?

TOM: I haven't had sex with anyone for over a year. But before that, it was everything.

ARTIE: What about now? Can you do everything by yourself?

TOM: If you have a good imagination. Never underestimate the power of the mind.

DAN *gets up, moves away from the table.* MICHAEL *follows.*

MICHAEL: Dan—what's wrong?

DAN: This kind of talk is so depressing. Look at the other people in here. We're talking about something they probably never have to worry about. Here we sit overlooking the Continental Divide, and when I think about what it is that really divides us from them, I just get angry.

MICHAEL: Can I get angry for you? Tell me what I can do.

DAN: Let's just finish dinner and enjoy the fact that we're in each other's company—and laugh.

MICHAEL: Could I kiss the breadcrumbs off your cheek?

DAN: You can even kiss my lips. You might get garlic, but you won't get AIDS.

MICHAEL *(kisses* DAN*):* Thanks for the dinner and the conversation and the company.

DAN: You're welcome. (DAN *returns to the circle. As he sits, all freeeze in position.*)

MICHAEL *(to audience):* A year later two are gone. (BOBBI *and* ROGER *leave the stage.*) The man from Colorado and the man who made the reservations. Looking back, I realize now that accepting that invitation to dinner that night was probably the first step in overcoming my fear. I could sit down to dinner with thirteen people with AIDS again. I could sit down with twenty. (*He moves to rejoin the circle.*) In fact, I think I could be a person with AIDS myself. It's not so bad to be a person.

He takes hold of the hand of the man to his left, then the man to his right. All soon join hands. When the last two men have clasped hands, MICHAEL *looks directly at the audience. Lights dim.*

Coyote VI:
The Sacred Dump
Murray Mednick

Coyote VI: The Sacred Dump was first presented at the Padua Hills Playwrights' Festival in Claremont, California, on July 16, 1983, with the following cast:

CLOWN	Priscilla Cohen
SPIDER WOMAN	Christine Avila
COYOTE	Darrell Larson
TRICKSTER	Norbert Weisser

Directed by Murray Mednick
Lighting by Karen Musser
Stage Manager, Matthew Goulish
Production Coordinator, Peggy Dobreer
Understudy, Assistant to the Director, Robert Behling
Set created by the company
Costume for Spider Woman by Michele Jo Blanch

The play, along with *Coyote II: The Shadow Ripens*, was subsequently produced by Sarah Lovett and Alice Sealy in Santa Fe, New Mexico, under the auspices of The Armory for the Arts, Ian Rosencrantz, Director. The production opened on September 23, 1983, with the same cast. Production Manager was Matthew Ghoulish, Production Coordinator Peggy Dobreer, set design and construction by Robert Behling, sound design by Don Preston.

The story of the Four Worlds is related by the Hopi Creation Myth and was first told in the Cycle in *Coyote II: The Shadow Ripens (West Coast Plays #7)*. This is the Fourth World.

The Germ God *(Muyingwa)*: god of regeneration and rebirth. In the play he is represented by a sort of enclosure constructed of branches, brush, bones, etc., which is at the same time visually representative of the face of this deity.

Massauwu: God of the Dead.

On the CLOWN: at this point in the Cycle she is beginning to recover her powers of speech, having arrived (in *I: Pointing*) with the audience as a lost, dazed, totally mute creature who succeeded in attaching herself to SPIDER WOMAN. Now, under SPIDER WOMAN's tutelage, she has firmly found her place in the ritual ceremony of the Cycle. At first her attempts to speak are halting and difficult, but by the end of the play she has fully recovered and speaks fluently. As further evidence of her increase in mastery and powers bestowed upon her by SPIDER WOMAN, CLOWN carries two "magical" instruments with which she controls the beats of the play: a wooden block, which she "knocks," and a Tibetan bell.

PHOTO: MARGARET VON BIESEN

THE SPACE: some twenty-five by seventy yards of open space. Extreme upstage right is a kind of ramp which has no useful function and reminds us of nothing. COYOTE makes his entrance on it. Up left is a round object which could be a meteorite—the "planet." There are other objects—as well as sources of light—that look like nothing we've ever seen. Poles fifty feet high, holes in the ground, fissures. Center stage, about thirty yards from the audience, is the Germ God, some six feet in diameter and twelve feet high. Down right from the Germ God is what appears to be the carcass of an American buffalo. Down left from the Germ God, about ten yards up from the audience, is SPIDER WOMAN's perch high up in a tree or tree-like structure. She is in the center of an enormous web, the lines of which extend in every direction.

Coyote VI:
The Sacred Dump
Murray Mednick

A strange sound in the space, reminiscent of "the singing of the insects" (in Coyote V). *A long wait as the sound builds in intensity and volume. It is interrupted suddenly by the eerie, chilling, and yet poignant cry of a huge wounded ant, whom we do not see. The sound of the insects begins to fade, and then, gradually,* SPIDER WOMAN's *face appears in the tree.*

SPIDER WOMAN: I am Gogyeng Sowuuti! *(She smiles.)* Some of you I know by your names! Some I know by—your actions! Others I know—by your thoughts! But all of you I know by your nature! *(Fiercely)* It was me who brought you here to this place! ME! *(Smiles.)* You can come out now, child! *(Pause. Gently)* Come out!

CLOWN *appears from within the Germ God.*

SPIDER WOMAN: Come down!

CLOWN *races downstage to the audience.*

SPIDER WOMAN: Remember, child, my instructions to you concerning the Fourth World?

CLOWN *mischievously shakes her head "no."*

SPIDER WOMAN: It was not all beautiful and easy like the previous ones. It had height and depth, heat and cold, beauty and barrenness.

CLOWN *shakes her head "yes."*

SPIDER WOMAN: What was this world called?
CLOWN *(half-signing)*: World com-pete!
SPIDER WOMAN: Good! World complete! It had everything to choose from! But it was up to the people to help carry out the plan of creation!
CLOWN *(half-signing)*: There are no butterflies playing in this place! There are no flowers singing here!
SPIDER WOMAN: No, there are no butterflies playing in this place. There are no flowers singing here.
CLOWN *(half-signing)*: There are no song birds here! There are no

little creatures who mean no harm!

SPIDER WOMAN: There are no song birds here. There are no little
creatures who mean no harm. Things are very abnormal here.
(Sighs.) I'll tell you what happened. The Third World failed. It
was flooded. I had to save the people who still had the song in
their hearts. It was ME who saved them!

CLOWN: I know that already! I know all that already!

SPIDER WOMAN: Oh, so you know that already. Well, then talk!

PHOTO: MARGARET VON BIESEN

CLOWN *and* SPIDER WOMAN (CLOWN *half-signs*): The people forgot why they were here and that Tiowa was their father! We had to move to a higher world! The sun turned red! The air got thick! The earth cracked! The buildings fell down! We heard footsteps in the sky! (CLOWN *is trying to act all this out at the same time.*) We thought we could escape up there through a hole in the sky! We'll build a bamboo ladder and send a bird up there to talk to whoever is walking around up there! A bird climbed up and flew through the hole in the sky and came back! He spoke to Massauwu, God of the Dead, who lives on the other side! He says it's okay! We can come up there and live! But we have to try and be real human beings! And we have to hurry up—the world is being flooded! The people are drowning! The Fire Clan goes up first and reaches the hole in the sky! The other clans follow! But there are Evil Ones among us! We kick down the ladder, so no more can come up! We're in the Fourth World! (*Pause.*)

CLOWN: The Fourth World! The Fourth World! Come on—I have a job to do here!

SPIDER WOMAN: Hold your horses! I know you have a job to do! I gave it to you! So, in the Fourth World, they went to Massauwu and asked him to be their leader. "No thanks," he says, "you go your way and I'll go mine." (*Laughs.*) He came over to me once while we were resting on one of the rungs of the Solar System. "Gogyeng Sowuuti," he said to me, "I know you are working for Earth Mother, and have to do your job, but those people you saved, they are carrying bad germs in them." "What germs?" I asked him. "The germ of fear; the germ of greed; the germ of too much thinking. They'll forget why they are alive and try to have power over the Spirit. They won't be able to see reality. You'll have plenty trouble. This world will be poisoned, and the Spirit withdrawn." He knew what he was talking about. He advised me to keep on friendly terms with the Germ God, Muyingwa.

CLOWN: He's my friend!

SPIDER WOMAN: It's true. He likes you very much. (CLOWN *beams.*) He'll come in handy later, when we start all over again. With a new Code. (*Laughs.*) The Fourth World, the World Complete, was punished and destroyed.

CLOWN (*of the audience*): Are there strange creatures in this place?

SPIDER WOMAN: Yes, but don't be afraid. They're only imaginary creatures now. They're ghosts. They're not real anymore. They just imagine each other being there.

CLOWN: What happens when they die?

SPIDER WOMAN: When they die, they don't join the Spirit World;

they go into crevices in the ground and become poisonous gases.

CLOWN: Ugh!

SPIDER WOMAN: You see, child, it's a very interesting thing. The Fourth World looks like it's still there. *(Laughs.)* Intact. They don't realize that the Spirit's been taken out of it.

CLOWN: What can we do?

SPIDER WOMAN: Do? Wait, I'll come down!

CLOWN: Oh!

SPIDER WOMAN *(chants, as she makes her spidery descent)*: Oh! Many stones! Many people together! They stored their goods and armed themselves! Water in the canyons! Oh! The cities! The towns! The great Kivas! The fire signals! The shine/shine! The screaming of the Cloud People! Huuu!

She has hit the ground, taking the warrior's posture. Now, as she speaks the following, she takes the series of positions indicated by OLD NANA *in* Coyote V.

SPIDER WOMAN: The people thought they had it all coming to them, just because they happened to get born. They didn't listen to their good spirits. They closed their doors. The water was poisoned. The air was poisoned. The earth was poisoned. And when the Hard Punishment came—some tried to escape through a hole in the sky! They didn't make it. They fell into everlasting silence. One of those was. . . Coyote! Some tried to escape through a hole in the ground! They didn't make it. They got burned alive! And one of those was. . . Trickster! Many others! They locked themselves up! They crawled into cellars and burrows and rooms! It was each one for himself! None of those made it either! They had become DERANGED INSECTS!

SPIDER WOMAN *and* CLOWN *scream "the singing of insects," sound from* Coyote V, CLOWN *taking a posture of supplication. . . .* SPIDER WOMAN *stops and goes to her.*

SPIDER WOMAN *(gently)*: Don't worry, they're all part of the chemical soup now. *(Laughs.)* And you, you're here with me.

CLOWN: I think someone else is around here too!

SPIDER WOMAN: Right! Coyote/Trickster is around here! I just experienced his presence. Now we have to call him out as a witness.

CLOWN: They won't come out! They're scared!

SPIDER WOMAN: I know they're scared.

CLOWN: They won't come out!

SPIDER WOMAN: They'll come out if we arouse their curiosity. The one thing they can't resist is women and curiosity. . . . We'll make a big hullabaloo.

CLOWN *(half-signing)*: Boo!

SPIDER WOMAN: Hullabaloo.

CLOWN: Boo!

SPIDER WOMAN: Say it. Hubbababoo. Never mind. This is what you do: hand these instruments out to some of these imaginary kids here. Then, when I give you the signal, start those kids waving them in the air. Then Coyote/Trickster will come out.

CLOWN *(hands out the instruments to kids in the audience)*: Okay!

SPIDER WOMAN: Wait! I have to get back up my tree! If they see me here, they won't come out!

CLOWN: Right!

SPIDER WOMAN *(climbing back into her tree)*: Okay! Start now!

CLOWN *conducts the kids waving the instruments. The sound is like the humming of strange insects. A few beats, then* COYOTE *howls, off.* CLOWN *intensifies her efforts. Another howl, and a groan from* TRICKSTER. TRICKSTER *is down right in the body of the dead buffalo.* COYOTE *scampers out onto the ramp up right, stops, howls.* CLOWN *chases the kids back into the audience.* TRICKSTER *groans and stands, shaking off the buffalo ·but still wearing his headress.* COYOTE *leaps from the ramp, bounding high into the air. They move about the space, quickly taking the series of postures given them by* OLD NANA *in V, finally meeting each other in front of the Germ God.*

COYOTE: Buffalo!

He scampers to TRICKSTER *and hugs him.* TRICKSTER, *confused, decides too late to respond. Now both are embarrassed.* COYOTE *retreats.*

TRICKSTER: Coyote!

Suddenly they become aware of themselves in the environment and are stunned, frozen to the spot. They look fearfully around. They look at the audience. They look again at each other. They try to run but CLOWN *knocks, holding them in place.*

PHOTO: MARGARET VON BIESEN

FIRST EXCHANGE

SPIDER WOMAN: You need something?

COYOTE: Yes. I need to give my pain room to stretch. . . .

TRICKSTER: I didn't have a bag for it. You need the right vessel. Like a net that you could hold it in, or a bag. A vessel. . . .

COYOTE: Pain is the vessel, and you hold on to it in order to float. . .?

A beat. They try to run, but CLOWN *knocks.*

SECOND EXCHANGE

SPIDER WOMAN: Tell us one thing that happens a lot.

COYOTE and TRICKSTER: I hang myself up in an embarrassing situation, and then later I say. . .

COYOTE: I did that on purpose, for the other person's benefit.

TRICKSTER: No way you can get caught, you tell yourself shit like that.

A beat. They try to run. CLOWN *knocks.*

THIRD EXCHANGE

SPIDER WOMAN: What were you doing out there?

COYOTE: I was looking for a woman who had no problems! I never found one!

SPIDER WOMAN: That's not enough.

TRICKSTER: I was dancing. I was dancing. I was dancing. That's what I was doing. Dancing. Something disturbed me. Dancing. I don't remember. Something disturbed me. Small. Like a fly. I shoulda just stomped on it. Squashed it. It was nothing! Nothing!

He flings away his headress in disgust. They try to run. CLOWN *knocks.*

FOURTH EXCHANGE

SPIDER WOMAN: What did you have?

COYOTE: We always had someone to dance with.

TRICKSTER: You could never step without stumbling!

COYOTE: We always had quarters for the juke box.

TRICKSTER: You could never fly without falling!

COYOTE: We always had cups of coffee.

TRICKSTER: You could never fart without hurting!

COYOTE: We always had clean sheets on our beds.

TRICKSTER: You could never eat without ripping your throat!

COYOTE: We always had great sex.

TRICKSTER: You could never have sex without catching a disease!

COYOTE: The maitre d' always seated you.

TRICKSTER: You could never laugh without crying!

COYOTE: We always had plenty tears.

TRICKSTER: You could never swim without drowning! It was a hell of a place! *(Pause.)*

COYOTE: I have nothing. *(Pause.)*

Again they try to run. CLOWN *knocks.*

FIFTH EXCHANGE

SPIDER WOMAN: Where were you going?

COYOTE: I was on my way. I forgot where I was going. I forgot why. I forgot my starting point. I couldn't remember. I was lost.

TRICKSTER: How could this be happening? How could this be happening to me?

COYOTE: It doesn't matter. It doesn't matter which way I go. I could go this way.

TRICKSTER: I could go that way.

COYOTE: It doesn't matter. I could keep right on going. *(Pause.)* The Fourth World is round.

They try to run. CLOWN *knocks.*

SIXTH EXCHANGE

SPIDER WOMAN: What was there?

TRICKSTER: There used to be a mountain, and another mountain, and trees, and birds singing, and a bunch of cars in the parking lot. *(Pause.)* And then there was a light. And fog came down on the mountain. *(Pause.)* Then it all went away.

They try to run for the last time. CLOWN *knocks.*

SEVENTH EXCHANGE

SPIDER WOMAN: What do you know?

COYOTE: Everybody knows how to run. Everyone knows how to feel sorry.

CLOWN *spits.* TRICKSTER *becomes entranced with the spit.*

COYOTE: Animals know when it's cold. That's all I know. Therefore I am an animal. (CLOWN *knocks.*) It's like we're all out on the street. *(Pause.)* I thought everything was all right, but the sidewalk blew up.

CLOWN *knocks.*

EIGHTH EXCHANGE

SPIDER WOMAN: What comes here?

TRICKSTER *(waking)*: The lost moments come here. This is where we keep them. That's why it glows. *(Pause.)* We don't really bring *that* moment here, we bring *this* moment here.

COYOTE: My father sits all alone in a room.

CLOWN *strikes the bell.*

NINTH EXCHANGE

SPIDER WOMAN: What happened to the Fourth World?

COYOTE: We had to get out!

TRICKSTER: We were all huddled!

COYOTE: Strangers grabbed my tail!

TRICKSTER: In a creek bed! But we couldn't breathe!

COYOTE: I had to lead them out!

TRICKSTER: Licking our wounds!

COYOTE: I had to jump very high!

TRICKSTER: Then the rain came! Felt like hot fire coming down!
Burning our coats! Stinking flesh, rotting bones!

COYOTE: Insects!

TRICKSTER: Stinking flesh!

COYOTE: I'll kill them all!

TRICKSTER: I'm not through yet! I've got plans! We few survivors!

COYOTE: I smelled it coming!

TRICKSTER: Walk our squat bones! Our empty eye-sockets!

COYOTE: They grabbed my tail!

TRICKSTER: I was a little bee, dying, covered with dust. . . .

COYOTE: I threw a rope through the hole in the sky!

TRICKSTER: There was talking, then everything stopped. And then I
remembered.

COYOTE: Then the rope broke and they tumbled down!

TRICKSTER: And then I forgot.

COYOTE: Like rain.

CLOWN *knocks.*

TENTH EXCHANGE

SPIDER WOMAN: Where would you go?

TRICKSTER: There's a big hole in the ground that I know. You can
travel through it to the center of the earth, but you have no control over where you're going. It just swallows you, like a seed,
like a germ.

ELEVENTH EXCHANGE

SPIDER WOMAN: What would you like to learn?

COYOTE: One day I will learn how to roll my own cigarettes. In the
meantime, I have to smoke Lucky Strikes, and smoke every single
one of them very fast. *(To* TRICKSTER*)* This morning I was on a
planet all alone, a perfectly smooth copper planet. I could run
around it in less than ten minutes. And there are no flies there.

SPIDER WOMAN: That's not enough.

TRICKSTER: I don't want to talk anymore! (CLOWN *knocks.*) As I
think it, it turns into nothing! (CLOWN *knocks.*) I have to learn
how to speak faster than I think! (CLOWN *knocks.*) I have to learn
to speak as I think! (CLOWN *knocks.*) I have to learn how to
speak!

CLOWN *knocks.*

TWELFTH EXCHANGE

SPIDER WOMAN: And before thought?

COYOTE: Before I became a human being, I, Coyote, was all creatures. First-born I was!

TRICKSTER: Everything around me was trying to eat me. Everything around me is trying to eat me to this day!

COYOTE: It was all in the seed of my Father, Tiowa, and I evolved into something really fantastic—I could fly!

TRICKSTER: I was an eating machine, like all the others. . . .

COYOTE: At first I could only glide. . . . And then I lost weight. . . . And then. . . I could fish! I could dive into the water, to the bottom, for food!

TRICKSTER: Feathers need careful maintenance! Jays and crows are particularly addicted to angry ants—they eat the other insects!

COYOTE: My arms had a feeling of lightness. My heart was empty and my belly was full. My head was a pair of eyes. I could see the inside of things by their nature, by their powers and colors!

TRICKSTER: A reptile, hitting the ground, avoiding a stall and a crash, its wings beating the heavy air. . . !

COYOTE: It's a simple question of flight control. Oh! I had a beak that could suck nectar!

TRICKSTER: Everything is alive! When it gets murdered, it stinks! I knew all these odors by their nature, by their powers and flavors!

CLOWN *gets the kids to start waving the instruments again, accompanying* COYOTE/TRICKSTER's *frenzy.*

COYOTE: I sing my song! It penetrates all thickets! And not only that —I will mate with my own! So all you rivals, you better answer me!

TRICKSTER: I rutted! I was in heat! I would fuck anything that moved!

COYOTE: I am a fine thing! I display myself! I am spectacular! I am a bird of paradise!

TRICKSTER: My wife's friends, my friends' wives, my daughters, my daughters' friends, my sisters, my sisters' friends, the beasts in the field and their shepherds! *(Stomps and bellows like a buffalo in heat.)*

COYOTE: My life is devoted to dancing! I am Coyote! All creatures of paradise, I am them all! I must be beautiful! And here is the climax of my performance! *(He is all puffed up.)*

CLOWN *stops the music. An awkward silence.* COYOTE *and* TRICKSTER *subside.*

THIRTEENTH EXCHANGE

SPIDER WOMAN: And now?

COYOTE *walks away.* TRICKSTER *tries to recover his poise.*

TRICKSTER: There's a very thin line drawn from that point to here. And you try to keep it, and it gets thinner as you come down... but it stays there....

COYOTE: Once it's happened, it's gone. It doesn't matter where you look. You have to look up, you have to look down. Once it's happened, it's gone.

TRICKSTER: You're connected, very thin, thinning out into just between my fingers, like so....

COYOTE: While it's happening, it's gone. Happening is gone.

TRICKSTER: You can't really trust your left side. It always wants to add something.

COYOTE: It happens to everyone. All we have is what we remember. We do what we know how to do. All we know how to do is die.

CLOWN *knocks.*

FOURTEENTH EXCHANGE

SPIDER WOMAN: How are you?

They hesitate. CLOWN *knocks.*

TRICKSTER: I'm talking and it don't sound right. I'm saying things for no reason. I don't mean it. I'm just saying things. It comes out harshly. Then I fall silent, stiff. I'm dead. People are embarrassed. They think I'm strange. Then someone makes a joke. I laugh like a corpse, ha ha ha.

COYOTE: I'm very sorry. I surrender.... I'm very ashamed. I meant it, but I'm still ashamed.

TRICKSTER: I don't talk right. The owls and the crows talk better than me. The sparrows talk better than me.

COYOTE: When I became a human being, I fell out of the womb of a woman. I had been implanted there. I fell out of a hole in the sky into the body of a woman, like a seed. I was an egg in the body of a woman. This woman, my mother, was also once an egg/seed. This was the beginning of a transformation—from seed, to female, to grotesque. It had all been prepared, in time, by the poison in the shell of the seed.

TRICKSTER: I don't walk right. The beetles walk better than me, the four-leggeds walk better than me. The wounded dogs walk better than me!

COYOTE: When I was a child everything was familiar to me and had power. The air had power, the earth had power, the sky had power. The power was the Spirit in all things and I knew it personally—me, Coyote!

FIFTEENTH EXCHANGE

SPIDER WOMAN: And then?
COYOTE *tries to speak, cannot.*

SPIDER WOMAN: And then?
COYOTE: In the twilight of the Fourth World, Tiowa withdrew the Spirit. I was on my own.

SIXTEENTH EXCHANGE

SPIDER WOMAN: What are you?
COYOTE *and* TRICKSTER: I am the living tip of the long line of the dead, like the head of a worm, the long line of the dead....

CLOWN *knocks.* TRICKSTER *sits at the foot of the tree.* COYOTE *kneels.*

SEVENTEENTH EXCHANGE

SPIDER WOMAN: Who brought you?
COYOTE: My father.
TRICKSTER (*as* COYOTE's *father*): Coyote?

PHOTO: MARGARET VON BIESEN

COYOTE: Hi, Dad.

TRICKSTER: You look the same.

COYOTE: You look the same.

TRICKSTER: You know what's happening to me?

COYOTE: Yes.

TRICKSTER: Yeah.... They all come to me now. Now they all come. It's very dramatic.

COYOTE: Me, too. I've come, too.

TRICKSTER: I got it coming to me. People, money, whatever. I got it now.

COYOTE: You got it.

TRICKSTER: Your sisters and brothers, your aunts and uncles, they're all coming to see me now.

COYOTE: What else?

TRICKSTER: I took care of my car. It's in the shop this minute. It's a Caddie. Right front tire bald on one side. Alignment's off. An imperfection. I'm taking care of it. Pay the man later, if he'll wait. (*Pause.*) I got the right number for you, finally?

COYOTE: What number?

TRICKSTER: 396-9216. Area code 213.

COYOTE: That's it.

TRICKSTER: Same number? That's the number?

COYOTE: That's my number.

TRICKSTER: That's the one I have!

COYOTE: You've had the right number.

TRICKSTER: Holy shit! All these years!

COYOTE: That's the number.

TRICKSTER: I thought you moved!

COYOTE: That's the number. So, how you doin'?

TRICKSTER: Well, you know. I'll be goin' to work.

COYOTE: Will you? That's great.

TRICKSTER: Oh, yeah! Sure! They can't do it without me. Run the show. I'm the one knows the machines. Sound and all. Especially the sound. Do that myself. Oh, yeah.

COYOTE: What happened?

TRICKSTER: One day I shit out my bowels. Stool covered with blood. Large intestine came out. Colon came out. Oh, yeah. Now they say it's in my liver. Oh, yeah. Big discussion. Your aunts and uncles. Your brothers and sisters. Chemotherapy. Oh, yeah, sure. We'll see. Makes you sick and your hair falls out. *(Pause, looking off.)* Did you see that?

COYOTE: What?

TRICKSTER: It rained! It rained for the flutter of an eye! Did you catch it? It was a fantasy! *(Laughs.)* Oh, yeah!

CLOWN *strikes the bell.* COYOTE *rises.*

COYOTE: I walked down to the road. Once I had been a child in this place. The world was shining in a bright light. There was the road.

CLOWN *knocks.* COYOTE *starts walking away.*

EIGHTEENTH EXCHANGE

SPIDER WOMAN: Who gave you life? (COYOTE *keeps walking.*) Who gave you life!

CLOWN *strikes the bell.* COYOTE *stops.*

COYOTE: My mother. It was her mother who created her—and so on, back to the beginning, the long worm of the dead. She, my grandmother, created my mother. . . a gargoyle. *(He looks up into the tree where* SPIDER WOMAN *has become the gargoyle.)* It wasn't easy. First with violence, then with coldness, and then with crazy indifference. And then she was ready. My mother was ready.

TRICKSTER: She never rolled over and put out! She never gave! Your mother had nothing to give but vengeance. She was already dead. *(Pause.)* And me? Your father?

COYOTE: *(to* TRICKSTER*)*: She beat me at dawn and she beat me at twilight. She used a coal shovel. *(To audience)* She was trying to beat the strength out of Coyote, but she was making him mad at the same time. *(Pause.)* This was in the twilight of the Fourth World.

TRICKSTER: And me? I was dead too. Finished. I would fuck anything that moved. Anything female. *(Pause.)* I suppose the animal was alive. *(Pause.)* She never put her arms around me with affection. She never eased my way. No help. And she was unclean. Unclean. I'd kill her, but what would be the point?

COYOTE: I took the coal shovel from her hands. I said, "You do that again, and I'll kill you." She never did it again. I was on my own. Time passed. She could no longer function. They had to put her away.

SPIDER WOMAN *(as* COYOTE*'s mother)*: Coyote, don't sign the papers! Don't let them give me treatments! Your father wants to kill me!

TRICKSTER: I couldn't sign the papers. I was illegal myself. Incompetent. A jailbird. An animal. *(Pause.)* They never asked me about it! They ganged up on me! They were out to get me! They put me in prison! They wouldn't take MY word for it! They took everybody else's word but mine!

COYOTE: I went on a long journey and I signed the papers. They gave her shocks. *(The tree shakes.)* And again. *(The tree shakes.)* And again. *(The tree shakes.)* They calmed her down. I felt guilty. They said it was all for the best. But she had been the source of terrific pain. . . . And she taught me the alphabet, in English, when I was small.

SPIDER WOMAN: I'm already dead. All three of my natures. Dead, almost from the beginning. Now I chew my pills, my chemical cud. Time passes. The government takes care of me. They owe me, for all I have suffered. The failures of men.

COYOTE: The gargoyle was completed.

Suddenly the ant cries out, off. TRICKSTER *jumps to his feet. The ant cries again.*

SPIDER WOMAN: There is a wounded ant around here. He is hurt bad. He needs help.

TRICKSTER: Yeah?

SPIDER WOMAN: Yeah. Only you can do it, Buffalo-Head. You have to find that ant and give it a helping hand.

TRICKSTER: Me? No!

SPIDER WOMAN: Yeah, you. You have to fullfill your mission. You have to bring that ant over to the Germ God. She is material for a new world. Then maybe the waterfall will come to earth.

COYOTE: You'd better do it.

TRICKSTER: No. *You* do it.

COYOTE: I wasn't asked to do it.

SPIDER WOMAN: He's got something else to do.

COYOTE: Oh? What's that?

The ant cries out, off.

SPIDER WOMAN: Buffalo-Head, you go and find that ant!

TRICKSTER: Wait a minute! I have a few more things to say here!

COYOTE: I thought you didn't want to talk anymore.

TRICKSTER: That was before!

SPIDER WOMAN: Say what you have to say and get moving! *(The ant cries out.)* Hurry!

COYOTE: What do you want to talk about?

TRICKSTER: I forgot.

COYOTE: Come on!

TRICKSTER: Kissing! What is this thing about kissing? Does it spread germs? Do you like kissing? I don't know if I like kissing or not anymore. I'm confused about it. What do you think? *(CLOWN starts throwing dirt at him.)* All right! I remember now. It's a story. There was this false preacher who spread a lot of lies. I want this on the record! He was part of bringing the Fourth World down! But he didn't know it. Or maybe he did, but he wouldn't admit it! He was talking about missionaries, spread all over the world, places where they couldn't fly flags! So they sat on beds! And stroked their flags! He was selling sex! And he wouldn't cop to it! He couldn't cop to the fact that he was talking about sex! He was a liar! He brought the Fourth World down!

SPIDER WOMAN: Okay. Thank you very much.

TRICKSTER: He had a lot of money that sonofabitch! He had built a palace made of glass! I saw him on TV last night, that fucking liar! I just wanted this on the record! All right, I'll go and find that ant now, and give her a helping hand. *(He wanders upstage, muttering to himself.)*

NINETEENTH EXCHANGE

SPIDER WOMAN: What did you bring me?

COYOTE: Nothing.

SPIDER WOMAN: What did you bring me?

COYOTE: Myself.

SPIDER WOMAN: That's not enough. You must bring me acceptance, as you would the living dead. I gave you life.

COYOTE: I am Coyote!

SPIDER WOMAN: It's you who wants vengeance now. To deny me. To rebuff me.

COYOTE: I'll send you money. Soon as I get a job.

SPIDER WOMAN: I'll take it! I need it! Send money!

COYOTE: I am Coyote!

SPIDER WOMAN: You are nothing. You have nothing, not even money. You're not even intelligent. Muyingwa, the Germ God, has more intelligence than you. Massauwu, the God of the Dead, has more power than you. Even the owl talks better than you. Even the beetle walks better than you.

The ant cries out, off. TRICKSTER *stops, sees it, takes his protective posture. He hesitates. Then, distracted by the fallen "planet" up left, he takes a left turn, goes to the planet, and stares at it, entranced.*

COYOTE *(to* SPIDER WOMAN*)*: What do I have to do?

TRICKSTER, *cracking up, pisses on the planet.* CLOWN *is mortified and the others amazed.* TRICKSTER, *still laughing, starts back downstage.*

TRICKSTER: Did you see what I did? There were millions of little beings running around on that planet! They were weird—screaming and yelling and carrying on! I pissed on 'em! Ha!

The ant cries out, off. TRICKSTER, *seeing it for the first time, stops. The ant cries out.* TRICKSTER *girds himself and goes off toward the sound.*

TWENTIETH EXCHANGE

COYOTE: What do I have to do?

SPIDER WOMAN: You must come near to me.

COYOTE: I can't come near you. Your odor is offensive to me. Your face is offensive to me. You live in filth. You are the dead alive.

SPIDER WOMAN: Come near to me.

COYOTE: I saw how you knocked on the neighbor's door: "You see! You see, woman! It's my son! My son is here! My son has come to honor me!"

SPIDER WOMAN: What's wrong with that?

COYOTE: I did not come to honor you. How could I honor you?

SPIDER WOMAN: I gave you life. Come and pick me up. Pick me up and carry me. Come on.

COYOTE: I can't!

CLOWN *knocks.*

CLOWN: Pick her up! *(Points to the Germ God.)*
SPIDER WOMAN: Come on. Bend a little. Bend your back. Stretch your pain. *(Laughs.)* Give it up.
COYOTE: HUUU!
SPIDER WOMAN: That's right! A warrior! A warrior has flexibility!
COYOTE: Don't kiss me.
SPIDER WOMAN: I won't kiss you.
COYOTE: Please don't kiss me.
SPIDER WOMAN: I won't kiss you. I'll turn my face away.
COYOTE *(struggling)*: All right then.

CLOWN *strikes the bell.*

COYOTE: I'll pick you up. I can't stand you, but I'll pick you up. You gave me life.
SPIDER WOMAN: Good then. Come and carry me. Take me to the Germ God, Muyingwa. I won't kiss you.
COYOTE: I'll come and pick you up. I'll carry you to the Germ God. You gave me life.

SPIDER WOMAN *mounts* COYOTE*'s back, facing away from him. Slowly,* COYOTE *carries her toward the Germ God.* CLOWN, *walking backwards, accompanies them.*

SPIDER WOMAN *(as the gargoyle)*: The insects! I heard them buzzing in the mountains / —very strong—talking to me / —And then the light went out of me / —One breath, that's all it takes, to go down / —And then you come up on the other side— / sweet—ah ah ah / —A man with a bandanna—and no hair / —coming to greet me—

CLOWN: The world didn't need anymore height; / it already had height. / The world didn't need anymore depth; / it already had depth. / The world didn't need anymore time; / it already had time. / The world didn't need to be made more complete; / it was already complete. / The world didn't need to be made more beautiful; / it was already beautiful.

As they enter the Germ God, TRICKSTER *appears carrying the wounded ant on his back. The ant is man-sized and cries out repeatedly. The Germ God dims up slowly.* TRICKSTER *and the ant are the last to enter.*

The Germ God becomes brightly lit. Music. Blackout.

Coyote VII:
He Brings the Waterfall
Murray Mednick

Coyote VII: He Brings the Waterfall was first performed at the Padua Hills Playwrights' Festival at California Institute for the Arts, Valencia, on July 13, 1984, with the following cast:

CLOWN	Priscilla Cohen
SPIDER WOMAN	Christine Avila
COYOTE	Darrell Larson
TRICKSTER	Norbert Weisser
BOY COYOTE	Jesse Shepard
BOY TRICKSTER	Morgan Weisser

Directed by Murray Mednick
Production manager, Matthew Goulish
Sets by Robert Behling
Lighting design by Karen Musser
Production coordinator, Peggy Dobreer

The complete *Coyote Cycle* was performed at the Audobon Randall Davey Center in Santa Fe, New Mexico, on September 29, 1984, produced by Sarah Lovett and Alice Sealey of Theater-in-the-Red, with the same cast (Dakota Fitzner playing BOY COYOTE) and crew, with the help of Kelly Stuart, Frederick Lopez, Chas Rundberg, Zoe Viles, Deborah Scharaga, Rhona Gold, and John Oldach.

Coyote VII:
He Brings the Waterfall
Murray Mednick

Darkness, about an hour before dawn. The Tibetan bell is struck.
SPIDER WOMAN *and* CLOWN, *in white costumes, appear in the distance. They approach slowly and majestically, accompanied by tones of the bell. Reaching the outer edge of the playing area,* SPIDER WOMAN *stops suddenly and takes a severe pointing posture. Then she drops it abruptly and rushes forward, shouting at the audience:*

SPIDER WOMAN: Now you're gonna get it! Now you're gonna get it! Trickster is coming for you now! *Pendejos!* He's coming for you! You think you got medical problems now? Don't tell me about your filthy medical problems! I know all the diseases possible for two-legged beings! I've had them all! *Cabrones!*

She takes the SPIDER WOMAN *posture. A beat, then she drops it, races to her right, changes direction, and races upstage left.* CLOWN, *trying to keep up, falls down.*

SPIDER WOMAN *(to audience)*: I have a boyfriend who will protect me! He has no hair and wears a red bandana! *(Laughs.)* But who will protect you, eh?! *Hijos de la chispiada!* Bones on a scaffold! You hear me?! You'll be bones! Less than bones! Bone ash! *(Laughs.)* I can't wait!

Suddenly she shows the five directions, each supported by a drumbeat. Then the steady rhythm of the drum continues as SPIDER WOMAN *and* CLOWN *make a procession down centerstage toward the audience.*

SPIDER WOMAN: I have seen the new colors in the sky! I have tasted the new flavors in the earth! It was not pleasant to me! It was not agreeable to me! *(*TRICKSTER *is heard off, as Owl.)* Wait! Listen!

CLOWN: Trickster is angry!

SPIDER WOMAN: Yes!

CLOWN: Divine is sunlight! Divine is Earthmaker's tent! Divine is the Spider Lady's posture!

SPIDER WOMAN: The fish have cancer! The bones have plague!

CLOWN: Trickster is merciless!

SPIDER WOMAN: Yes! *(*COYOTE *is heard off, as Blue Jay.)*

CLOWN: Divine is thunder! Divine is lightning. Divine is Coyote's journey from beginning to end!

SPIDER WOMAN: Yes!

CLOWN: Everyone is pleading for mercy!

SPIDER WOMAN: Yes! We have to kill all the people now with a destroying fire! After that a big man will come walking over the Earth! He will go around planting new people! *(They stop in front of the audience.)*

CLOWN: I love Trickster, but he has a magnificent vengeance. Everyone will suffer and die! *(Pause.)*

SPIDER WOMAN: I had better go among the people now.

CLOWN *(amazed)*: What for?

SPIDER WOMAN: To protect them from the wrath of Trickster.

CLOWN: But you don't like the people very much!

SPIDER WOMAN: I have to keep my personal feelings out of this. *(She goes to her place just left of the audience. To* CLOWN *)* You take over here.

CLOWN *(fearfully alert)*: Right!

SPIDER WOMAN *(to audience)*: Earthmaker said, "I will send messages to the Earth by the spirits of the people who reach me but whose time to die has not yet come. They will carry messages to you from time to time. When their spirits come back into their bodies, they will revive and tell you their experiences."

COYOTE *appears in a distant tree as "Blue Jay." He squawks and flaps his wings.*

SPIDER WOMAN *(to audience)*: Now don't be afraid, that Blue Jay over there is really Coyote. Don't pay any attention to him or he'll steal your power. That's the kind of thing Blue Jay likes to do. Don't pay any attention to him. . . .

CLOWN *points. "Blue Jay" disappears.*

SPIDER WOMAN *(to audience)*: We have gone to the Planet of the Spider People and to Other Side Camp. We have brought the material for a new world into the body of the Germ God, Muyingwa. . . . And you can let that Ant go now, Child.

CLOWN: Oh, the Ant!

SPIDER WOMAN: Yes. Let her go.

CLOWN *fumbles in a tiny purse and then gingerly, gently, puts the tiny Ant on the ground with a finger.* TRICKSTER *appears in a distant tree as "Owl." He hoots and flaps his wings.*

SPIDER WOMAN *(to audience)*: When the Owl is heard, someone dies. So try not to listen to that Owl. That's Trickster in that Owl. Try not to listen. . . that's how Owl will steal your power. . . don't listen. . .

CLOWN *points. "Owl" disappears. The tiny ant seems to be crawling up* CLOWN's *leg. She jumps.*

SPIDER WOMAN *(laughing)*: That Ant is frightened! I don't blame her! *(Laughs.)* Anyway, now it's up to Coyote to bring the waterfall to earth. *(Cackling.)* While we're waiting, let me tell you another thing about the Chinese! If you happen to be at an intersection, you'd better be really careful when a Chinaman is coming down the road because the Chinese can't tell red from green and they have no side vision at all!

She cracks up. COYOTE *comes running into the space. The drumbeat ceases.*

COYOTE: Hello!

CLOWN: Hello!

COYOTE: My name is Brown.

CLOWN *(offering her hand)*: How do you do?

COYOTE *(sniffing her hand)*: I do everything well, thank you.

SPIDER WOMAN *(to audience)*: That person there is really Coyote.

COYOTE: Have you seen a Buffalo around here?

CLOWN: No, I haven't!

SPIDER WOMAN *(to audience)*: He doesn't look like much, but it's Coyote all right. *(*COYOTE *smiles at the audience.)* He's trying to act charming. Don't fall for it, that's how he steals your power. Just watch him out of the corner of your eye.

CLOWN *turns to keep* COYOTE *in the corner of her eye. He follows. They make a complete turn.*

COYOTE: You must be the queen of this planet, otherwise known as Spider Woman?

CLOWN: No, I'm not.

COYOTE: Oh. Have you seen an Owl around here?

CLOWN: Yes, I saw an Owl!

COYOTE *(alerted)*: Where?

CLOWN *(pointing)*: There!

COYOTE *takes his protective posture, then becomes* "COYOTE." *Silently, slowly, he looks intently all around, making a complete turn. Satisfied that "Owl" is not near, he drops it, starts to go, changes his mind and returns to* CLOWN.

COYOTE: By the way, you look very familiar to me, only different. Are you a relative?

CLOWN *(insulted)*: No, I'm not!

COYOTE: What's your personal history?

CLOWN: I came into this life a human being, with parents. I didn't know if I could do it. I hit the road. I ate many powerful substances and took a lot of abuse from people. But now I'm Clown-Divine.

COYOTE: So what is your place around here?

CLOWN: I am the Chief Clown! I am boss of all the Clowns!

COYOTE: Do you consider yourself a mythological figure now, like me?

CLOWN: I am the Chief Clown! I am boss of all the Clowns!

COYOTE: Show me something then.

CLOWN *(pointing)*: Mister! Did you see that?

COYOTE: What?

CLOWN: It rained! It rained for the flutter of an eye! Did you catch it?

COYOTE: No.

CLOWN: It was a fantasy!

A single drumbeat. CLOWN *points to a spot in the ground center-stage.*

CLOWN *and* SPIDER WOMAN: A deep unease, there, under the gravel! Under the rock! Disturbed! Unhappy!

TRICKSTER *appears upstage behind some rocks and dead branches. He speaks as* COYOTE's *father (as in* Coyote VI: The Sacred Dump).

TRICKSTER *(a mournful wail)*: COYOTE!

COYOTE *(kneeling)*: It's my father, dead in the ground, buried in the arms of Massauwu!

TRICKSTER: I was a bad man, Coyote, a stupid man, a slave to lust, a helpless man! Now all my chances are gone forever, and my bones lie in the darkness of Massauwu!

COYOTE: The nose is gone, the ears are gone, the eyes are gone, the sex organs are gone.... His bones lie in the darkness of Massauwu!

TRICKSTER: She has forgiven me, Coyote, she has forgiven me all... that I'd done...but she weeps, Coyote, she weeps day and night....

COYOTE *(backing away)*: It's a trick!

TRICKSTER *(rising)*: Ha! It's time now for revenge! Revenge for it all! All the stupidity and the filth! Revenge for the torture! Revenge on the know-it-alls! Revenge on the grabbers! Revenge on the hysterics! Revenge on the fuck-you guys! The smug! Those smegma-heads! The ambitious! The who-gives-a-shits! Revenge on the petulant and the ones with grievances! Revenge on the company guys and the patriots, the big wheels and the profiteers! Revenge on the ordinary! Revenge on the teachers, the knuckle-beaters and baby-fuckers! Revenge on all the lying sonsofbitches! Revenge! I want it all! Heh, heh, watch out for the Owl, Coyote, watch out for the Crow!

TRICKSTER *becomes "Crow," cawing as* COYOTE *runs off howling.*

SPIDER WOMAN *(to audience)*: There he is! Watch out now, watch out!

TRICKSTER *drops the "Crow" and slowly, menacingly approaches the downstage playing area and the fearful* CLOWN.

SPIDER WOMAN *(to audience)*: Remember, that person there is really Trickster. He is pretending to be cool, but he knows you're there. Remember, he wants to steal your power, he wants to kill you! That's how Trickster goes around. Just watch him out of the corner of your eye....

CLOWN *looks at* TRICKSTER *out of the corner of her eye and he drops the stone he was going to bash her with.*

TRICKSTER: Heh, heh. My name is Smith. . . . Who are you?

CLOWN: I am Chief of all the Clowns.

TRICKSTER: What? You can't be a Chief!

CLOWN: Why not?

TRICKSTER (*guffawing*): You're a woman!

CLOWN: I am boss of all the Clowns!

TRICKSTER (*laughing*): Okay, show me something.

CLOWN *shows him her breasts. He gazes at them a moment.*

TRICKSTER: No. That doesn't make me feel any better. That's no
answer to the problem. That's just stinking flesh. That doesn't
get it. (CLOWN, *hurt, turns away.*) Show me something else.
(CLOWN *does nothing.*) That's no good. That's nothing. Nothing
is nothing. It's not funny. It's not funny at all. (*He finds a large
club.*) I am going to crush you now!

CLOWN: (*falling to her knees*): Spider Grandmother! Spider Grandmother!

SPIDER WOMAN (*to audience*): No one move! Not a muscle! Not an
eyelash!   .

TRICKSTER *begins circling her fiercely, pounding the earth with
his club.*

TRICKSTER: Tell me about these here bones!

CLOWN: Bones?

TRICKSTER: The bones! The bones!

CLOWN: Bones! Especially of a limb! Any part or piece of the hard
tissue forming the skeleton of most full-grown vertebrate animals, especially a piece between two joints! The hard tissue is the
skeleton, hence—the body, living or dead!

TRICKSTER: The bones! The bones!

CLOWN: A bone-like substance or thing, a thing made of bone or
bone-like material! Flat sticks used as clappers by end-men in
minstrel shows for keeping time to music! (*Pause.*) The end-man
in a minstrel show himself! (*Pause.*) Dice! (*Pause.*) I feel it in my
bones! (*Pause.*) I have a bone to pick! (*Pause.*) Make no bones
about it!

TRICKSTER *quickly makes a large circle around her with glowing
white sand.*

CLOWN: Bone ash! A white porous ash prepared by burning bones
in the open air, and consisting chiefly of calcium phosphate!
Used as fertilizer!

She is near tears. TRICKSTER *picks up his club and prepares to charge her.*

TRICKSTER *(fierce)*: Now you will help pay for the sufferings of Earthmother!

SPIDER WOMAN: Dig, Child!

CLOWN *frantically digs in the ground, uncovering a large, shining Buffalo Skull.* TRICKSTER *is mesmerized by it.*

TRICKSTER: I went down, down. I came to a lake. There on the other side of the lake was the man, standing on a buffalo head, pointing at me. The buffalo head was shining white, white as the salt flat, hot white. The man was pointing at me. I looked up. It was the roof of a cave, sky-blue. . . .

COYOTE *appears in the distance, upstage center.*

COYOTE *(pointing)*: DON'T KILL ME!

TRICKSTER *takes his protective posture.* COYOTE *disappears.* BOY COYOTE *appears off in the bushes, right, as "Blue Jay."* TRICKSTER, *sensing him, points.*

TRICKSTER: There!

The young "Blue Jay" disappears. TRICKSTER *growls.* CLOWN *cowers.* TRICKSTER *eyes the audience. He stomps. He is enraged. He prepares to charge the audience.* BOY COYOTE *rushes into the space.*

BOY COYOTE: Buffalo-head!

TRICKSTER *(wheeling about)*: What?!

BOY COYOTE: Do you remember how it was, Trickster?

TRICKSTER *(amazed)*: When?

BOY COYOTE: *(moving cautiously around him toward the* CLOWN*)*: When you were young and Earthmother was young, and the air was sweet, and the water was sweet, and the world was in a bright light and all things had power? Do you remember?

A beat. TRICKSTER *breaks down and cries.* BOY COYOTE *scrapes away some of the circle of white sand with his foot, releasing the* CLOWN, *then takes his protective posture.*

BOY COYOTE: Don't kill me, Trickster.

TRICKSTER: I won't kill you. I can't kill you. *(He begins pounding the earth with his club.)* But I am going to kill all of the two-leggeds, especially the white-eyes! I am going to kill them all! I am going to kill them with a destroying fire! I am going to evaporate them! My vengeance will be magnificent! *(Pounding the earth, he approaches the audience.)* Not only will I destroy their flesh, but their memories also! And that of their fathers! And their fathers' fathers!

BOY COYOTE *runs off as* TRICKSTER *charges the audience, full tilt. A sharp clang—it's as though he has rammed himself into a steel wall.*

PHOTO: MARGARET VON BIESEN

SPIDER WOMAN *(to audience)*: I've put an invisible shield up over here, to protect you! That's just one example of my power.

TRICKSTER *(furiously)*: First they put me in irons! They put shackles on me! They beat me around the head! They kicked my rib bones in! They kicked in my solar plexus! They stabbed my liver! They tortured me with needles! They poured acid rain on me! They poisoned me with rays! They broke my heart! And now they've put up a fuckin' shield! Another fuckin' shield! *(He begins backing off, right.)* Well, I'll be back! I'll be back. *(He becomes "Crow.")* I've got plans! *(Cawing, he vanishes.* COYOTE *runs in, left, startling the* CLOWN.*).*

COYOTE: No need to be afraid of me, Clown-Divine! I am Coyote! Coyote is light! He goes about with leaps and bounds!

CLOWN: Bully for Coyote!

COYOTE: I can see that you're not feeling so secure at this time,

because of that other guy around here. Well, not to worry. . . .
(He leans against the "shield.") I can handle him all right. (BOY
TRICKSTER *appears in the bushes, left, as "Crow."* COYOTE
points. BOY TRICKSTER *disappears.* COYOTE *smiles at the audience.)* Today, I realized that the person I was when I was going
around and walking and talking with people is the person Coyote
is as far as other people are concerned when I am going around.

CLOWN: And?

COYOTE: I always thought I was somebody else going around in
whatever body I happened to be in at the time and that that
somebody was a secret known only to Coyote.

CLOWN: And?

COYOTE: He is *really* a great guy, that one! *(CLOWN is appalled.*
COYOTE *smiles, looks up.* CLOWN *looks up.* COYOTE *looks at*
CLOWN.*)* Why are you trying to turn a quiet moment into a
tragedy? *(CLOWN is doubly appalled.* COYOTE *smiles at the audience.* TRICKSTER *appears, up right.)* Here comes something.
Ahem. *(Going to* TRICKSTER.*)* In order to be a bona fide warrior,
first you have to be a human being. I did that.

TRICKSTER: What's a fuckin' warrior?

COYOTE: A warrior always knows what time it is.

TRICKSTER: I am a hunter, a stalker, and a spy!

COYOTE *and* CLOWN: Three things, huh?

TRICKSTER: Right! *(CLOWN whistles.)*

COYOTE: You remember pissing on that planet?

TRICKSTER: Which one?

COYOTE: Which one?! The one you pissed on!

TRICKSTER: Oh, yeah, that one.

COYOTE: Then you got nothin' to talk about. A guy who goes around
pissing on other people's planets has got nothin' to talk about.

TRICKSTER: It was a tiny planet.

COYOTE: So?

TRICKSTER: So, nothin'! What are you, some kind of good guy?
(Goes behind an upstage bush to take a leak.)

COYOTE: I am a very nice guy! And I'm handsome, too, and quite
talented. (BOY TRICKSTER *appears from behind the bush, but-
toning his fly.)*

BOY TRICKSTER: You are a flea-bitten, canine bag of bones, and I'm
going to cut your balls off and feed them to the crows!

COYOTE *(amazed)*: Why?

BOY TRICKSTER *(throwing gravel at him)*: Because you want to steal
my women, that's why!

COYOTE: I don't want to fight, I want to eat. I've become a human
being.

BOY TRICKSTER: Eat? Eat what? The fish have cancer, the bones have plague.

COYOTE: I think I'll eat you.

BOY TRICKSTER: You don't have the stomach for it.

COYOTE: I love buffalo meat! Buffalo meat is my favorite food to eat! *Numero uno!* (SPIDER WOMAN *laughs.*) That woman sure laughs a lot! She also has the habit of asking a lot of questions! That kind of behavior is rude!

BOY TRICKSTER: Yeah! And she's put a shield up over there! But as soon as that Spider Lady has to take a leak, I'm going to kill all those pople she's got with her!

SPIDER WOMAN: Ha! When the Spider Lady takes a leak, the world turns upside down, you little twirp.

BOY TRICKSTER: Did you hear that?

COYOTE: Yeah. But you don't want to kill all those people. If we kill all the people, the white-eyes especially, we'll just be adding to the pile of bodies, the long line of the dead. What we have to do now is bring the water. (*He makes the spiraling gesture as* BOY TRICKSTER *becomes "Owl."*)

BOY TRICKSTER: I don't see it that way.

COYOTE: You don't?

BOY TRICKSTER: No. Now I think we have to accomplish some vengeance.

COYOTE: Hmmm. (*Backing away.*) Time was when people woke up in the morning and were happy to join me in my work. That's how I came to be called First Worker. (*He becomes "Hare."*) Nowadays people wake up in the morning and brush their teeth.... (*He rushes off, right.*)

CLOWN (*to* BOY TRICKSTER): Hi, Mr. Owl!

BOY TRICKSTER: What is that idiot Rabbit talking about?

> BOY COYOTE *enters as "Hare." A freeze as "Owl" and "Hare" face each other. Then they drop it.*

BOY COYOTE: Hi.

BOY TRICKSTER: Hi.

BOY COYOTE: How ya doin'?

BOY TRICKSTER: I'm having a good time. I'm getting ready to kill all of the two-leggeds.

BOY COYOTE: And then what?

BOY TRICKSTER: Then I'll lie in the arms of Earthmother for a long time.

BOY COYOTE: I'm gonna take a long rest, too. And then I'll keep on going around. (*He looks up.*) But I won't be back here for a

PHOTO: MARGARET VON BIESEN

while. *(Looking at the audience.)* You'll never get through that shield. That Spider Lady has got strong legs. I don't know why she does that. She doesn't like them very much but she still protects them.

BOY TRICKSTER: I don't understand it either. They gave the fish cancer. They gave plague to the bones of our fathers. They...

BOY COYOTE: Who is "they"?

BOY TRICKSTER: *(angrily)*: They is they! Them! The white-eyes! The two-leggeds! Them! All those ones going around that are not us!

BOY COYOTE *(pointing to the Buffalo Skull)*: That Buffalo Head Bone is attached to the Long Line of the Dead. I believe that if we can play the game of pulling that Buffalo Head around that circle, we will bring peace to the bones of our fathers.

BOY TRICKSTER *(considers)*: There is no way on earth that I would ever do anything you suggest to me, either now or in the future. *(Starts off, stops.)* But I'll think about it.

BOY COYOTE: Sure thing.

BOY TRICKSTER *goes off.* SPIDER WOMAN *charges the space, chasing* BOY COYOTE *off.*

SPIDER WOMAN: Sure thing! Sure thing! *(Gasping.)* Come here, Clown-Divine!

CLOWN: *(approaching her)*: Here I am, Spider Grandmother!

SPIDER WOMAN: Good. I want to tell you something. *(She indicates where* CLOWN *should sit.)* One day I woke up to a morning bright with power. The air was scented with flowers and green grass; sweet water flowed in the streams; the four-leggeds were at peace; the insects were singing quiet songs; the flower-beings were happy in the sunlight. Then I saw a two-legged white-eyed woman walking in the field near my cave. This woman had a right hand made of two knives cutting, and she was going around stabbing the flowers with her right hand, killing them. She sang while she was killing them. Then she gathered up the corpses of the flower-beings and took them into her hut and put them into water so she could look at and smell the corpses of the flower-beings. That's when I knew... that's when I knew in my heart ...that these two-legged, white-eyed...creatures...were INSANE.

Maddened with anger and grief, she eyes the audience, then races toward them.

SPIDER WOMAN *(to audience)*: Massauwu is coming for you now! That's right! It's time, now! At last! Time to clean up the mess! It's time! *(Stops herself.)* But Coyote said, "sure thing," and Trickster went off thinking! Ha! Trickster can't think! His head will start to vibrate and he'll come back worse than before! *(Pause.)* Good! *(To* CLOWN*)* Do you know why I say, "Good!"?
CLOWN: No, why?
SPIDER WOMAN *(laughing crazily)*: Because I took off the shield, that's why! No more shield.
CLOWN: Oh, no!

Still laughing, SPIDER WOMAN *goes up right for a good view of what might happen next.* COYOTE *comes running into the space.*

COYOTE: I said, "sure thing!" I said, "sure thing!" Why did I say that? "Sure thing! Sure thing!"
CLOWN: Coyote! Don't let him come back. Don't let him come back!
COYOTE: Oh, sure thing. *(Does a take on himself, then prepares to approach the Buffalo Skull.)*
CLOWN: What are you doing?
COYOTE: I have to bring him back.
CLOWN: Oh, no!
COYOTE: I'm going to sing my death song now, and bring him back.
(He kneels above the Buffalo Skull.)

Divine is sunlight.
Divine is Earthmaker's tent
Divine is the Spider Lady's posture

Divine is thunder
Divine is lightning
Divine is Coyote's Journey
    From beginning to end

I became a human being
And walked among the two-leggeds
I saw the new colors in the sky
I tasted the new flavors in the earth

It was not pleasant to me
It was not agreeable to me

I saw the bones of my planet
Whitening in Starlight,
On a scaffold in Starlight
    Made of a subtle wind
    Singing a subtle song

Deep as all the dead together
Deep as all the dead together

At once!

A single drumbeat. TRICKSTER *rushes in to attack* COYOTE *with a large rock.*

TRICKSTER: Sing it then! Because now you die! *(He stops above* COYOTE *ready to bash his head in, but is paralyzed. A beat.)* I can't kill you! *(Another beat.)*
COYOTE *(standing)*: Did you get anywhere with your thinking?
TRICKSTER *(dropping the rock, in extreme frustration)*: I don't know what to think! I can't think! Vengeance is all I have left! That's all there is!
COYOTE *(offhand)*: Don't resent yourself, Trickster.
TRICKSTER *(incredulous)*: What?
COYOTE: The trouble with you is your background.
TRICKSTER: Background?
COYOTE: Abuse.
TRICKSTER: WHAT THE FUCK ARE YOU TALKING ABOUT?
COYOTE: All I'm saying is, we can't get through the Spider Lady's shield. *(Indicating the audience.)* That shield is made of powerful stuff.

TRICKSTER: What's it made of?

COYOTE: Uh, time. It's another time. We can't get. . . through.

TRICKSTER: Time? Time? (*He picks up his club and gets ready to charge, but can't help asking one more question.*) What is this here abuse?

COYOTE: Don't distract me, Trickster. Everybody has a background of abuse. My advice to you is to put your vengeance into that Buffalo Head Bone.

TRICKSTER: Why?

COYOTE (*very annoyed*): Why? How many times do I have to tell you?!

TRICKSTER (*furiously*): As many times as you want to! (*He prepares to charge.*)

CLOWN: No, wait!

SPIDER WOMAN: Go ahead! Charge! (*Laughs.*)

CLOWN (*to* SPIDER WOMAN): You stay out of this!

TRICKSTER (*to* CLOWN): Now what?

COYOTE *has become curious about the "shield," decides to inspect it with his nose—quite close to the audience.*

CLOWN: Listen, Trickster, that bone I dug up for you is attached to the Long Line of the Dead.

TRICKSTER: I've been told that already. I don't want to think about it.

CLOWN: Don't think. Just listen. That line goes back through all time and it all comes together here. Right here. Right here is the center of all. See?

TRICKSTER: No! What I see is murder, greed, cruelty—and abuse!

SPIDER WOMAN: Right!

TRICKSTER: And I'm not gonna sacrifice my pure rage for the sake of these puny two-leggeds!

CLOWN: They may still have a chance, Trickster.

TRICKSTER: They've been having a chance for a million years now! Fuck 'em!

SPIDER WOMAN: Fuck 'em!

TRICKSTER: Now they've got no more chances!

SPIDER WOMAN: That's the way they want it!

TRICKSTER: I LIKE it! (CLOWN *spits.*)

CLOWN: I can't waste my time here. (*She joins* SPIDER WOMAN *as Coyote returns to the scene.*)

CLOWN: It's not for them, Trickster. It's for yourself. You can take care of all your vengeance at once and you won't have to spend anymore energy in that direction.

TRICKSTER: No! You don't tell me nothin'! *(He clubs* COYOTE, *turns to audience.* COYOTE *springs up.)* You don't give me no fuckin' advice! *(Clubs him again, turns to audience.* COYOTE *springs up.)* A fuckin' good guy all of a sudden! *(Clubs him again, turns to audience.* COYOTE *springs up.)* I'm taking care of the problem! *(Clubs him again, goes for the audience.* COYOTE *springs up.)*

COYOTE: You're right! Let's do it!

TRICKSTER *(stopped)*: Huh?

COYOTE: A good guy I'm not. Let's GO!

TRICKSTER: Wait a minute. . .

COYOTE: Yeah?

TRICKSTER: This is MY vengeance!

COYOTE: Fine. I won't take any credit for it.

TRICKSTER: Let's go then!

COYOTE: I was just thinking.

TRICKSTER *(stopped)*: What were you thinking?

COYOTE: If we do it this time, we'll only have to do it again next time.

TRICKSTER: And?

COYOTE: If we do it my way, we do it for ALL time, once and for all. . . . There's just one drawback.

TRICKSTER: What's that?

COYOTE: It takes a big man to accomplish such a mission.

TRICKSTER: I'm the man! Come on!

COYOTE *(looking up)*: Oh!

TRICKSTER: What?

COYOTE: Look up, Trickster! *(*TRICKSTER *looks up.)* Earthmother has sent out feelers!

TRICKSTER: Yeah! *(All four characters reach to the sky as if touching many strands of light.)*

COYOTE: They go all the way up to the stars!

TRICKSTER: Yeah!

COYOTE: She is feeling around up there for help. . . . *(*TRICKSTER *starts to cry. A beat.)* Listen. There's only one thing to do. You have to put all your vengeance into that Buffalo Head Bone. And I'll pull that bone around that circle. And then the waterfall will come to Earth. That's all that's left.

TRICKSTER *(going to the Buffalo Skull)*: That's all that's left.

COYOTE: That's it.

TRICKSTER: That's it.

COYOTE: HUUU! *(*TRICKSTER, *undergoing a terrible inner struggle, is brought to his knees above the skull.* SPIDER WOMAN *and* CLOWN *move further up the hillside.)*

SPIDER WOMAN: We traveled in the Germ God...

CLOWN: Muyingwa!

SPIDER WOMAN: A long way we traveled...

CLOWN: In an instant!

SPIDER WOMAN: With the material...

CLOWN: For a new world!

SPIDER WOMAN: An ecstatic journey we made...

CLOWN: And we saw the bones! (COYOTE *is ready now to pull the Buffalo Skull.*)

COYOTE: Let's go.

SPIDER WOMAN: They came to this land, and this is what they said!

COYOTE (*as he starts to pull*): This is what they said.

TRICKSTER (*with great force, reflecting tremendous inner conflict*): This land is Paradise. This place is a boon to mankind. We got freedom here. We can worship whatever we want here. Oh, the water is sweet. Oh, the air is sweet. And there is every kind of food here in abundance. We can have time here. We can worship what we want here. First we'll clear the vermin off the land. Those ones that are not us, that don't believe as us. Then we'll cut up the land in pieces, and everybody can own a piece of land. And we'll clear the land and plant food in the land, because the game won't last forever. We can worship what we want here. We'll buy and sell the land we cut up. We'll buy and sell the food we grow. We'll have cattle ranches and stockyards. And we'll create wealth. We'll get wealth out of the land and out of the ground. And we'll create power. We can worship whatever we want here. And we'll find energy. We'll cut into the land for energy and power. And we'll get energy from the water. And we'll keep the vermin out of the way. Those who don't believe as us, who aren't one of us, who aren't in this thing with us. We'll fence 'em and we'll feed 'em, but we'll keep 'em out of the way. Because there's nothing like this land, and there's nothing like this wealth, and there's nothing like this power. And we can worship what we want here. And we'll cut our way through mountains and cross the rivers and valleys, and we'll be moving, we'll be on the move, we're moving, moving, creating wealth, creating power, and it has to be fed, it has to be fed with ENERGY! WE'LL FIND THAT ENERGY. WE WORSHIP WHAT WE WANT TO! WE'LL CUT INTO THE LAND FOR ENERGY! WE'LL DAM THE RIVERS! WE'LL CUT THROUGH BEDROCK! WE'LL CUT THROUGH MATTER! WE'LL FIND MORE! MORE! WE WORSHIP WHAT WE WANT!

TRICKSTER *collapses as* COYOTE *completes the circle with the Buffalo Skull.*

SPIDER WOMAN *and* CLOWN: LET'S GO!
COYOTE *(helping* TRICKSTER *to his feet)*: Come on!
SPIDER WOMAN *and* CLOWN: LET'S GO!
COYOTE: Wait a minute! (TRICKSTER *can barely walk.*)
SPIDER WOMAN: What are you making such a big deal out of it for?
CLOWN: Big deal!
SPIDER WOMAN: What you did is nothing!
CLOWN: Nothing!
SPIDER WOMAN: Child's play! Nothing!
CLOWN: Child's play! Nothing!
SPIDER WOMAN: Let's go!
COYOTE: Give us a helping hand!
SPIDER WOMAN: No way, fool! You ain't done nothing until you can climb up the side of this hill now! Come on!
CLOWN: Come on!

COYOTE *and* TRICKSTER *struggle to a higher level, regaining their strength.*

ALL TOGETHER *(as they climb toward the rim)*: This is what Earthmaker says: Coyote and myself, we will not be seen again until Earthmother is old and dying. Then we will return to Earth, for it will need a change by that time. Coyote will come along first, and when you see him you will know that I am coming. When I come along, all the spirits of the dead will be with me. There will be no more Other Side Camp. All the people will live together. Earthmother will go back to first shape and live as a mother among her children. Then things will be made right.

They form a tableau on the rim of the hill and make a keening sound. A bright light appears behind them. The waterfall comes to earth as the sun rises.

Coyote Comes Full Cycle Under Stars

Robert Koehler

Six years after the presentation of the first Coyote *play, the full, completed* Coyote Cycle *was presented in Santa Fe, New Mexico, starting at 7:30* P.M. *on September 29, 1984, and running until dawn the next morning. The following account was written by Robert Koehler for the* Los Angeles Times *and appeared in that paper's Sunday Calendar section on October 14, 1984. The previous* Coyote *plays are available in the following issues of* West Coast Plays: Coyote I: Pointing; Coyote II: The Shadow Ripens; *and* Coyote III: Planet of the Spider People *in* West Coast Plays #7. Coyote IV: Other Side Camp *in* West Coast Plays #9. Coyote V: Listening to Old Nana *in* West Coast Plays #13/14. *The interview referred to in the article is "On the Creation of the Coyote Cycle" by Barry Barankin in* West Coast Plays #7.

Coyote is the legend of our beliefs, strength of our strong.
—Dennis Banks

Santa Fe—In the beginning, the Creator (playwright/director Murray Mednick) took a small band of actors (Darrell Larson, Norbert Weisser, Ellen Blake) into a remote clearing in a place called Padua Hills. They peered up into the trees, smelled the air, and perused the ground under their feet. They began moving around, feeling the planet's gravitational pull, prowling each other in a love/ hate hunt.

The Creator said to the two men: "You will be Coyote/Trickster —one from the mountains above, the other from the earth below. And you"—pointing at the actress—"will be Spider Woman. If the other two get out of line, whip 'em back into shape."

Thus—or so we might imagine, under the spell of Mednick's playwrighting voice—*The Coyote Cycle* was born.

Seven parts of the Cycle have emerged year-by-year at the Padua Hills Playwrights' Festival in California, where Mednick is artistic director. But not until a recent Saturday night had an audience been invited to witness, meditate with, and sleep to the entire *Coyote* saga. They had come to the foothills beyond Santa Fe to put themselves through a test. The test was a challenge to concentrate from seven o'clock in the twilit eve to the break of dawn the next day.

It also asked a willingness to surrender to what Mednick called "the grammar of these pieces"—their mythic, coy language; the exercises and movements that act as a code for each section; the audience's own exercising as they hiked from one performance to another (a Padua tradition). The flow would have been felt a little more this night but for the numbing, chilled air that reminded us, with a vengeance, that we were in the Sangre de Cristo mountains. Note-taking was out of the question. Stay warm. Don't wander off the trail. And listen.

With survival comes its rewards. The great reward as dawn emerged was the realization that *Coyote*, all seven parts of it, was of a piece. The fear that it would be unconnected plays in search of a center was dashed to the ground. For once, an ambitious idea had realized startling fruition.

For all its ambition, to say nothing of its circuitousness, *Coyote*'s basic dramatic line is as clean and bold as an Indian painting. Larson's Coyote is on a mission from Earthmaker "to destroy the evil spirits afflicting mankind. . . to make the waterfall come to earth." Weisser's Trickster—not just Coyote's alter-ego but his other half— erupts out of the ground, up from one of his customary subterranean journeys, in what is surely one of the most hilarious and theatrical—uh, stage entrances?—ever.

Coyote is equal parts bumbling and wise. He gets no help from Trickster, who cons, shadows, and nearly outfoxes the poor critter. The wonder isn't that it takes Coyote so long—eleven hours (including intermissions)—to bring the waterfall to earth. The wonder is that he gets the job done at all.

Above both of them is the spell and power of Spider Woman (Christine Avila, who took the role over from Blake a few years ago). She isn't to be read as a sexist image of a black widow spider ensnaring any susceptible male. Rather—and it gets us to the overriding concern of *The Coyote Cycle*—she weaves the interconnecting web that links all the disparate adventures and desires together. Avila's majestic presence belies a feminine aura of guiding, nurturing, and healing, most clearly with her prodding of her aide, Clown (Priscilla Cohen), into maturity and womanhood.

What Mednick is after is nothing less than an ecological view of existence. It infuses everything, from the constant web-image to the physical process of actor and audience involvement. (There's nothing worse in this saga, for character or listener, than if, as Coyote says, "your sense of place is dead.")

The paramount concern of the characters—even when they want to bash each other's brains in—is that the earth is dying. We're told by way of tales which Mednick invented or borrowed from, among others, Hopi and Eskimo creation stories, that the planet has died before and has been made over. The hope, a poignant one in the nuclear age, is that it can be made over again. But you sense, especially, Spider Woman's impatience. Might Earthmaker not just give up on us?

The fun at Santa Fe was picking out and following any number of the many strands of Mednick's ecological web to see where they led. And the complete *Coyote*, even with the specter of ecocide haunting it to the final coda, is tremendous fun—especially when witnessed in a clean environment. For instance, in part three, *Planet of the Spider People*, Coyote/Trickster refer to the Milky Way. Look up, and there it is. You couldn't do that at Padua.

One strand that struck this freezing viewer at about 2:30 A.M. was the theme of growing up—becoming a human being. If the waterfall is the exterior goal, this was the interior one. And if this is the odd goal of animals, then it's one of the many oddities we accept here. At Coyote's lowest ebbs—be they losing his wife in the Land of the Dead or quarreling with his uncooperative penis—what eggs him on is gaining humanness. Clown begins the Cycle with a torrent of mumbles and guttural spewings (she's a dope addict) but evolves, with the guidance of Spider Woman, into a capable, adult conjurer. There's hope for the human ecology, at least.

Another strand is everyone's need to tell a story. In many ways, the Cycle is one long string of successive tales, told to make a point or declare one's existence. Parts one (*Pointing*), two (*The Shadow Ripens*), four (*Other Side Camp*), and six (*The Sacred Dump*) are especially thick with tales. Instantly, links are made between the Gaelic *Mabinogion*, the Native American myths, and the Icelandic sagas. The work is rife with Westernisms as well. But Mednick takes us so far West that we're in the East, carried across a conceptual Bering Strait into the land of Zen where "arrows go clear through you." All this exemplifies *Coyote's* great contribution to contemporary theater: Mednick has created a new kind of anthropologic time capsule.

In an interview in 1980, Weisser revealed rule number one for *Coyote* actors: "Don't get lost in the words and in the characters. Pay attention to the energy that comes through your feet—all the time, all the time." Through the night we follow the words and the characters, but we also follow the cast's feet. They are in constant motion, adhering to the exercises and choreography Mednick and the actors have developed together. The Cycle can be seen as an increasingly sophisticated series of movement/exercises, heightening tidally toward the climaxing waterfall.

Most of the crowd made it through to dawn, though no one avoided nodding off (sleep, Mednick suggested between sets, is one way of experiencing the Cycle). No one, that is, except the players and Mednick, who played an appropriate rhythm drum during scenes.

Robert Wilson projects aside, could there be a more epic marathon group performance than this? Larson, Weisser, Avila, and Cohen not only stay with their characters, they grow stronger in them as the hours go by and the temperature drops. The coyote-strength that Dennis Banks refers to seems to be with them. *Other Side Camp* involves a deal where Weisser and Larson will exchange their cloaks—their only protection—for Spider Grandmother's wisdom. Now *this* is environmental drama.

When you see *Coyote* through, you forget specifics and remember Mednick's paradoxical way of combining holy man's language with streetwise talk (Avila is a master here). Also the shotgun wit, Robert Behling's variegated sets that work up a train of dazzling images, and the stars above. Wherever you see *Coyote* (and hopefully there will be more chances), be sure you can see the stars.

Aspects of Padua

The Seventh Annual Padua Hills Playwrights' Workshop and Festival took place at the California Institute of the Arts in Valencia, California, under the artistic direction of Murray Mednick. This seventh year was marked by the move from Claremont to Valencia (and the subsequent changes in performance spaces); the presentation of the largest company of playwrights, actors, apprentices, students, and (for want of an appropriate theater title) "facilitators" to date. The following notes, impressions, memoirs, and maxims were solicited from a random selection of participants by Susan La Tempa.

PHOTO: DEBRA RICHARDSON

The Question of Where
Susan Champagne

Having spent my fourth summer as a student/apprentice at the Padua Hills Playwrights' Workshop/Festival, I feel the need to reflect on what makes Padua such a necessary place for me and others.

Padua is a six week program where students, writers, actors, directors, and technicians live and work together to create plays for specific outdoors spaces. In writing workshops we're stirred by an image, an association, a succession of words, a place—and we're encouraged to try to communicate something of our experience.

The concern with space is primary in that it connects us with the sensual: with where we have been, with where we are. In some way, this connection can't help but concern us with our heritage: with what our past tells us of where we have come from and with how we will determine where we'll go. This brings us to the idea of "home."

"How do I get back to my own tribe and see the real world?" is a question Coyote often asks in Murray Mednick's *Coyote* plays. This question might be the key to Mednick's approach to playwrighting and playmaking. The question of "where" we are, and our vision or our self-deception about how we behave in this world and in our own specific spaces within it provides us with a primary dramatic as well as a *real* question. Padua is a place to explore this.

Maxims to Make Plays By

Stephen Bauer

Paper isn't stone.

Five cooks with five cats can make five meals, and each one will be cat soup.

Try to know when to shoot the shit.

You may light off a lot of ideas before you find the gas.

Sometimes you've got to let a person be his own idiot.

A day at a time you chop rehearsals—apples, oranges, bananas, melons—and in the end, you have fruit salad.

Pragmatism can be as valuable as creativity, vision, diplomacy, finesse, and sweat.

If you know you're right, find a bigger bat.

Style is something you mine.

Some actors really can perform the phone book.

Keep a boot on the throat of your critic.

Sometimes you need to shine a light on it to see it.

Inspiration can be cocaine: it's here, it's there, and then what?

You don't write a play, you write a theater.

Language is an animal thing—it has tongue, teeth, lips, air, and an appetite for live meat.

If you paste it with a bumperstickers, it's not in the race.

Your budget always doubles.

My eye is my eye.

A pencil and a hoe are different tools.

A pencil, a hoe, and an actor are different tools.

If you use all the good stuff, the play will be six hours long.

You don't bitch if you don't care.

Writing is a physical activity is a way of thinking is work. So is rehearsal.

Listen to the language fresh and stop listening to yourself.

You can't learn karate from a book.

What is unknown is alive; what is known is gone, dead.

You don't grow a cornstalk until you bury the kernel.

The word "director" is only an anagram for the word "audience."

Even if it doesn't apply, eventually it will apply.

Spraypaint ain't tuckpoint, and talk ain't caulk.

If you feed a jackal your left leg today, what do you feed him tomorrow?

A good garden needs a lot of shit.

Pathology is never easy.

Black Humor and Kinetic Psychosis

Roxanne Rogers

John O'Keefe's offering this year at Padua, *Mimzabim*, became an investigation of the consumerized psychology of the 1980s with each character a microcosm of the young urban professional. Through exercises, improvisation, and experimentation, we (I was one of the actors) dilated the ideas and emotional tone of the script into fast-paced and athletic movement, voice, and gesture. The total performance came at the audiences from all sides and on all levels.

We created a visceral style of acting by tearing each scene or character apart to find its essence, before restructuring it into a rhythm more suited to rock 'n' roll than to the "well made play."

Our goal was to make *Mimzabim* more than a psycho-horror show
—to make it a real comedic investigation of the darker side of our
own greed, selfishness, and violence. Before we were done, most
scenes had been significantly changed and most of the script
reordered to create a visual and aural cacophony which made the
audience's subconscious bristle with fear.

O'Keefe is one of the few playwright/directors who welcomes
the opportunity to muck around in the lower depths long enough to
see what humor lies there. In addition, O'Keefe is a tremendous
actor himself, with unending resources for guiding actors through
the rather grisly "research" demanded in his work. In order to get
to the core of *Mimzabim*, we had to develop a method of getting to
and working within intensified mental and physical states. Some of
our tactics are enumerated below.

Our first decision was to work as an ensemble, establishing a
"tight but open anarchy" where everyone's suggestions were
considered and more often adopted than not. From day one,
rehearsals began with a rigorous vocal and physical warm-up. This
gave us ready access to our finer impulses which we constantly
drew upon to inquire into the bare bones of a scene or character.
Scenes that weren't working were repeated again and again until
an internal rhythm was pinpointed. Then another set of exercises
was developed to keep the trickier scenes primed at their apex.

Characters were explored through accelerated movement until,
again, a rhythm was established, at which point the character was
reintegrated into the scene. As actors, we switched roles in order to
watch others rehearsing our own scenes. This little trick let us see
which aspects of our characters were coming across, as well as how
other members of the ensemble viewed each characer in the context of the play.

We developed a disciplined lunacy in rehearsal which facilitated
the unique stylization of the piece. Some of the images throughout
the play were so hard-edged and terrifying (i.e., highly realistic
dummies falling onto the stage from seven stories above, or Sara's
blood-curdling hysteria blasting through the closet door) that
audience members were unsure whether to scream or laugh. Our
acting had to balance on a fine edge between black humor and
kinetic psychosis in order to summon the audience into the blustery
world of *Mimzabim*.

We continued to radically rework elements of the play during
the three weeks in which we performed, often performing new,
untried ideas right on top of bits that worked well from the beginning. Constant simplification became essential as the original

special effects in the script were very ornate, while our budget and production capabilities were extremely limited. We all contributed directing, dialogue, and acting ideas freely. Everything was subject to change, if need be.

So it was through the "tight but open anarchy" of our ensemble effort that we were all able to contribute fully, proving that seven minds *are* better than one *if* working together. However, this well-balanced band of artists was created after John O'Keefe had worked with most of the cast members in numerous prior pieces. We were able to sculpt a visceral performance out of all our talents under the keen eye of O'Keefe and his uncanny ability to infest an audience's subconscious with throbbing gothic imagery.

I Wandered Through
Jack Hollingsworth

The Padua Hills Playwrights' Festival opened its theater doors and I wandered through six incredible weeks, soaking up its magic, and I'm still spinning.

The festival was defined by you. It was there, coming alive, and you pretty much chose what you wanted to be a part of. Plays were growing up all around. Walking across a field or down a hall you might be stopped by a playwright, and, by saying yes, you became a part of his or her creation. Thus I became a part of three vastly different plays. But I was living in such a cross-fire of plays and people that I came to know a good portion of them all. If something interesting was happening on someone else's set, I'd hear about it and check it out.

By going to the different rehearsals I came to see how the playwrights approached their work. A lot of misconceptions were ripped away and, in general, theater became de-mystified. The glamor was drowned in the constant sweat and work of what it really takes to make a play play.

I came to have a profound feeling for the actresses and actors and how often they make what is written better, more alive. And how this life, this living character, changes the scribblings in ways undreamed—a truly remarkable part of the magic.

I saw a myriad of theatrical problems solved, often through unique solutions suited only to that particular play. I saw how a playwright might scalpel out some dead part or how some other playwright might expand their piece.

Through the weeks, a feeling for the group grew. This feeling has continued beyond the festival. And this has a way of expanding, of helping me take new directions and avenues that weren't open to me before.

Padua breeds talent and hope.

Observations on the Festival
John Steppling

The Padua Hills Festival has always focused its energy inward —publicity was relatively ignored and the natural intimacy and immediacy of the experience coveted.

"The instant the criterion of authenticity ceases to be applicable to artistic production, the total function of art is reversed. Instead of being based on ritual, it begins to be based on another practice—politics." Walter Benjamin.

The festival has always been a place for its artists to discover the unnecessary.

The true festival serves to nurture new desires which can cultivate the possible conditions for a transformation of theatrical practice.

Temporary utopianism at work against the atomizing of people this society encourages. Leisure life is now private life. Our experience of culture is ever more separate.

"The capitalist order can survive only by ceaselessly fabricating a new past for itself." Guy Debord.

Padua has looked for ways to overcome the prevailing conditions in southern California—the lack of a genuine critical community and an audience uncomfortable with anything not easily labeled and measured. The feelings of familiarity so cherished, of agreement and identification—the exhibition value. Theater today has ceased to have any connection to what Baudelaire called "Correspondences" (Benjamin designated "Correspondences" as the data of remembrance, not historical data but the data of pre-history).

"Identification is the lowest form of appreciation." Genet.

Today's "reviewer" trivializes by possessing only fragmentary judgements.

The "Aura" of a work of art, says Benjamin, is in its here and now, a quality of unapproachability, born of the ritual and magical context where all art originates.
"The origin is the goal." Karl Kraus.

Padua has aimed at establishing a sense of tradition, of a certain experience rooted in tradition, "Erfahrung," of the authentic.

"The cold stone floor of Greek tragedy." Robert Bly.

The real combative posture is elusive; the value of this festival is not in its individual works but in the collective sensibility—the spirit rather than the product. The content of the Padua Hills Festival is in the form of the festival.

Adolescent Urges
Leon Martell

SCENE ONE

The PLAYWRIGHT *on the phone.*

PLAYWRIGHT: I was wondering if you were coming to Padua this summer and if you would be in my play?

YOUNG ACTOR: What's it about?

PLAYWRIGHT: It's. . . about adolescent urges. *(Pause.)* Playing. . . adolescent urges. . . .

YOUNG ACTOR: Uh huh.

PLAYWRIGHT: Or like, why I'm a grown man but I still want to go to Clint Eastwood movies.

YOUNG ACTOR: 'Cause they're fun.

PLAYWRIGHT: I'm gonna need your help because you're, you know, *in* adolescence, or just been through it.

YOUNG ACTOR: Yeah.

PLAYWRIGHT: Like I was wondering. What kind of music do you listen to? Do you listen to. . . Quiet Riot?

YOUNG ACTOR: No. Some guys my age do, though. Heavy metal kids.

PLAYWRIGHT: What do they like about it?

YOUNG ACTOR: That the adults hate it, mostly.

PLAYWRIGHT: What do you listen to?

YOUNG ACTOR: Oh, the Police. Bruce Springsteen.

PLAYWRIGHT: That's what I listen to! *(Pause.)* You'll probably be playing younger than you are. . .

SCENE TWO

The PLAYWRIGHT *on the phone.*

TV PERSON: Now, where do we reach you next week?

PLAYWRIGHT: In the dorm in Valencia.

TV PERSON: Oh, right. *(Pause.)* Why are you in a dorm in Valencia?

PLAYWRIGHT: I'm doing the playwrights' festival. The Padua Hills Playwrights' Festival.
TV PERSON: Oh, right. *(Pause.)* Where's Padua Hills? In Valencia?

SCENE THREE

A rehearsal room in Valencia, California.

PLAYWRIGHT: So! That's what it's about. It's a quest. It's about magic, but I don't ever want to say "magic." It's the way of seeing magic in places and things that most of us see as normal. Does this seem...to make sense?
THE CAST: Oh yeah! Great. Sure!
ADULT ACTOR: Uh, when do we get a...script?
PLAYWRIGHT: Monday. *(Pause.) Really.* The entire first draft. I promise!

SCENE FOUR

A sidewalk near a cement wall.

PLAYWRIGHT: I've got another rewrite.
THE CAST: ACK. GAG. NOOOOO! NOT ANOTHER ONE! Can we have a copy?
PLAYWRIGHT: I wrote it late last night so there wasn't anywhere to make a copy before now, but I typed up another so if we bunch around we can read off these two.
THE CAST: OK.
ADULT ACTOR *(reading)*: "Wakasecauheah? Askiddin' Askidin'?"
PLAYWRIGHT: Yeah—it's like: "Wait a second here. I'm kidding."
ADULT ACTOR: OK. *(Reads.)* "Wakasecauheah? Askiddin'. Comahbak! Wekebeefrez?"
PLAYWRIGHT: Oh—the last one's a typo.

SCENE FIVE

On the set

STAGE MANAGER: I'm going to warn you, I've never run lights before. I never really wanted to. I'm afraid of it. I'm just the sort of person who panics under stress. *(Pause.)* But I'll do it.
PLAYWRIGHT: Don't worry, this will be easy. If you can't see the actors, bring up more lights. It'll be that simple. These are just like wall dimmers....
STAGE MANAGER: LIKE WHAT?! LIKE WHAT?!
PLAYWRIGHT: LIKE DIMMERS! People have them in their houses to dim the lights. You know—a knob you turn and the lights dim.

STAGE MANAGER: Oh, yeah.

PLAYWRIGHT: These are *just* like that, only bigger. Turn 'em *up*, *more* light. Turn 'em *down*, less light. Simple. Only, when you're patching it together...

STAGE MANAGER: WHAT?! WHAT?!

PLAYWRIGHT: When you're *putting* the light set-up *together*, *plugging* the lights in, you have to put the thousand watt light into its own...

STAGE MANAGER (*interrupting*): What's that noise?

PLAYWRIGHT: THE SPRINKLERS!! I'LLGETTHELIGHT-BOARD YOUGETTHELIGHTS!!!

STAGE MANAGER: WHICH LIGHTS?

PLAYWRIGHT: THE ONES ON THE GROUND! *THAT ONE!* THE WATER'S SHOOTING RIGHT INTO IT!!!

SCENE SIX

In the parking lot.

ADULT ACTOR: I just wanted to know, now that the show's over—when is Tavish getting his skateboard back?

PLAYWRIGHT: He didn't get it back *yet?*

ADULT ACTOR: No.

PLAYWRIGHT: Oh god. Don't worry. He'll get it back.

ADULT ACTOR: I'm not worried.

PLAYWRIGHT: He loaned it to us on good faith that we'd take good care of it. That was pretty generous for a seven-year-old. Really generous. I'll see that he gets it back right away. Don't worry.

ADULT ACTOR: I'm not worried.

PLAYWRIGHT: That's right, Jesse was going to give it to Morgan!

ADULT ACTOR: Morgan doesn't have it.

PLAYWRIGHT: Oh god, I'll find it. Don't worry!

ADULT ACTOR: I'm not worried.

SCENE SEVEN

The PLAYWRIGHT *on the phone.*

TV PERSON: So, how was your thing?

PLAYWRIGHT: Great! Great!

TV PERSON: No problems?

PLAYWRIGHT: A million problems! But I got to do what I wanted to do, so how can I bitch, eh?

TV PERSON: I guess.

PLAYWRIGHT: I worked with some brilliant young people. The

kids really show you. When the writing is good, they make it great. When it's bad, it falls apart.

TV PERSON: Hmmm.

PLAYWRIGHT: So you really see what you've got, no bullshit. They don't know how to fake it, so you can't either. I learned a lot.

TV PERSON: So you made it through.

PLAYWRIGHT: Oh, I was on the edge of quitting for the first week, but my friends reminded me, "This is an experiment. It doesn't have to work, it just has to be an experiment."

TV PERSON: And it worked!

PLAYWRIGHT: *That* made me wonder if it was a big enough experiment.

TV PERSON: You theater guys are sick.

Family Portrait
Beverly A Smith

Family Portrait was first presented at the Lorraine Hansberry Theater, San Francisco, on May 18, 1984, with the following cast:

TANDY	Norman Dwight Huntsman
CARYL	Tonya-Marie Amos
FRANCINE	Talibah

Directed by Steven Ronald Dawson
Set design by Barbara Henley
Lighting design by Doug Nelson
Sound design by Shyworks Sound
Produced by SEW Productions
Photographs by Allen Nomura

CHARACTERS

TANDY: Black, 32-year-old husband of Francine
FRANCINE: Black, 36-year-old working mother and wife.
CARYL: Black, 20-year-old daughter of Francine.

Family Portrait
Beverly A Smith

Lights up on TANDY, FRANCINE, *and* CARYL *downstage center, posing for a picture.* FRANCINE, *wearing a nice dress with a jacket or a suit, is sitting in a chair. Standing to her right, dressed in a three-piece suit with his left hand on her shoulder, is* TANDY. *Sitting at* FRANCINE's *feet on the edge of the stage, dressed in her high school uniform—white blouse, short pleated plaid skirt, matching cardigan, and penny loafers—is* CARYL. *They are all smiling out over the audience. A burst of light flashes (like a flashbulb) and the scene fades to black.*

Lights up on three areas of the stage. Each area could be on different levels, and has a straight-back chair. The mid-stage right area has a small work table. This is TANDY's *space. The center area has a night stand. This is* FRANCINE's *space. The mid-stage left area has a floor speaker. This is* CARYL's *space. Each person is seated in his or her space.*

TANDY (*picking up cigarettes from table and lighting one*): I don't know why I agreed to having this portrait done. I could be home watching the game.

CARYL (*with leg up on chair, straightening her socks*): Every year, since I can remember, we've had to do this portrait business. But it's only been for the past seven years that I've had to wear my high school uniform.

FRANCINE: You'd think that I asked them to put on blindfolds and stand against the wall to be shot! I had to nag them for three hours just to get them down here on time.

TANDY: Well, as long as it makes her happy. My daddy used to say to do what little thing you could to make the woman happy so that you can do the *big* things that make *you* happy.

CARYL: Of course my stepfather wasn't in any of these pictures until he married my mom. That was when I was thirteen.

FRANCINE: My mother used to try to get all of us together to take a family portrait. Every year she'd try to do it, and my father would always act up and we'd never get to go.

TANDY: That old man. Now he wasn't a saint. He messed around a lot, and hit on my mom a little—just a little, because there were four of us sons around. But he still worked hard and brought most of his money home to Mom.

CARYL: I never saw my real father. My mom used to tell me that he was killed in a car accident. But my cousin April said. . . .

FRANCINE: There were six girls and two boys in my family. Could you see all of us crowding into a family portrait?

CARYL: She heard my Aunt Cloteal talking about how my father lived with my mother for three years, and when my mom got pregnant with me. . . .

FRANCINE: We never had an ounce of privacy. I was the youngest, and I think it was when I was a little girl. . . .

CARYL: He moved out and married someone else. . . I wonder if my mom will ever forgive me for that.

FRANCINE: That I decided I would never have more than one child. . .and even that was too much.

TANDY: So my mom—no matter what my old man did—she stayed with him. She'd always tell my two sisters. . . .

CARYL: I never told Mom what I heard, but maybe if my real daddy were here, Mom would feel differently about me.

TANDY: "The man is *always* the head of the house. Without a man, nothing is important." That's why my sisters always helped look after us sons.

FRANCINE: I was so tired of being crowded up that I left home at thirteen—just so I could get a breath. There were so many of us I just got lost in the shuffle. No one paid any attention to me.

TANDY: They'd cook and wash and iron for us. They even had to clean our rooms for us because my mom felt that men had more important things to do.

FRANCINE: How does a thirteen-year-old girl survive in the world? Well, luckily I ran into Tomas. He was a street brother—about thirty years old—but he took me in.

CARYL: I always wish I had known my father. We don't have any pictures. I think my mom burned them or something.

TANDY: Which we did. My brothers were able to play some pro ball, but I went the academic route. . . .

FRANCINE: Tomas was what most people call a "pretty nigguh"—light-skinned with wavy hair. We were together for three years. . . .

TANDY: And got an MBA. Both my sisters got married, and they have a bunch of little kids. Went right from my daddy's house to their husbands' houses. They're still taking care of their men.

CARYL: If it weren't for my cousin April, I wouldn't know anything. She told me my father was "cute". . . too cute for my mom. At least that's what *her* mother said.

FRANCINE: And we wouldn't have been together that long if I hadn't followed what my mother always told us. . . .

CARYL: He supposedly had children all over town. Which means I have brothers and sisters I've never seen.

FRANCINE: "In order to get ahead in this world, there has to be a leader and someone to follow. The man leads, so the woman *got* to follow." *(Laughs and turns to* TANDY, *then to* CARYL.*)* Tandy, Caryl, come on now! We've got to sit for another picture!

She moves chair down center. This time, TANDY *sits,* FRANCINE *stands at his left, and* CARYL *sits on the edge of the stage to his right. They smile, looking out over the audience. A light flashes, followed by a fade to black.*

Lights up on FRANCINE's *area only.*

FRANCINE *(standing by chair)*: See, nobody likes to talk about sex. And that's a lot of what Tomas and I were about. I didn't see him very much, but we made love every chance we could. I knew that Tomas was into some shady business, but as long as he never brought it around me, I didn't care. We always seemed to have enough money, and I didn't ask for much. And I'd stay home and keep the apartment together. I had so many plants in the place, Tomas used to call it "Eden." *(Pauses and changes tone.)* But there was a snake in the garden. I mean, it wasn't anyone's fault. We took precautions—Tomas always used a rubber—but one must have been defective. I didn't realize for three months that I was even pregnant. Tomas was furious! He blamed everything on me. He left me when I was in my seventh month, and went off and married some eighteen-year-old girl across town. One of his friends, who had been trying to get into my face, told me. *(Lights up on* CARYL's *area. She is sitting facing the audience.)* If I'd have known then what I know *now*, I would have gotten rid of the "snake in the garden."

CARYL: I must admit, Mom has been good to me. She made sure that I went to the best schools, and she bought me everything she felt I needed. I know her life was rough. . . .

FRANCINE: I was on welfare the first three years because I was too young to get a job, and I had no education. So I went to school and got a high school diploma, joined the WIN program to get some training, and was able to get a job in the State Personnel Office.

CARYL: But my life hasn't been so great either. Whenever Mom had a free moment, she spent it looking for a father for me. . .or so she said.

FRANCINE: After I was working and doing okay for me and Caryl, then I let my family know where I was. I didn't want any of them to shake their finger in my face and tell me, "I told you so!"

CARYL *(to* FRANCINE*):* But all I want is my *real* father. You never tell me anything about him. It's almost as if he never existed. . . .

FRANCINE: So I told them the story that I had been married, but Caryl's father had been killed in a car accident. Well, I didn't tell all of them that. I told my sister Cloteal the truth. . .because we've always been tight.

CARYL: And if my father never existed, then neither do I.

Lights fade out on CARYL, *and up on* TANDY.

FRANCINE: But it's not right for a woman to be alone in the world. I was still young, in my early twenties, and I must say, I still had a lot on the ball.

TANDY: I majored in management. I have good ideas and I can work well with people. And I must admit, I love the feeling of being in control. I mean not only being in control of my own life, but in control of other people. . . in the work environment, that is.

FRANCINE *stands and looks at herself in an imaginary, full-length mirror.*

FRANCINE *(touching her body as she talks)*: I did develop early. Tomas said that I must have been *born* a woman. I had big breasts that he loved to touch. He'd say he'd never have to worry about a place to lay his head.

TANDY: I got a job right after grad school with IBM. Of course, I had to go into their executive trainee program first, so that I could be molded into the company's image.

FRANCINE: And I had nice smooth hips and big legs. But the best part is my waist. Tomas' fingers could meet around my waist, and he'd hold me that way whenever we made love. My waist is still pretty small.

TANDY: We had to eat, sleep, and breathe IBM. You know, for the longest time we could only wear navy blue or black suits. We all looked like we were going to a funeral five days a week. I was the only one that ever smiled at people. I guess that's why they put me in personnel.

FRANCINE *(sitting)*: So luckily I still had my looks, and I have a job that gave me a lot of public contact. Many nice men came into the office, and a lot of them would ask me out. I thought it was important to go out and get to know people so that I could find a man who would be a good father for Caryl, and a good husband to me.

TANDY: There are a lot of fringe benefits when you work for IBM. One is that you suddenly become attractive to the women. Even a janitor can get over if he says, "I work for IBM. . .". Never mind that he cleans *bathrooms* at IBM. But after a while a man gets tired of many women and starts looking for *the one*, you know? And I found her. I was out being bored by the usual "unusual" sights, when I saw this lady sitting in a group of women. For what it was worth, she could have been sitting with a gorilla, because I only noticed her.

Fast dance music comes up. Lights flash in FRANCINE's *and* TANDY's *areas.* TANDY *is looking at* FRANCINE. *He stands and walks toward her. Lights fade out in* TANDY's *area, and fade up on* CARYL, *with her feet on the speaker, head set on, sitting in the chair, and rocking to the music.* FRANCINE *is laughing and tapping her foot to the music, as if she is sitting in a disco.*

TANDY *mimes asking* FRANCINE *to dance, and she accepts. They move downstage and dance. After a few moments, a slow song comes on. They slow dance, miming conversation.* CARYL *turns and watches them dance for a minute, slipping the head set down to her neck. When she starts to talk, the music fades out and the lights fade out on* FRANCINE *and* TANDY. *They continue embracing.*

CARYL: She didn't come home that night. In fact, she didn't come home all weekend. Oh, she called and told the sitter to drop me off at a friend's house. My mom is always responsible. And she even called me Sunday morning to apologize for not being able to take me to see "The Wiz" like she had promised. I was almost twelve years old then.

Lights up on TANDY's *and* FRANCINE's *areas.*

TANDY: Francine was just what I'd been looking for. I mean, she's four years older, but that is what was good about it. She had a lot of experience, and I felt I could learn from her. She was the kind of woman my old man used to say was hard to find. . . .

FRANCINE: Tandy didn't mind that I had a child. He loved me for what *I* am. Even though he is four years younger, he seemed to have his head on straight. He was responsible, and he respected the fact that I am a responsible person, too. My momma was right. . . "Age don't make the man."

TANDY: She is a lady in public, and a wild woman in private. Although she dressed and acted conservatively, you could feel the carnal fire burning underneath. She's got strong desires, and she was about taking care of business both in and out of bed.

CARYL: I don't think my mother and I ever had a real relationship. Everything with us was just appropriate—nothing more. She treated me as if I were another piece of business, an obligation. Whenever I tried to talk to her about anything personal, she would shine me off, tell me she was too busy to deal with foolishness.

FRANCINE: Caryl, I know you didn't want to come today, but would you mnd getting over here so that we can get this over with? You too, Tandy.

TANDY *(lighting another cigarette)*: Why don't you do a mother-daughter shot this time? I'm just the newest addition to the family.

FRANCINE *(waving CARYL over)*: Well, come on. Just don't stand there.

CARYL *and* FRANCINE *move downstage center.* FRANCINE *sits and* CARYL *stands to her left. They assume a pose. The light flashes. All lights fade to black. Lights up on* TANDY's *area.*

TANDY: As a man on the executive track, I need a supportive woman. The women that I met and dated in the company used to get on my nerves real quick. They always talked about how important their careers are, and then they would proceed to charge the meal on *their* American Express cards. It was like I didn't count for anything as a man. But Francine was different. When I talked about myself, she listened, I mean really listened. And she always let me pay our way when we went out. She always had a way of knowing what I wanted at the time. You know, after you spend time getting your manhood kicked around by a bunch of impotent white men every day, it made you feel good to come home to someone who cared about *your* welfare. Yeah, I can hear the women's libbers groaning in their graves, but our relationship was so good that Francine could take care of *my* needs *and* her own. *(Lights up on* CARYL's *area.)* Who ever heard of a black feminist? It's a contradiction of terms. Black women are too individual to fall into that "feminist" trap. There's nothing like a black woman.... Anyway, after a year, Francine and I decided to get married.

CARYL: It was quite a wedding. Since it was my mom's first real wedding, she went all out. I was one of her four bridesmaids, and I was paired up with one of my stepfather's nephews.

TANDY: My father was a little concerned at first because Francine already had a daughter. He said, "A man should be careful 'bout gettin used goods." But my mom liked her right away because she knew a woman's place—to support her man. And Caryl was perfect! She's very intelligent and mannerable. Most of the time she was so quiet, you'd hardly know she was around.

CARYL: At first things felt really good. We moved into a three-bedroom house, and I got to fix up my room any way I wanted. And my mom even started treating me better. We'd go shopping together and she was more interested in what I was doing at school. I'd always been an honor student, and I had joined the track team. But most of all, I was finally going to have a father. He was nice. He'd make it a point to have all of us go places together...vacations, movies, dinners. Sometimes, when my mom didn't feel up to it, he'd take me places himself. He treated me like his own daughter.

Lights down on CARYL's *area.*

TANDY: You know what? Within three months after getting married, I was promoted to Corporate Affirmative Action Officer. You know why? Because being married made me a more stable member of the corporate family.

Lights out on TANDY *and up on* CARYL *and* FRANCINE *in* FRANCINE's *area.* CARYL *is seated, holding a hand mirror, while* FRANCINE *is styling her hair.*

FRANCINE *(combing* CARYL's *hair):* Now how did you say you wanted this?

CARYL *(looking into the mirror):* I want to see what it looks like piled up.*(Long pause.)*: Momma, why do I have to start wearing a bra?

FRANCINE: Well...so that it will...help support your breasts so that they won't sag.

CARYL: Momma, I don't have anything *to* sag!

FRANCINE: Well, they also keep your breasts covered so that they don't show through your clothes.

CARYL: Well, can't I just wear a T-shirt or something? I feel stupid wearing a bra with nothing to fill it.

FRANCINE: Well, don't your friends wear them?

CARYL: Yes, but they need to. Did you know Twyla's fourteen years old like me and she wears a 34C bra? And she wears make-up? And stockings? And has pierced ears with three holes in each ear? And all the boys are crazy about her?

FRANCINE: Honey, everyone is different. You'll be at that point soon. Look, tomorrow's Saturday. Let's go shopping for some beautiful lacy bras, and maybe some colored stockings. Does that sound okay? (CARYL *nods her head.*) Now how does this hair look?

CARYL *(looking in mirror)*: I like this! Maybe I could get my hair cut and styled?

FRANCINE *(putting the comb and bobby pins into the nightstand drawer)*: I'll think about it.

CARYL: Mom, when I'm rich, I'm going to build this big house so that you and Tandy can live with me.

FRANCINE *(laughing)*: Um-umm-umm. When you're grown, I intend to live on the other side of the country from you. You're on your own! And I don't intend to be a babysitting grandma, either!

They laugh. CARYL *puts the mirror in the drawer and starts rummaging through the drawer, trying on earrings, opening bottles of perfume, and playing with tubes of lipstick.*

CARYL: Mom, have you decided about the dance? It's next Friday.

TANDY *comes into the area.*

FRANCINE *(taking the earrings, make-up, and perfume, and putting them back in the drawer)*: So you want me to drop you and your friends off and pick you up? *(Pause.)* I don't know. Friday's are so bad for me.

TANDY: How are my favorite ladies? *(He hugs* FRANCINE *and musses* CARYL's *hair.)*

CARYL: Stop! Mom just fixed it!

TANDY: I can take Caryl and her friends, *and* pick them up . . . if you feel it's okay for her to go to the dance.

FRANCINE: Well . . . I'm not sure . . . (TANDY *and* CARYL *make pleading faces.*) Okay! Okay! You can go! Double-teaming me like that!

CARYL *(hugging* FRANCINE*)*: Thanks, Mom. I'm going to call Twyla and Ruth Ann now. *(She starts to leave.)*

TANDY: Hey, don't I get one of those, too?

CARYL *hugs* TANDY. *Then she returns to her own area, which is in darkness.*

TANDY: She's getting to be quite a lady! They grow up before you know it. *(He pokes* FRANCINE *in the ribs.)* Makes you feel old, doesn't it?

FRANCINE *(laughing and moving away):* No! You're only as old as you feel, so I'm *never* going to feel old.

TANDY: Come here.

FRANCINE: Why?

TANDY: Come over here. I've got something for you.

FRANCINE: Bring it over here.

TANDY: Uh uhn. You've got to come and get it.

FRANCINE: Let's compromise. At the count of three, let's both meet in the middle. *(They line up to get ready.)* One, two, three. . . go!

Neither one makes a move to go. They stand looking at each other, then burst into laughter. They move to each other and embrace. Lights fade to black. Lights up on the three areas and the downstage center area.

CARYL *(studiously rolling a joint):* Mom, why don't you two get a picture together? Reaffirm your wonderful relationship. *(She lights the joint.)*

TANDY: Sounds like a good idea to me. Let's look at each other with loving admiration. . .like we used to do.

TANDY and FRANCINE move to downstage center area. She sits. TANDY stands, grabbing her hands, and they look at each other full of love. CARYL smokes and watches them. Light flashes, then all lights fade to black. In the dark, the sound of someone sniffing cocaine is heard.

Lights up on TANDY's area only. He has a rolled dollar bill in his hand and a mirror with white powder on the table. He wipes his nostrils before speaking.

TANDY: I don't know when it all went wrong. And it didn't just go wrong. It fucked up royally! I guess it started when I began sneaking things onto my expense account. When I got my promotion, I had to travel a lot—go from office to office to make sure the corporation was in compliance with the Equal Employment Opportunity guidelines. So like I was in New York one time and I called up a buddy of mine. We wanted to go and see "Sophisticated Ladies," so I got us a couple of tickets and put it on my expense account—along with dinner and drinks. You know, I thought it wouldn't be a problem because a lot of other people did it. One dude had gotten himself an entire home computer with word processing and printer capabilities, and he didn't have to pay a quarter. So I figured a good night on the town was nothing. Well, nothing happened, so I figured everything was all right. I'd pad my expenses a little here and a little there. It took them a while, but they caught up with me. Almost $7000 later. But what makes me so mad is I didn't have anything to show for it! Some of the white boys got personal equipment, and even new cars at the company's expense—and they still got their jobs! I should have read the signs. No more equal opportunity here, bru-thuh! So I lost my job behind some chickenfeed. And you know, like I can't find another job like that—not under Reagonomics! *(Lights up on* FRANCINE's *area.)* How the fuck is a man supposed to take care of a family without a decent job?!

FRANCINE: It's been over three years since Tandy lost his job. Oh, he's had other jobs—not as good as what he had at IBM—but he either ends up being fired or walking off the job.

TANDY: I didn't invest all those years in school and at that goddamn company just to have some stockboy tell me what to do! Yeah, I left my last job because some boy that supervises the mail room was going to tell me how to do *my* job. . . and we didn't even work in the same area! But what tore it was that my boss was on *his* side! I told them, "Fuck this job. Get my paycheck ready so I can go!"

FRANCINE: It doesn't bother me that he's not working steady now, because we're doing okay on what I make. I know Tandy has a lot of pride. And that's what's been the problem for our black men . . . someone is always trying to take that pride away from them. So I feel it's my duty to be supportive and help in any way I can. *(Lights down on* TANDY's *area.)* I don't know about other men, but it seems that Tandy equates his job with his manhood. The lower the job, the lower his estimate of himself. But I don't feel the same way. I love him too much for that. He's still the same man. Except. . .*(Lights up on* CARYL's *area. She is reading through "Essence" magazine.)* Our sex life hasn't been the same. I mean we still make love, but not nearly as often or with the same feeling. Then he started that cocaine, and I don't know if that has anything to do with it either. I don't know what to do, other than be patient. I'm sure things will work themselves out.

Fast music comes up in CARYL*'s area. Lights out in* FRANCINE*'s area. After a moment, the phone rings.* CARYL *turns off the music and answers the phone.*

CARYL: Hello?... Hey, Twyla! What's going on?... Yeah this phone is great! I'm glad Mom got it for me.... What do you mean she didn't have a choice? Shut up, girl, I don't stay on the phone *that* much.... Well, at least I've never burnt a phone *out* like *you* did.... Who's pregnant?... Not *her*, she's always on the Honor Roll! Who's the daddy?... Oooooh.... Well, I hope that baby doesn't take after his big-head daddy 'cuz she's sure going to have a hard delivery.... I'm supposed to be studying for my Trig class. I swear, girl, I hope this class doesn't keep me out of college.... I haven't decided yet. I *want* to go back East.... Ruth Ann said Tandy is what!!... *(Laughing.)* I don't want to have to kick her behind about my mother's husband—talking about Tandy's super fine.... Who's been asking about me?... Girl, you'd better tell me or I'll never speak to you again!... Is he somebody I like?... *Yes*, I *do* like some of the guys in our neighborhood. It's just that I'm busy trying to keep my grades up, and then there *are* other things to do besides hang out all the time.... Girl, are you going to tell me who asked about me, or what?... I don't want to hear about who asked *you* out.... *(Exasperated)* Okay! Who asked you?... Cecil?... Nothing's wrong with him. He's just—too tall!... Well, I was slow dancing with him one time at Ruth Ann's house, and he was holding me tight and trying to roll *(Laughing)*—and his "thing" was almost up to my chest!... Who told you he could kiss? I let him kiss me once—just once—and I tell you, you'd best be prepared to swim! My face was wet from my nose to my chin!... Now tell me, who asked about *me*?... Is he cute?... Wait a minute. Let me turn on some music because if it's who I think it is, I'm going to scream! *(She puts the phone down and puts on "Watchin' You" by Slave. Then she goes back to the phone.)* Okay! Who is it? *(She screams.)* How do you know?... Benny told you? How does *he* know?... Wayne asked your brother Benny about me directly?... Well, what did he *say*? And what did *Benny* say? You really think he's going to ask me to the party next weekend? *(She screams again.)* Look, I'm going to have to get off this phone.... I'll stop by in the morning so we can walk to school together.... My denim skirt?... You've still got my blue sweater!... That's why you want it? You're a mess. Yeah, I'll bring it. Later.

She hangs up the phone and screams again, jumping around with excitement. Then she turns up the music and starts to dance. TANDY *comes over and stands just in the light, watching her. She dances for a few moments before seeing him.*

CARYL: Oh... I'm sorry.... Was the music too loud?... I didn't hear you come in.

TANDY *(moving into the area):* That's very nice. What do you call it?

CARYL: Oh... It's Slave... "Watchin' You"....

TANDY: No, I mean the dance.

CARYL: Oh!... That's nothing. Just something we're doing at school. I don't even know what it's called.

TANDY: Maybe you could show me how to do it. You know, I like to keep up with the latest dances.

CARYL: Well, I haven't learned it well enough myself yet....

TANDY: Well, I'll take a rain check.

CARYL: Oh... Okay. *(*TANDY *keeps watching her.)* Well... I'm going to have study... I have a lot of homework.

TANDY: Okay, I'll see you later.

He goes back to his area. CARYL *watches where he exited. Then she moves downstage in her area to talk to the audience.*

CARYL: That was the first time he ever made me nervous. It was creepy. I was about seventeen then. I'd come in from school, and he'd be here because he wasn't working. He'd watch me from the moment I came in. And even when my mom was home, I'd look up to find him watching me.

Lights up on TANDY's *area. He's watching* CARYL. *She turns and looks at him. He smiles. She turns back to the audience.*

CARYL: So I'd go to my room just to get away from his eyes.

TANDY *(still watching* CARYL): I don't know what it was. Really, that first time I came in to tell her to turn down the music a bit. But when I saw her dancing, it was like seeing her for the first time. That short skirt moving around her strong thighs....

CARYL: He used to come into my room without knocking, and make small talk. And he'd watch me all the time. Oh, he used to watch me before, but it was more with fatherly pride or something like that. This was different.

TANDY: And her smell! She was dancing around and getting really sweaty. She wore a light perfume, but her own smell was stronger. It wasn't that musky animal smell most women have, but clean and fresh. I started thinking about what it would smell like between those thighs.

CARYL: So I started locking my door. The first time he tried the knob and found it locked, he went away.

TANDY: And the white blouse was thin enough so that her sweat would make it stick to her skin. I could see her plain white bra through the blouse, and I found myself wondering if she had chocolate-brown or copper-colored nipples.

CARYL: But he became more persistent. He would knock, and I'd try to put him off by telling him I was sleeping or changing clothes, or studying. I was getting worried, but I was afraid to tell Mom. What could I say? Tandy's been coming to my room to see how I'm doing?

Fast dance music comes up. CARYL *is dancing. Lights fade out on* TANDY's *area as he walks over to* CARYL's *area. He stands just in the light.*

TANDY: Well, you ready to give me that dance lesson yet?

CARYL: Well. . .sure. . . . Now's as good a time as any.

CARYL *nervously starts showing* TANDY *the dance. After a while, a slow song comes on.* TANDY *pulls* CARYL *to him and starts dancing with her.*

TANDY: You slow dance much, Caryl?

CARYL: Well. . .at school dances and houseparties.

TANDY: You don't have a boyfriend yet, do you?

CARYL: Well. . .I. . .I go out sometimes. . .but. . .there's no one special. . . . School keeps me pretty busy.

TANDY: Don't be so stiff! The key to slow dancing is to relax. *(They dance for a few moments.* TANDY's *hands start roaming and he presses* CARYL *closer.)*

CARYL: I'm. . .I'm going to have to study now. *(*TANDY *keeps holding her. She struggles a bit.)* I've got to go! Let me go!

TANDY *grabs* CARYL *hard and kisses her until she stops struggling.*

TANDY: I've wanted to do this for a long time. *(He runs his fingers through her hair.)* Don't worry. It'll be all right.

As TANDY *goes back to his area, lights come up in* FRANCINE's *area.* FRANCINE *is putting on make-up, getting ready to go out.* CARYL *walks just to the light in* FRANCINE's *area. She watches* FRANCINE *for a moment.*

CARYL: Momma. . . .

FRANCINE: Oooh!... Girl, you nearly scared me to death!...
What do you want, Caryl!

CARYL *(moving more into the area)*: You getting ready to go somewhere?

FRANCINE: Tandy asked me to go out dancing tonight. It's been
months since we've gone anywhere. *(TANDY crosses to FRAN-
CINE's area.)* Maybe things are going to get better.

CARYL: Momma, I want to tell you. . . .

TANDY *walks past* CARYL *to* FRANCINE. *He grabs* FRANCINE *from
behind and kisses her on the back of the neck. She turns to him
and they kiss.*

TANDY: How are you doing, Caryl?

CARYL: Fine...I'm...

FRANCINE: What do you have to tell me, Caryl?

CARYL *(looking from* FRANCINE *to* TANDY*)*: I just wanted to say...
have a good time! That's all I wanted to say.

FRANCINE: Thanks, honey. You'll be okay tonight, won't you?

CARYL: Sure, I'll be fine...I'm just going to visit Twyla for a
while. I'll be back by ten.

FRANCINE: Okay. You have your key?

CARYL: Yes...Yes, I do.

TANDY *(still hugging* FRANCINE*)*: Have a good time.

CARYL *nods her head and goes back to her area. Lights fade out
in* FRANCINE's *area.* TANDY *returns to his area.*

CARYL: I couldn't make myself tell her about Tandy. He started becoming more attentive to Mom, and I didn't want to spoil her
happiness. But mainly I was afraid that she would choose him
over me, and probably put *me* out of the house.

TANDY: I had a real struggle with myself about Caryl. She *is* my
wife's daughter. She was only seventeen, and only a dog would
do what I was considering doing.

CARYL: So just to be safe, I started staying at school later, or visiting
girlfriends until it was time for my mom to come home. I was so
nervous I couldn't eat, and I lost about ten pounds in a week.

TANDY: So I tried not to think about her. I still loved Francine, so I
concentrated on her. But it was like someone telling you not to
think about monkeys. You start thinking about them all the time.

CARYL: After a while, he started watching me again. And when I
was anywhere near him—at the dinner table, passing in the hall,

anywhere—I could feel the heat from him.

TANDY: I thought about Caryl all the time—even when I was making love to Francine. I kept thinking about the way she smelled that first day—all sweaty! So finally I said, "Fuck it!" I was going to have it all. Besides, it wasn't as if she were *my* daughter.

TANDY *goes to* CARYL's *area, standing just in the light. Lights fade out in* TANDY's *area.*

CARYL: One afternoon, Mom came home late. She had a special project to work on at her job, so that when I came home, Tandy told me that she would be working most of the evening. Tandy and I ate dinner together. He drank a lot of wine, and tried to make me drink a glass. I finished eating and went to my room. I forgot to lock the door. *(She looks up at* TANDY, *startled to see him at the door.)* I . . . I was just going to study.

TANDY: Don't let me stop you. *(He moves into the area and stands facing her.)* You know, you are a beautiful young woman. I enjoyed holding and kissing you that day. Remember? *(She backs away from him. He follows.)* You haven't had a man kiss you like that before? There's more. . . much more than that.

He grabs her. She cries out and tries to get free. He pulls her to him.

CARYL: Please don't hurt me! Please. . . .

TANDY: Don't struggle. Don't struggle and it won't hurt. *(Lights fade out in* CARYL's *area and up in* FRANCINE's *area.)* Oh, Caryl, you are so beautiful! I've wanted you for a long time.

FRANCINE: I don't know what it was, but Tandy really came around.

TANDY *(in the darkness)*: Don't be afraid! Just touch it. It won't hurt!

FRANCINE: He still hadn't found a good job, but he was out looking. And our sex life got better and better.

CARYL *screams in pain, and then whimpers.*

TANDY: OOOH! It's in! It's in! . . . It's all right now. Don't cry, it's all right. Uhmmm! Uhmmm!

FRANCINE: But Caryl, I didn't know what her problem was. She'd slink around the house like a ghost. *(CARYL goes to* FRANCINE's *area and stands just in the light.)* I was hoping that she hadn't got strung out behind some no account boy. . . .

CARYL: Mom. . . I . . . I have to talk to you.

FRANCINE: Come on in! You look like death warmed over! (CARYL

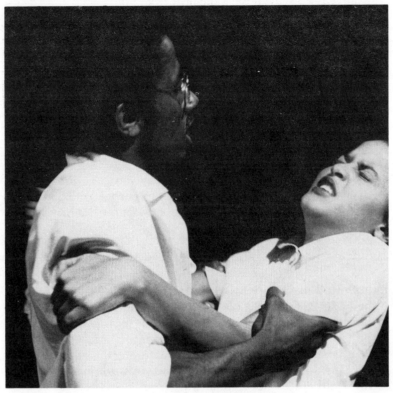

comes into the area.) What's the matter?

CARYL *(crying)*: Momma... Tandy... Tandy raped me!...

FRANCINE: What the hell did you say?

CARYL: He... he... raped me!...

> FRANCINE *slaps her. They stare at each other a moment. Then* FRANCINE *slaps her again. Then she grabs* CARYL *by the shoulders.*

FRANCINE: You let some boy put his hands on you, and you're going to stand here in *my* face and tell me my husband *raped* you?!! Who the hell do you think you're playing with, huh?!!

CARYL: But Momma... it happened... the other night when you came in late....

FRANCINE: Don't let that lie come out your mouth again or I'll beat all the black off you, you hear me?

CARYL: But Momma... please....

FRANCINE: You think you're grown enough to fuck around in the streets and then come and lie in my face?! Then you get your ass in the streets and stay there! Now get out of here. Don't let me see your face for the rest of the day!

Lights up on CARYL's *area as she returns to it.* FRANCINE *reaches into the drawer of the night stand, takes out a shot glass and vodka, pours herself a drink, and dashes it down. Lights out in her area.*

CARYL: He kept saying it wouldn't hurt. It hurt like hell. I thought I was going to die. But the day I tried to talk to my mother was the day I really died. *(She shakes her head.)* I don't know. Something snapped inside of me. My mother didn't give a damn about me. There was no one who cared. You know that feeling you get with cocaine? Some of the kids at school say you get "froze." Well, that's how I felt. . . and I haven't thawed out yet. And that pain I felt at first soon became a burning between my thighs.

TANDY *goes to* CARYL's *area as the lights come up on* FRANCINE's *area.* FRANCINE *is sitting, staring straight ahead, twisting a belt in her hands.*

CARYL: He came to my room whenever Mom was away. And. . . and I let him. Each time it became better and better. After a while I started looking forward to these visits. *(Pause.)* One night he came to my room after Mom had gone to bed.
TANDY *(coming into the area)*: How you feeling tonight?
CARYL: I'm. . . I'm not sure. We're not going to do anything to-night, are we? What if Mom wakes up?
TANDY: Don't worry about it. Besides, I've got something you might like. *(He goes over and kisses her. She hugs him. He takes out a bag of cocaine, a mirror, and a rolled-up dollar bill.)* You ever get high? *(She shakes her head "no.")* This is cocaine. It'll make you feel better. See, I take a line of it and sniff it into my nose with this rolled-up dollar. *(He turns his back to the audience and demonstrates for her.)* Now you try. *(She turns her back to the audience and sniffs. Lights off in* CARYL's *area.)*
FRANCINE: You know, when you've slept with a man for a while, you start to miss him when he's been out of the bed too long. I rolled over and found his side of the bed empty and cold. I had no idea where he was so I got up. . . *(She rises.)* And went out into the hall. That's when I heard noises coming from Caryl's room. *(Lights up on* CARYL's *area. She is alone.)*
CARYL: Tandy had put some cocaine on his dick. He said it would keep him hard all night, and he was really going at me.
FRANCINE: It sounded like a lot of moaning and groaning. And I thought that Caryl had sneaked some boy into the house while

we were sleeping.

CARYL: Momma burst into the room, and she caught Tandy in mid-stroke, with his ass in the air. He said, "Oh, oh, shit!" And then he came. Momma reached for his belt at the foot of the bed, and he started apologizing. But Momma kept looking at me. She was going to kill me! She told Tandy. . . .

FRANCINE *(still holding the belt)*: Get out! Get your black ass out now!

CARYL: And he got out—to pack his clothes probably—and he left me in there with her. She started cursing at me and beating me with the belt.

FRANCINE *is still in her own area, lashing out with the belt as if she is hitting someone.*

FRANCINE: You bitch! I lost one man over you. I'm not going to lose another one!

CARYL *(reacting as if she is being hit)*: Don't, Momma! I tried to tell you. . . . It's not my fault! It's not my fault!

FRANCINE *(still hitting)*: Don't you know I'll kill you? That man is married to *me*!!

CARYL: Kill me then and get it over with! Go ahead and kill me! Kill me!

FRANCINE *(still hitting out)*: You think you can get *my* man by cocking open your legs like that? You bitch, you bitch. . . .

Lights out in FRANCINE's *area.*

CARYL: She beat me so badly, I couldn't go to school for three days. I still have a scar on my stomach where she hit me with the buckle. Why didn't you just go ahead and kill me?!!

Blackout. Lights up on TANDY's *and* FRANCINE's *areas.* FRANCINE *is drinking the vodka.*

TANDY: I don't know. I just let things get out of hand. You know, I guess losing my job was like losing my manhood. Caryl was a way for me to get that back. Naw. That's too easy. I don't know what it was. I just know that when Francine found out, that was it. So I went to the bedroom that night and started packing my clothes. *(He stops in his tracks and looks at the audience.)* You know, I never realized how crazy that woman is. She came into the bedroom later and begged me to stay with her, told me I could do whatever I wanted as long as I spent my nights with her. Now here I was sleeping with her daughter and she was begging me not to go! If it had been *my* daughter and I had caught some nigguh on top of her, I'd have shot him dead in his ass! But here she was practically giving me her daughter so I could stay. *(Lights out on* TANDY's *area.)*

FRANCINE: What else could I do? What kind of woman does that make me if I can't keep a man? If it weren't for Caryl coming in the first place, I'd probably still be with Tomas. And I love Tandy—and I know he loves me. And I know that no matter how strong a man may be in other ways, when a woman opens her legs for him, he's going to take what's offered. Now just because Caryl's my daughter doesn't mean she's not a woman. She was seventeen at the time, and I had had her at sixteen.

She continues drinking. Lights fade out on FRANCINE's *area and up on* CARYL's. CARYL *is holding a packet of birth control pills.*

CARYL: My momma didn't want me to get pregnant because she didn't want to ruin her image. I mean, what would that say about her as a mother? So she gave me three packets of her pills— just to start. She didn't tell me how to use them. She just said take one a day. So I did. But the kind she gave me were the 21-day pills, the purple ones, where you take one a day until they're gone, wait seven days for your period, then start a new pack. Well, I took them every day—non-stop—and didn't have a period for two months *plus* I was sick as a dog. I thought I was pregnant and it wasn't until she took me to the doctor that we found out what the problem was. So now I take the 28-day pills, with the little orange ones that let you have your period. Once Tandy had found out how badly my mother had beaten me, he made her promise not to ever lay her hands on me again—part of the bargain. I managed to finish high school, but I didn't go on to college. Like I said, I died a long time ago; and all my dreams died, too.

Lights up on TANDY's *and* FRANCINE's *areas.* TANDY *lights a cigarette and* FRANCINE *keeps drinking, bringing another bottle out of the night stand drawer.*

FRANCINE: I've never been one to bite my tongue. See, I *need* a man in my life. For thirteen years, while I was raising Caryl, I went without one. Oh, I did spend time with quite a few during those years, but they weren't permanent.

TANDY: You know that night? I could have just packed my bags and walked out. But everything was such a mess! How could I just walk out and leave them like that? I mean, I love them both, and I was afraid that if I left, Francine might hurt Caryl or herself.

CARYL: So Tandy sleeps with me during the day—when he's not working—and with my mother at night—another part of the bargain. I only have one more year before I'm twenty-one. Then I guess I'll move out and get a job and place of my own. As long as I stay here, I get whatever I want to keep me happy—that's a part of the bargain, too. My mom's afraid that if I leave, Tandy would follow me—and what kind of woman would that make her?

FRANCINE: Oh, I accomplished a lot by myself. I raised a daughter, worked myself up to a well-paying job. . . all of that! But I'm thirty-six years old with a grown daughter!. . . I have *finally* found someone I love, and who loves me.

TANDY: Look at me! Trying to justify this shit! I mean, I was never raised like this! But this situation seems to satisfy *something* in me. Maybe if I weren't able to live *this* way, I'd be out in the streets chasing whatever came along. . . and what would I have to show for it?

CARYL: I don't have any place to go! And I don't have any friends anymore. . . . Well, how can I talk about the way I live to anyone?! Whenever I go anywhere alone, I feel so cold. I shiver and feel as if I'm going to throw up. At least here at home, I feel. . . safe.

TANDY: So at least I have something now. And you know, I almost hate to admit it, but it's kind of exciting living with these two attractive women like this. I mean they are both *women* now. If the Lord didn't give them anything else, he gave them free will. If they don't like being here. . . well, they can always leave. . . or tell *me* to leave. So things go on. It's comfortable.

CARYL: And look at me! A twenty-year-old woman wearing her high school uniform. Well, Mom makes us take these silly-ass pictures every year so that she can try to believe that we still have a normal family. And *my* life had only been normal while I was still in high school; therefore this get-up! Tandy you got anymore of that coke? I could sure use some now.

TANDY *goes into* CARYL's *area. He draws up some lines on the mirror and stands in front of* CARYL, *blocking her from the audience while she "blows." When she finishes, he puts everything away, and they kiss.*

FRANCINE *(putting the empty glass and bottle on the night stand)*: I'm tired! And I don't want to gamble anymore!. . . I don't want to run the risk of having to spend the rest of my life alone. . . without anyone. So what's my crime, huh? That I have chosen to love *myself* more. . . just this once? For thirteen years I sacrificed my own happiness. So now I am happy. *(She shouts.* CARYL *and* TANDY *watch her, stunned.)* I AM HAPPY, DO YOU HEAR THAT?!! *(She starts to cry and lose control.)* And I am not going to give that up anymore. Not anymore, not anymore, not anymore. . . *(*CARYL *and* TANDY *go to her.)*

TANDY: Come on, Francine. Let's put these bottles and shit away so we can finish up these pictures.

CARYL *and* TANDY *assist* FRANCINE *as they all move downstage center, bringing the chair to pose for more pictures. The lights fade in all the other areas. After the first flash, they shift positions. After the second flash, they shift positions again. After the third flash, there is a blackout.*

Vacuum
Chris Hardman

Vacuum was first performed at the Pacific Micro Systems Warehouse in Sausalito, California, on April 16, 1981, with the following cast:

WALTER the door-to-door salesman	Ernesto Sanchez
MARY the housewife	Michele Larsson
OLDER HOUSEWIFE	Michele Larsson
ATTENDANTS	Chris Tellis
	Martin Bates

Direction, stage design, and lighting by Chris Hardman
Music and sound design by Alfred Agius-Sinerco
Script compiled from interviews, questionnaires, combined with written dialogue and narration by Chris Hardman
Costumes by Gail Spaien
Interviews conducted by Martin Bates, Chris Hardman,
Al Agius-Sinerco
Produced by Antenna Theater

Also presented at the San Francisco Museum of Modern Art, Intersection Theater, and Margaret Jenkins Dance Studio, San Francisco; Julia Morgan Theater, Berkeley; Marin Community Playhouse, San Anselmo; Bolinas Community Center, Bolinas, California.

European Premiere: Lantaren Theater, Rotterdam, Netherlands, June 6, 1981; also presented at the American Center, Paris, France; Mannheim International Theater Festival, West Germany; Tubingen, Ulm, Konstanz, and Karlsruhe (all West Germany).

Vacuum was presented at the Rhode Island School of Design in February, 1982, and in New York at The Performing Garage, in March, with the following cast:

WALTER	Ernesto Sanchez
MARY	Annie Hallatt
OLDER HOUSEWIFE	Annie Hallatt
ATTENDANTS	Chris Tellis
	Ray Myslewski

The text (right hand pages) is a recorded soundtrack constructed from taped interviews. The accompanying action, performed by masked actors who never speak, is described on the facing pages. In *Vacuum*, salesmen talk about selling, housewives talk about buying, a scientist talks about vacuums, a psychiatrist talks about rejection, a bartender talks about drinking... many other aspects of selling, vacuums, and the lives of people who deal with these things are discussed by the people themselves. Some of the material in *Vacuum* was written by Chris Hardman to tie together the interview material into a cohesive narrative line. To record these passages, Antenna turned to people whose professional lives reflect the voices required.

WALTER is spoken by Jimmy Romanella, a former Kirby salesman.
MARY is spoken by Katy Volz, a Marin County housewife.
NARRATOR comments are spoken by Scott Beach, a San Francisco radio and TV personality.
SCIENTIFIC INFORMATION is read by Stewart Brand, scientist and editor of *The Whole Earth Catalog* and *Co-Evolution Quarterly*.

MASKS

All performers in *Vacuum* wear masks designed by Chris Hardman, modeled after real people. These models are:

WALTER: Paul Stuppi, Electrolux sales manager
MARY: Shelby Brough, Marin housewife
OLDER HOUSEWIFE: Mrs. Marjorie Miller
The ATTENDANTS wear silverized faceless masks.

SET

The set is a clear stage 25' deep, 35' wide, with a 4'x4'x7' "wall unit" at either side which serves as a wing for the props. These props—all of which are carried on and off by the performers—are used to create settings (living room, bar, street, etc.). Three lights are also on the stage, and are used to create shadow effects on the rear wall, which is a continuous sheet of photographic background paper. The recorded sound-and-music-and-voice track is quadrophonic and played over speakers behind and before the audience. Additional sound effects are created onstage by the action of the props (doors slamming, vacuum noise, etc.). Introduction begins as house lights fade.

Vacuum
Chris Hardman

INTRODUCTION

SALESMAN 1: That time that we were having a contest—and this was in San Francisco, there used to be—a guy called in, he says, "Hey I want, I want ten vacuums, Kirby vacuum cleaners, and I want you to deliver them up to the Mayflower Hotel in San Francisco." And the sales manager says, "OK, I'll take the order, and I'll send a man out at 2 o'clock in the afternoon." Prior to that we were all sitting at a sales meeting here, all ten of us, and the sales manager come in, he said, "Hey I've got a contest here. Anybody who can go out this morning and get one sale, I got him a bonus here, a delivery in San Francisco—for *ten sales* to the Mayflower Hotel." Jeeze we ran out of this place I'll tell you—I went up there, I knocked doors and everything like that and man I finally got a sale—I found an easy one. And you know I came back and I called the office and I says, "Hey, has—has Mark Johnson called in?" He says no. "Listen, put me down for 11 o'clock, I got this sale." He says, "Great Ray, you won them ten sales." I ran down to the office here, and I got in here and I looked at the scoreboard, and damn I was the first guy in here. So I waited another hour and it was 2 o'clock—it was 11 o'clock at this particular time, and the appointment was for 2 o'clock—and the sales manager Dean Fry says, "Here Ray, here's that delivery up to the Mayflower Hotel up in San Francisco." But he said, "Don't forget the demonstrator, 'cause they're not that easy." So I went up to San Francisco, I went to the—I had a heck of a time finding this place—finally I, I found this hotel. And I went in and knocked at, told the—there was a gal at the desk and I says I'm looking for the manager of the hotel, I'm s'pose to come up and demonstrate a Kirby. "Well, he's in the back room there, you can, I'll—what's your name?" I said Ray Buddovitch. "Well go on and knock at the door." So I knocked at the door and said, "Hey, Ray Buddovitch here from the Kirby Company; I want to show you a Kirby." The guy says, "Hey I got no appointment right now." I says, "Hey, I'm here. You remember you called for an appointment?" He says, "No, I haven't got time." So I put down the kit and I started demonstrating and I polished the floor and I cleaned the carpets and I was doing the drapes and he says, "Gee that's great!" He says, "I never seen a product like that before!" I says, "Well listen, how many do you want—do you want the ten right now?" He says, "No, I tell you what I'll

TITLE DANCE

ATTENDANT *enters rolling a four-foot diameter Disc—the V-A-C-
-U-U-M Disc—by a white handle attached to its center. The Disc is
upholstered in salmon colored rug liner. A white line drawn across
the face forms a soft V or tight U. The* ATTENDANT *carries in his
other hand a flat white stick two and a half feet long. As the* NAR-
RATOR *announces V, the* ATTENDANT *stops the Disc in the V position, then he drives the Disc forward one half revolution and slaps it
with the stick horizontally forming an A. The Disc is rolled back a
quarter turn to the C position. The two U's are similar to the V. The
M is made like the A but with the stick laid vertically.*

do—I'll take twelve of those Kirbys." Holy Mackerel, I was so excited I ran down to the office. I only had the one machine, and I made out the order and everything like that—and I handed it in. And everybody was excited, and it was just—hey, it was just pandemonium. And my sales manager came up to me and he says, "Hey, Ray, where'd you sell these Kirbys?" I said, "Mayflower Hotel." He says, "You should've been at the *Mayfair*—the guy's still waiting."

TITLE DANCE

NARRATOR:

V

A

C

U

U

M

As the V-A-C-U-U-M Disc rolls across stage and out, WALTER
enters, Briefcase in hand. The Briefcase is a flat, lightweight, sharp
rectangle, tan leather on one side, dark brown on the other. When
flipped it changes dark to light, light to dark. The Briefcase has
WALTER by the hand, guiding him, showing him the territory. It
flys forward and WALTER follows. It moves with confidence,
WALTER follows reluctantly.

WALTER KNOCKS ON DOORS

An ATTENDANT enters shouldering an articulated Parallelogram
which is ten-feet long when closed upon itself like a pole. The AT-
TENDANT carries it closed but when the NARRATOR says "door-to-
door" he springs the Parallelogram open and stands it vertically. In
this configuration, the Parallelogram resembles a doorway. The AT-
TENDANT collapses the Parallelogram back into a pole, lays it on the
floor and exits.

The halves of a simple house shape two-feet high by two-feet wide,
divided at the roof peak to form two Half Houses, are worn like hel-
mets by the two ATTENDANTS as they enter and dance. They spin,
then come together to form a complete house image, then break
apart only to reform as another house in another spot. WALTER
traipses in front of this appearing-and-disappearing suburban land-
scape, still guided by his Briefcase.

WALTER KNOCKS ON DOORS

NARRATOR: Could it be that a man just discharged from the Marine
Corps, and just enrolled in night school—could such a man who
is young and just married, and whose brother-in-law is regional
director for a vacuum sales force—could he try out for a job as a
door-to-door salesman?

Shoeshine.
Scoring.
Cufflink.
Dodge Dart.
Street map.
Tie clasp.
Hair cream.
Parker pen.
"Just ate."
"Luncheonette."
New Guy.
First Try.

As the HOUSEWIFE *speaks of her typical salesman, an* ATTENDANT *comes forward with a Flip Face, a square of plywood with the painted profile of a sleazy salesman stereotype hinged vertically to the center. The profile flips from side to side shiftily. The face remains the same. When the* HOUSEWIFE *talks of the type of salesman she likes, the Flip Face is turned to its back where an arrow appears pointing towards* WALTER.

The two House Heads form into a house image directly behind WALTER. *This is the place, the right house.*

Scissor-hinged white infant gates extend horizontally from the wings stage right and left. They float to the ground, there to stand upright representing a picket Fence. MARY *enters stage left and* ATTENDANT *enters stage right, each hidden behind a wooden venetian Blind, held closed. They take up positions behind the Fences. As* WALTER *passes between the Fences the other* ATTENDANT *lifts the Parallelogram, forming a doorway.* WALTER *summons up his courage, approaches the dooor, and knocks. As he knocks the door spins away. The Blinds click open and shut, and* WALTER *spins off-stage left. Gray out.*

HOUSEWIFE 1: The... typical vacuum cleaner man... is usually elderly; he's always dressed in a suit. He comes with a vacuum cleaner in hand, and he wishes to demonstrate how good this vacuum cleaner is. And "if you just give me a moment more of your time"—and he keeps asking for a moment more and a moment more. Meanwhile you have stuff on the stove that's burning, and you're trying to politely tell the man to go but he doesn't. And then he throws stuff on your rug, and just starts vacuuming in order to show you how super this vacuum cleaner is. And then I have the type that I would like to see, which would be a younger person, dressed casually, not so pushy, but just asks for one moment, and takes it, and that's it.

SALESMAN 2: This house was the one that you always searched for all your life. If you get a green house, with a red shingle roof—yeah. Every door-to-door guy looks for a pale green house with a red shingle roof. They're an absolute lead-pipe cinch for making a sale. I don't know *why*. But every one you go and check on, you'll find they got a set of encyclopedias, fire alarms, pots and pans, and usually a door-to-door type cleaner.

SALESMAN 1: Prospecting for customers huh, let's talk about *that*. How does a guy get a customer for to buy a vacuum cleaner. Well, in the vacuum cleaner business you have, what we have is incentives for people to let you in the house—steak knives, carving food knives, uh, five pounds of coffee, or something like that —a case of Cola. We'll go to the door, "How are you," knock at the door. "Hi, how are you? My name is Ray Buddovitch, I'm here to give you a free case of Cokes just to come in and shampoo your carpets. How's that sound? Great, here's your Cokes, just take me a second." I walk in, I set up my equipment, I clean the rugs, I shampoo it—I show her the need, I show her the desire, I show her how, the financing, how she can get it—and the rest is up to her.

MARY SHOPS

The Parallelogram is returned to the floor and one Blind exits. The other advances upstage center. From behind it MARY *peers between the slats. The sound of a car passing is heard as* MARY *hands off the Blind to an* ATTENDANT *and starts her I Love To Shop Dance.*

MARY SHOPS

MARY *(thinking)*: That suit coat has to go—I should probably find a new one. What am I missing? Groceries? Butter, coffee, vegetable.

NARRATOR: She rarely went out. But when she did, she'd go to a store, or to a market. People were there and they were for the most part nice to her. These people helped her find the things she thought she needed. Sometimes, they'd talk to her about things. All *kinds* of things—whatever seemed to be of mutual interest. Other times, they were too busy. These were places she could go and people would talk to her. People never came to her house to talk. She went out only when she needed something. What was it that she needed? Could it be that she needed to talk, or that she needed to get out? Often she came back carrying things. These people who had wrapped them had asked her to return. They said, "Thank you. Come again."

MARY VACUUMS

MARY *returns home to vacuum. She steps forward, admiring her machine. Inside this '50s style streamline Silver Vacuum is a fluorescent tube.* MARY *flips on the light, then lifts and dips the slick machine in sync with the sound of a vacuum cleaner whooshing back and forth. Soon the Silver Vacuum is swirling through the air, barely held in check by* MARY.

MARY VACUUMS

TV CARPET SALESMAN: The carpet selection of styles and colors in your choice of all wool, nylon, and ultron. The carpet selection of styles and colors in your choice of all wool, nylon, and ultron. Sales prices include carpet plus regular custom tack—and installation.

MIX WITH SALESMAN 2: Every door-to-door guy looks for a pale green house with a red shingle roof. They're an absolute lead-pipe cinch for making a sale.

TV SALESMAN: The carpet selection of styles and colors in your choice of all wool, nylon, and ultron.

HOUSEWIFE 2: I use the one that you use for dusting, that sort of round brush that you use for dusting, and I use that for the lampshades and some of the materials, like the drapes and stuff. And then you just put, uh, you use the hose and go around the corners, because the, the part that you put on for the carpets doesn't actually get as close to the sides as you want. So you just take the hose and go up and down along the baseboards. Then you put on the other, the beater, and let it beat—and vacuum.

WALTER *enters and knocks, first hesitantly, then more insistently.*
MARY *finally hears the pounding over the Vacuum rumble and
turns off the machine. Lights come up as vac sounds fade out and*
MARY *walks to the Parallelogram doorway, held by an* ATTENDANT.

*The doorway is snapped into the pole configuration and removed
by an* ATTENDANT. *Blackout.*

WALTER'S REJECTION

An ATTENDANT *gripping a lit fluorescent Circle appears stage
right. The eerie blue/white light reveals* WALTER *standing center
stage. From* WALTER's *gut slowly pours a thin white cloth. As it hits
the floor an* ATTENDANT *grasps it, and, pulling it across the stage,
feeds it through the fluorescent Circle.* WALTER *clutches his end and
tries to stuff the cloth back inside. A fight ensues. The glowing Circle seems to suck out* WALTER's *energy.* WALTER *collapses. Blackout.*

SALESMAN 3: I believe, and I believe very strongly, that the sale is made within thirty seconds of when you first meet somebody. That first impression—that's what used to get—we used to drive across just how important it is for that man or that salesman to utter the right words that first thirty seconds, and his appearance.

WALTER *(after knocking at door, to* MARY*)*: Hi. How are you this morning? I—I'm Walter Krekowski, and I'm here, to give you a free case of Cokes just to come in and shampoo your carpet. How's that sound?

MARY: I already have a vacuum.

WALTER: Yes, but—maybe it's not doing its job. If—if you could just let me in, I can check and. . .

MARY: You're new at this, aren't you? Next time, tell them to send a salesman. Bye.

WALTER'S REJECTION

SALESMAN 3: It's not an easy job. And it is one that requires a great deal of persistence. You—you meet, continuously, rejection.

SCIENTIST *(mixed with* NARRATOR *who interjects* "rejection" *whenever vacuum is mentioned)*: A vacuum/rejection/theoretically is space without matter. A perfect vacuum/rejection/has never been obtained. The best man-made vacuum/rejection/contains about 100,000 molecules of vapor in each cubic centimeter, compared to about 20 billion billion molecules in air at sea level. The most nearly perfect vacuum/rejection/exists in intergalactic space, where it's estimated that on the average there is less than one molecule in a cubic centimeter. Commonly, but incorrectly,

A standard Spot illuminates WALTER *from across the stage. The Spot is in a porcelain base and behind this rig the* ATTENDANT *holds a one-foot diameter Disc. As the* ATTENDANT *walks toward* WALTER, *he tips the Spot up. When vertical it resembles a glowing cocktail glass on a circular tray.* WALTER *hoists the Spot and guzzles.*

MARY *has entered unlit in the background.* WALTER *points to her with the Spot and an* ATTENDANT *slips the Disc before her face. He flips it over. On the other side is a target. Blackout.*

a vacuum/rejection/is thought to cause suction. Actually, the apparent suction caused by a vacuum/rejection/is the pressure of the atmosphere tending to rush into the unoccupied space/rejection.

MARY: You're new at this, aren't you? Next time, tell them to send a salesman.

WALTER DRINKS

BARTENDER *(over sounds of clinking glasses, conversation, and other bar noise)*: It seems the bar is the place where everybody comes to either cry or laugh. But then they get to this point where they're completely out of control about what they're doing; and then they forget that they're in a public place—that they're not in their house, they're not in their office where they can yell and scream. It, it's a public place, and there's other people in there wanting—wanting to enjoy themselves. And they seem, well a drunk person forgets that.

SALESMAN 3: A salesman is born, not made. It's, I, I kinda—I, I have to—you have to be born with certain characteristic traits, you know. *But* I, I believe salesmen can be made—if taught properly.

BARTENDER: Drunk, out of hand, swearing, people are complaining. You're trying to calm him down. He's telling you he wants to talk to the owner, and the owner doesn't want to talk to him. You make the decision. Uh, all the way from you stole my twenty dollar bill—when they're drunk, there's no talking to them.

SALESMAN 3: Over the years, very very seldom—I could count on one hand the number of doors that I've had closed on me. But I always felt, the first time, it hurt. And when I analyzed it I realized maybe there was something wrong inside the house... and I was intruding at the moment... see, so a rejection always could be a momentary rejection, rather than a total one.

HOUSEWIFE 3: There's a certain quality of ego that says, "I want that sale!"

WALTER: That woman's going to buy a cleaner from me yet. I'm not about to be laughed at.

MARY CLEANS HER HOUSE

Lights fade in slowly to reveal House Heads assembled as a house upstage right. MARY, *armed with a spray can, is misting the stage with evergreen scent. Flinging the aerosal away, she sinks to her knees before the house and diligently starts to clean it with a rag.* ATTENDANTS *holding four-foot long Tubes filled with sawdust enter in single file formation: step, pivot, dump sawdust; step, pivot, dump sawdust. They arrive behind the house and smother it beneath a sawdust downpour.* MARY, *dust pan and whisk broom in hand, rolls away, then pops up. She madly starts sweeping up piles but by now the* ATTENDANTS *are flinging sawdust everywhere. An* ATTENDANT, *having off-loaded his sawdust, returns with the Vacuum Bag. The Vacuum Bag is an upright vacuum with a handle on one end and a horizontally hinged door on the other. The bag is packed with variously shaped, multi-colored wood fragments. The* ATTENDANT *flips open the door and lays out a wood chunk pile in a diagonal slash across the stage. The other* ATTENDANT *rummages through the debris locating the letters D-I-R-T strung together. He lifts these up by their string tail as if they were a dead rat.* MARY *flings her sawdust filled dust pan. All freeze while the dust settles. The stage is now covered in filth.* MARY *counters with a larger Dust Pan. She sweeps wood chunks and sawdust onto it from every corner of the stage but this Dust Pan has a handle which acts like a fulcrum. An* ATTENDANT *stamps on it catapulting the chunks and dust high into the air. All freeze while the dust settles.*

MARY CLEANS HER HOUSE

SALESMAN 2: It was always great if you could have a grandmother there or something like that, I mean if there was a young baby in the house. That's because after you show them all this dirt, the main thing that you tell them is, "You're not going to allow your child to crawl around the floor in this filth, you know, you're not that kind of parent, I can see that, right? You wouldn't do that would you? No way would you do that! And you're certainly not going to let it go on any longer are you? I mean, I know it's going to be a late evening, but I'm sure you're going to want to clean before you go to bed tonight, because you're not going to go in that bed, and lie in all that dead skin you saw, that we just vacuumed out of there, are you? So I know you want to clean your mattress, want to clean your floors, and everything else!"

NARRATOR: Question: what is it that is noticed only when it isn't there? Answer: a clean house. With a husband working all day and late into the night, she had found herself with a house and time. Could it be that her house was sinking in a sea of dirt? She constantly had to move things to clean behind them—and whenever she looked behind them, there was something to clean. If she moved to the right, there was dust. If she moved to the left there was. . . . What could happen if she ever got her house *clean?* Could dirt be keeping people from coming to the house? Could dirt be filling up the places where people and friendships might go? If she could get her house empty of dirt, maybe it would be filled with feelings.

OLDER HOUSEWIFE: You walk in a dirty house, you just cannot be comfortable, and when you walk out, you've got to go home and take a bath.

HOUSEWIFE 4: I guess I was brought up in a household where sanitary. . . was a heavy word.

OLDER HOUSEWIFE: I just got some kind of a phobia about dirty houses. Gives me some kind of. . . heebee jeebees. /In a dirty house/phobia of dirty houses/heebee jeebees.

An ATTENDANT *graciously supplies* MARY *with a Vacuum Cleaner, a working model, hand held with long nozzle and even longer hose trailing off stage. She flips the switch and commences cleaning. Dirt and dust are sucked up.* MARY *senses the first glimmer of hope, when in steps the other* ATTENDANT *holding the open exhaust end of the Vacuum hose. What is sucked from the stage spurts into the air.* MARY *becomes frantic. An* ATTENDANT *enters with a Push Broom and with bold strokes starts sweeping. The other* ATTENDANT *drops the hose and joins him. They sweep wildly as* MARY, *entangled in the hose, stabs her Vacuum in the air. Two* ATTENDANTS *sweep the sawdust, wood chunks, House Heads, Vacuum, and* MARY *off stage. Blackout.*

HOUSEWIFE 1: Is a...

NARRATOR: ...housewife...

HOUSEWIFE 1: ...a woman...

HOUSEWIFE 2: ...married...

NARRATOR: ...to a house?

HOUSEWIFE 3: I think a housewife's job is cooking, cleaning, taking care of the children, that's her job. They're a mechanic of all trades—they've got to do a little bit of everything—I think, you know. They have to be a good manager, be a good housekeeper, be a good...cook, and, uh—babysitter, and a good *wife*. Cleaning lady, cleaning lady/ cleaning lady, cleaning lady/ cleaning lady, cleaning lady/ cleaning lady, cleaning lady/ cleaning lady, cleaning lady/ cleaning lady/ they're cleaning ladies/ manager of the home/ babysitter, and a good *wife*.

OLDER HOUSEWIFE: You walk in a dirty house, you just cannot be comfortable.

NARRATOR: What could happen if she ever got her house *clean*? Could dirt be keeping people from coming to the house? Could dirt be filling up the spaces where people and friendships might go? If she could get her house empty of dirt, maybe it would be filled with feelings.

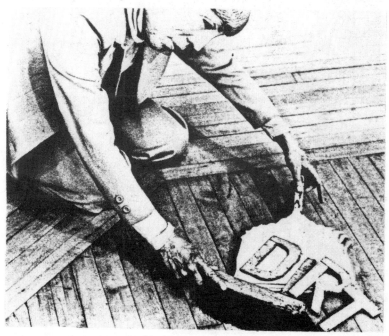

WALTER ATTENDS SALES COURSE

The Flip Face of the sleazy salesman is lit stage right and underneath appears a contraption—the Salesman Printing Device. This instrument consists of a one-foot by two-foot rectangular plate with two salesman profiles cut through it. Behind this plate is a roll of black plastic about sixteen feet long. An ATTENDANT *with a spray can of rug cleaner shoots the foam through the silhouettes' slot onto the plastic creating the printed profiles of salesmen in rug cleaner white. After each spraying the other* ATTENDANT *advances the plastic by pulling it across the stage until all sixteen feet are printed with profiles.*

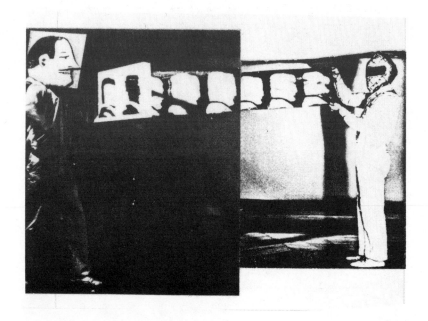

WALTER ATTENDS SALES COURSE

ACE SALES TRAINER: Title of my talk tonight is nothing happens until somebody *sells* something. *Nothing happens until somebody sells something.* The first thing I want to sell you men and women tonight, is basic and fundamental: unless you, and I— those of us engaged in selling, retail and wholesale, printed and personal—*understand* what we do, and understand it in terms of benefit to others than ourselves, we will never do it well. We will always be vulnerable. The first thing any man's going to realize on the great potential, or capabilities he has in selling, the first thing he's got to do, is to understand what he's doing. *Why . . .* selling. Lot of people talk that, about filling needs. Lot of people think of us sel . . . ourselves in terms of filling needs. Skip it. Not so. We haven't been a needy people for fifty years in this country. We're a prosperous people; we're not a needy people. We're not engaged in filling needs, we're engaged in something far more important than that. We're engaged in making people *want* things. We're *want* creators, not need fillers. Think of yourselves in terms of the most important people in America. If you're a professional salesman, you're a salesman twenty-four hours a day, seven days a week. You don't just put it on when your body's in front of the prospect and take it off when you leave his office. You don't put it on at nine and take it off at five. You're a salesman *all* the time. You eat, work, think, sleep, thrill to the prospect of being a *want* creator. It's the fundamental motivating force behind all human progress.

WALTER *marches behind this ribbon of salesmen, his face obscured by the others. The Printing Device is detached from the black band which is then free to march across the stage back and forth, up and down, as* WALTER *intertwines with it. The plastic is laid down and a ladder—the Ladder of Success—arrives and is set vertically center stage.* WALTER *tries to scale it but it tilts under his weight.* WALTER *backs off to observe the* ATTENDANT *lift the salesman ribbon over the top rung and then start pulling from behind. Each salesman rises to the top and, as the last profile completes its ascent,* WALTER *attempts to follow. Blackout.*

SALESMAN 1: If you were looking for a selling job I'd prob'ly tell you to go down the street and get a job at the 7-11 or something like that; but if you were coming in here for a *career*, and wanted to learn selling, then you're indeed the guy I want to talk to. "What am I, what am I going to get out of selling vacuum cleaners?"—that's what you're going to ask me, right? "What a dumb job, selling vacuum cleaners." Well let me tell you, the first thing I'm going to do is, I'm going to explain to you the possibilities to become as successful in this business as *I* am, to you; and how you can get up what we call the ladder of success in a short relative time with very little money. You don't need any money in this business; it's all you need is the guts, and the excitement, and the desire to get ahead. And in the vacuum cleaner business, they'll show you how to get there—to the top. And if you want to go to the top, and, when you get to the top, the first thing you think about is money and riches—well it's there. I mean, the numbers I can't draw because, I don't know how hard you want to work, or how much you want to get—and that's the way it was presented to me, and that's what I did. I went right to the top. I went from a door-to-door salesman to a sales manager to a crew manager where I took out guys door-to-door. And then they said, Hey Ray would you like to be an Area Distributor—that's being under a distributor, and buying machines off of him and *you* hiring two or three guys. And I did that. And finally I says, Hey, that's not for me. I want to go to the *top*. And so I said, the guy said to me, "Listen: sell 500 Kirbys, in six months, and you can be a distributor." 500 Kirbys!?

·

WALTER KNOCKS ON DOORS

Lights up. ATTENDANTS *each hold up venetian Blind props at head level.* WALTER *enters. Between each speech, he holds his Briefcase before one set of Blinds, knocks on the Briefcase as if on a door, swings the Briefcase away—and the Blinds snap shut to reveal a "yes" or "no" answer.*

WALTER KNOCKS ON DOORS

SALESMAN 5: If you summed it up in one word—enthusiasm. There's more of anything sold by enthusiasm than there is knowledge. Knowledge'll come. I know guys who've sold and sold and sold and sold and sold—because they were *enthusiastic. (Blinds snap closed:* "No.")

SALESMAN 3: It's not an easy job—and it is one that requires a great deal of persistence. *(Blinds snap closed:* "No.")

SALESMAN 1: And—if you do the basics, show your product, show the desire, show them the need, and—ask them to buy *(Blinds snap closed:* "No.")

SALESMAN 5: Without a positive attitude, you're dead. Absolutely dead in the water. *(Blinds close slowly:* "No.")

SALESMAN MIX: If you summed it up in one word—enthusiasm/ great deal of persistence/ show your product, show the desire, show them the need, and—ask them to buy. (WALTER, *hesitating, suddenly walks away without knocking, dejected. He resolves to try again; goes up to the venetian Blinds; knocks and gets his first* "Yes.")

SALESMAN 1: The thing is, not being a professional salesman, and being trained, and you just, you've only been out in the field let's say for thirty days, and you go in a home and you show your product; you're sincere, you're enthusiastic, and you, you really, you really put it down. And the woman gets excited, or the customer, and she *buys* it—the greatest thrill is walking out of that home. I don't care whether I've made one cent on the sale as far as commission, or I made my commission of fifty dollars or one hundred dollars; it's that personal satisfaction—I sold something! Gee, that's great!

WALTER *exits; blackout.*

MARY SHOPS FOR SHOES

Lights come up on an ATTENDANT *center stage holding a flat one and a half foot Square.* MARY *steps in and walks over to admire this Square. She runs her hand slowly along the edge. The Square floats down towards her foot. Then the Square breaks apart like a jigsaw puzzle into two pieces—the positive and negative images of a high-heel shoe. Both images are admired by* MARY *as the* ATTENDANT *bearers kneel before her. Blackout.*

MARY SHOPS FOR SHOES

HOUSEWIFE 5: You feel like you've had somebody pampering you.

HOUSEWIFE 6: Salespeople I find, uh, very helpful and very pleasant, and uh, very easy to get along with.

HOUSEWIFE 5: Those that're good salesmen, who're fast and entertaining and have a, a fine line, are indeed fun to watch; and it doesn't make any difference whether you know that you're going to say yes or no to their product. It is fun to watch them run through their routine.

NARRATOR: Shoes were particularly fun. She liked to buy shoes. It wasn't so much for their style or color, but because of the *way* they were bought. It felt so good to have someone kneeling before you. "How does it feel? Too tight? Would you like to walk around and look in the mirror?" These people cared about her— how she felt and how she looked. She liked them. They were helpful and understanding. They were almost always enthusiastic. Lawyers and doctors never seemed to act like that. Could it be that she should've married a salesman? Then maybe her life could be as pleasant as her shopping. It seemed that she always needed new shoes.

WALTER KNOCKS ON DOORS

Lights pop up on WALTER *and* ATTENDANTS *again holding Blinds. In this sequence,* WALTER *is energized and enthusiastic.*

SALESMAN 4: You begin to feel like you have complete control of everything. *(Blinds snap shut:* "Yes.")

SALESMAN 5: When I made a sale, I did it in such a way that it looked like the person was taking it away from me. *(Blinds snap shut:* "Yes.")

SALESMAN 1: I sold—one month I sold thirty-nine Kirbys. *(Blinds snap shut:* "Yes.")

SALESMAN 5: It's a terrific feeling. It was, it was a euphoric high. *(Blinds snap shut:* "Yes.")

SALESMAN 3: Gee, I'd say 85 percent of the reason that a sale is made is that the customer likes you. *(*WALTER *exits; lights fade out.)*

INTERLUDE

OLDER HOUSEWIFE *enters with her Vacuum Sweeper. It is comprised of a long crooked handle leading to a two-and-a-half foot long, four-inch diameter drum. Wrapped around this drum are four strips of heavy white cotton. She takes a sweep with her Vacuum Sweeper and out rolls a swath of white cloth. When she pulls back, the white cloth rolls onto the drum.* OLDER HOUSEWIFE *vacuums back and forth, laying out and reeling in strips of white. She continues to clean in this manner until the stage is covered with the four cloth strips neatly arranged side by side from downstage to up. She spins her Vacuum Sweeper in the air while admiring her handiwork. The two* ATTENDANTS *lift the strips from their corners and slowly, carefully wrap* OLDER HOUSEWIFE *into the cloth. The fluorescent Circle light appears in the corner. She is drawn towards it. Blackout.*

INTERLUDE

OLDER HOUSEWIFE: Well, I, I get the vacuum sweeper out of the utility room, and then I have to bring it upstairs. . . and uh, then I, uh, start vacuuming the upstairs *first*. And I vacuum very thorough because I want to get in the corners, and get everything up, because this carpet has, it gets—it shows all the dirt. So I have to do it almost every day. What I, what I think about is, when I'm vacuuming, is just how beautiful that carpet looks. You take a swish of the vacuum sweeper, and—what a difference: what the vacuum sweeper has run over and what it's *got* to run over. Well this Kirby, this Kirby vacuum sweeper tells you slant, you know, to slant one way, and then slant the other way, and it tells you not to push it forward. It's to kind of *slant*, and I think that gets the carpets, uh, cleaner, than if you just push it forward just any old way. But if you take a lot of pride and just sort of push it slanting it, you know, sideways, back and forth and back and forth, and then forward—that's what the directions are on this new Kirby. But it, it's strange, the directions tell you, it says, do not push it completely forward, turn it to the side, and then turn it to the side, and uh, it does. It works. It picks up a lot better then. That's why I like to vacuum my home is because it never looks dirty after you get it vacuumed. I think it's the most important part of, uh, housekeeping, is vacuuming to keep your house clean. . . . Thinking about just how good the house is looking, and, uh, how wonderful it is that they invented the vacuum sweeper, and uh, maybe I think sometimes about what I'm going to do, for the day: whether I'm going to. . . play golf, or—well, I just think that the vacuum sweeper is the greatest invention that was ever created for the housewife. I mean you can wash your clothes by hand, you can dry them on the line, you can wash your dishes by hand; but boy, you sure—if you sweep a rug, the dirt remains. And when you have wall-to-wall carpeting, the only way you can get it out is—by vacuuming. A person just *cannot* go without a vacuum sweeper. You can go without a lot of things, but if you have carpets in your home, you cannot live without a vacuum sweeper. . . . Well, if you, you know, like if you were at a nice lake where it's so, uh, the water is so calm and green and pure and clean, and you look at that lake and you think, oh it's the cleanest thing, cleanest lake I've ever seen; why, I think a carpet reminds me of that after it's been, after I've finished vacuuming. It's so clean, it's so, uh, perfect.

SCIENTIST: Nothing deteriorates because, uh, in a vacuum, because there's nothing there.

WALTER RETURNS TO MARY'S HOUSE

Lights fade up. Once again the Parallelogram is centerstage but this time it is hovering inches above the stage. It begins to sway slowly at first, then, as the arc widens, the tempo quickens. The ATTENDANT *twists it into the air and runs it through many of its possible permutations: vertical, horizontal, diagonal, thin as a sliver, fat as a door, jerked fast and swirled slowly.* WALTER *enters, adjusts his tie, then, hefting his Briefcase, he sinks to the stage floor and crawls across it while the Parallelogram whips around. He reaches the other side, gets to his feet, and once again cinches his tie.* MARY *has entered downstage.* WALTER *watches her. An* ATTENDANT *thrusts the target Disc in front of her face. The Parallelogram lands between the two of them and* WALTER *boldly walks up and knocks.*

WALTER RETURNS TO MARY'S HOUSE

STATE LEGISLATOR: State of California, Business and Professions code section 17523, says: Solicitation at residence of prospect should have a statement of purposes, contents, penalties, remedies, and defenses. Subsection A: It is unlawful for any person to solicit a sale or order for sale of goods or services at the residence of a prospective buyer, in person or by means of telephone, without clearly, affirmatively, and expressively revealing at the time the person initially contacts the prospective buyer, and before making any other statement, except a greeting, or asking the prospective buyer any other questions, that the purpose of the contact is to effect the sale by doing all of the following:

One: stating the identity of the person making the solicitation;

Two: stating the trade name of the person represented by the person making the solicitation;

Three: state the kind of goods or services being offered for sale;

Four: and in case of in-person contact, the person making the solicitation shall, in addition to meeting the requirements of paragraphs one, two, and three, show or display identification which states the information required by paragraphs one and two, as well as the address of the place of business of one of such persons so identified.

Under Subsection B: It is unlawful for any person, when soliciting a sale or order for sale of goods or services, at the residence of a prospective buyer, in person or by telephone, to use any plan, scheme, or ruse which misrepresents his true status or mission for the purpose of making such sale or order for the sale of goods. Under Subsection B: It is unlawful for any person, when soliciting a sale or order for the sale of goods or services, at the residence of a prospective buyer, in person or by telephone, to use any plan, scheme, or ruse which misrepresents his true status or mission for the purpose of making such sale or order for the sale of goods or services.

WALTER *(after knocking at* MARY's *door):*Hello! My name is Walter Krekowski, and I'm here as a representative of the Kirby Company, and I'm here to offer you something that could significantly change your life: a complete home renovation system.

MARY: I told you last April that I just bought a new vacuum. Now you don't think that I need a new one already. *(*WALTER *enters through the door.)*

WALTER: When you closed the door on me a year ago, I thought I was finished in sales—but I kept on trying. And since then I've made a lot of homemakers happy. So if I could just have a moment of your time, I'm sure I could show you at least ten different reasons why the vacuum I'm here to show you today, is the best there is on the market. *(To himself)* I've seen this kind before. If she moves to the right, she's lost interest in her husband. If she moves to the left, he's lost interest in her. (MARY *moves left.*) Just as I thought. Now if she crosses her arms and places her hand on her chin, then that means she is interested in a vacuum cleaner. But if she puts her hands on her hips, she's not. (MARY *puts her hands on hips.*) Just as I thought. If she doesn't offer me a cup of coffee, it'll mean she wants to be alone. But if she does, it means she wants me to stay. And if she says it's freshly made, then that means she doesn't want to buy anything—she just wants to talk.

MARY: Would you like a cup of coffee? *(Her hand trembles as she offers the cup.)*

WALTER *(thinking)*: And if her hand shakes when she brings it, and if she turns away after I accept the cup (MARY *turns away.*) it means that for her the pretense of buying is one of the few ways she has to relate. And if I say, "Thank you," then that means I understand, and that under the ruse of a business transaction, I will listen to her, and she to me. And if I say, "This is a nice house you have, ma'am," that means I will proceed to convince her to buy a vacuum. But on the other hand, if I say—*(To* MARY*)* Mary, both you and I know that neither of us are interested in vacuums.

HOUSEWIFE 3: They've found that the best salesmen had a quality of empathy, that he could identify with his customer, so that he could literally put himself in the customer's shoes, and feel and think what that customer was thinking. That way, he knew how to turn his next phrase, because—he could feel it.

NARRATOR: Move to the right, move to the left—put those hands on hips. Now feel the air move between you. The lungs suck air in. It moves to the left lung, and it moves to the right one—this air is full of feeling, and this air feels *good*. Feel this air move through you, and feel you moving. Move it—and let yourself be moved by it.

WALTER and MARY *dance.* WALTER *uses his Briefcase in the same manner as the jigsaw Square as a background for* MARY's *shoes.*

A *Large Target, three-and-a-half feet in diameter, rolls across stage, then back again.* MARY *freezes as it passes.*

An ATTENDANT *enters with the Parallelogram. He repeatedly opens it; then slams it shut.*

MARY *steals* WALTER's *Briefcase.* WALTER *doesn't protest as* MARY *puts it into the hands of an* ATTENDANT *and sends him away. An* AT-TENDANT *carries in a large Breakaway Target similar to the rolling one and holds it up behind* MARY. *She plucks out the red center.* WALTER *takes it from her as she breaks out the first white ring and slips it on like a bracelet.* WALTER *gently removes it from her wrist as the next ring becomes a hat and the next a necklace.* WALTER *takes off each ring and rolls them away. The final one slips all the way down her body onto the floor. Blackout.*

HOUSEWIFE 6: It's difficult for me to put off a salesman who *is* nice, but it, on the other hand, I mean, I feel as if I can't be rude to them in other words, uh—I don't wish to be rude to anybody, so I end up listening to everything they have to say. If the person gives a *hard* sell, I'm much more apt to say, be very direct and say, no thank you very much, and, and shut the door. But a soft sell, that continues on and on, I will end up listening to and listening to even though I know in the end that I'm going to say no.

SOUND MIX WITH MUSIC: In the end that I'm going to say no. *(Slam.)* That I'm going to say no. *(Slam.)* No. *(Slam.)* No. *(Slam.)* No.

HOUSEWIFE 6: Well they're trying to sell something first, so they've got to sell themselves. And to do that, they're going to flatter you, they're going to please you, they're going to say all sorts of nice things—whether you believe them or not. They're going to, you know, uh, usually they're pretty intelligent people, and they have a good command of the English language, usually—a good salesperson; and uh, they're just fun to be around. Much more interesting than an accountant, or a bookkeeper...yeah, I like salespeople. A lot.

SOUND MIX: I like salespeople. A lot./ A lot./ A lot./ A lot./ A lot.

NIGHTMARE

MARY, *in a red robe, appears from behind a black Screen which rises above and then sinks behind her. Her face is covered by the small Disc which slides down her body to her belly, then flips over—the target. Blackout. The hand held Spot illuminates a Dirt Tube with sawdust gushing out. Blackout. The same image of spilling sawdust repeats in another position. Blackout.* MARY *is caught in the glare of the hand-held Spot and an* ATTENDANT *spears her stomach with a collapsing Dirt Tube which seems to pass through her. Blackout. The hand-held Spot catches her again. She moves as if to scream. An Arrow consisting of a solid triangular head and a taut cloth shaft ushers from directly behind her mouth. Blackout. Arrow image repeats but travels in opposite direction.* WALTER *quickly spins in. Blackout. Arrow flies again, halts in front of* WALTER. *He shoves it away. Blackout.*

Once again WALTER *is caught by a hand-held Spot from across the stage. He walks toward it, possibly in hope of turning it into a glass of booze. It goes off before he gets there.*

WALTER DRINKS

NARRATOR: Those things he had told her, they were thoughts he
hadn't told anyone—not even his inner self. Now he had. He
had the possibility to sell everyone, even the woman who had
first turned him down. But instead of selling another vacuum, he
had sold himself. He had always known that a part of him was in
every sale, but now he knew that vacuums were nothing, and
that he was *all* of it. He'd have to stop selling. He'd have to go
back to her. Without the vacuum.

ABORTION

A white hospital curtain is drawn across three quarters of the stage.
MARY's *shadow plays back and forth on the curtain. A Doctor enters*
and motions MARY *onto a table. He leaves.* MARY's *silhouette begins*
to rise and grow larger. She seems to become airborne. The Doctor
returns with the fluorescent Circle. The Circle moves toward her.
Blackout.

ATTENDANT *holding Spotlight alternately spotlights* MARY *and*
WALTER *who stand at opposite sides of the stage.* WALTER *ap-*
proaches MARY. *When he reaches her,* MARY *turns away violently.*
Door slam is heard.

ABORTION

DOCTOR: Some people may, uh, subconsciously feel that a pregnancy would do something for their lives. But when it really happens, and they're faced with the reality of having to care for a new baby, and what it would really do to their lives, when they have to face that part of it, instead of dealing with their fantasies about babies, they make it, they make a different decision.

Sound mix of clinic doctors.

NURSE *(sound mix)*: Barbicane, Valium, Demerol. Herpedan, Barbicane, Valium, Demerol. Herpedan, Barbicane, Valium, Demerol. Herpedan, Barbicane, Valium, Demerol./ It's a drum-like arrangement, clear plastic or glass material. Underneath, a metal container, metal pump, metal motor, and it has hoses connected to it, long hoses which are also clear plastic, uh, connected to then a plastic curette./ OK, this table's hard.

PSYCHIATRIST: Usually, this is a generality, but usually, salespeople are very outgoing, gregarious. Uh, they're happy, they're self-confident, um; they try to sell their confidence in their product to the customer. They may flatter the person, uh, they—they're certainly going to be upbeat. And, what we find is that when a salesperson, a professional salesperson is trying to deal with someone who's depressed, they're more likely to offer platitudes, say things are going to be better, and point out the positive things rather than allow that person to deal with. . . their sadness.

WALTER'S CAR RIDE

WALTER *points handheld Spot at himself and turns it on. He stands up and scans the stage. The Fences shoot in at askew angles imprisoning* WALTER *between them. The Parallelogram is set as a doorway.* WALTER *walks up and knocks.* MARY *spins in and slams the door shut. The Parallelogram spins out.*

The fluorescent Circle enters jerking up and down and heading directly towards WALTER. *It shuts off just moments before impact.*

The Ladder slides in and WALTER *lifts it, holding the rungs like prison bars. He sets it up and tries to climb it, but without support it falls away.*

WALTER'S CAR RIDE

PSYCHIATRIST: Most people cannot accept rejection.

SALESMAN 1: And in the vacuum cleaner business, they'll show you/ and in the vacuum cleaner business, they'll show you how to get there—to the top.

SALESMAN 2: They're an absolute lead-pipe cinch for making a/ they're an absolute lead-pipe cinch for making a sale.

SALESMAN 1: Hey, you've got to sell, you've got to sell, you've got to sell—you've got to sell yourself.

SALESMAN 4: Without a positive attitude you're dead—absolutely dead in the water.

SALESMAN 2: Absolute lead-pipe cinch for making a sale.

MARY: You're new at this, aren't you? Next time tell them to send a *salesman.* Bye.

SALESMAN 3: It's not an easy job—and it is one that requires a great deal of persistence. You meet, constantly, rejection.

SCIENTIST: A vacuum is/ rejection/ theoretically space without matter in it. A perfect vacuum.

SALESMAN 1: They'll show you how to get there—to the top.

SALESMAN 4: Positive attitude you're dead—absolutely dead in the water.

SALESMAN 2: They're an absolute lead-pipe cinch for making a sale.

SALESMAN 1: And in the vacuum cleaner business, they'll show you how to get there—to the top. You've got to sell, you've got to sell, you've got to sell *yourself.*

The Blinds enter, one shoots back and forth across the stage, the other flashes: No...No...No. *The Large Target Disc rolls by.* MARY *spins in; stands center stage. The Parallelogram lands in front of her but whirls away as* WALTER *approaches. The two House Heads enter from opposite wings, slowly moving toward an eventual meeting.* MARY *stands directly behind where the meeting will occur.* WALTER *moves toward* MARY *but the two House Heads crash together before he reaches her, forming a solid wall. Blackout.*

The ATTENDANTS *enter wearing Spots at waist level and carrying three-foot long closed white Fans.* WALTER *stands between and behind them. With the first clap of thunder and barrage of rain the* ATTENDANTS *sweep their Fans from side to side in unison. The Fans suggest windshield wipers, the Spots headlights, and the Ladder in front suggests a grill. As the storm intensifies the* ATTENDANTS *sweep the Fans open and the ribs appear as multiple after images of wipers caught by headlights, street lights, and stoplights. The car image disintegrates as the Fans attack* WALTER *transforming into whips, prison bars, wheels, and other images.* WALTER *takes the Ladder in hand, first spinning it like a steering wheel, then crashing its edges against the ground, and finally smashing into two. Blackout.*

SALESMAN 4: Without a positive attitude, you're dead. *(Applause.)*

SALESMAN 1: If you were looking for a selling job, I'd prob'ly tell you to go down the street at the 7-11 or something like that—but if you were coming in here for a *career*, and wanted to learn selling./ First thing I want to tell you men and women tonight/ let me tell you, the first thing I'm going to do is, I'm going to explain to you the possibilities to become as successful in the business as I am, to you, and how you can get up what we call the ladder of success in a short relative time with very little money. You don't need any money in this business, all you need is the guts, and the excitement, and the desire to get ahead, and in the vacuum cleaner business, they'll show you how to get there—to the top/ to the top/ lead-pipe cinch/ lead-pipe cinch/ You've got to sell you've got to sell you've got to sell yourself/ Without a positive attitude you're dead—absolutely dead in the water.

WALTER: Mary, both you and I know that neither of us are interested in vacuums.

PSYCHIATRIST: And, Walter it seems, he's, he's having this resurgence of feelings./ He's having this resurgence of feelings./ He's having this resurgence of feelings./ He's having this resurgence of feelings.

MARY: You're new at this aren't you? Next time, tell them to send a *salesman*. Bye.

PSYCHIATRIST: He's having this resurgence of feelings./ *(Slam.)* He's having this resurgence of feelings./ *(Slam.)* He's having this resurgence of feelings. *(Slam.)* He's having this resurgence of feelings.

WALTER FACES THE VACUUM

An ATTENDANT *holds the lit fluorescent Circle center stage.*
WALTER *lifts his head and stares. He's attracted to it. He holds up his*
arm. The Circle slides slowly up to his shoulder as WALTER *intently*
observes. Vacuum sounds rise. WALTER *suddenly wrenches his arm*
free. Blackout.

WALTER KNOCKS ON DOORS

Lights fade up on WALTER *holding his Briefcase. He test runs some*
of his Briefcase maneuvers. A house enters (assembled House Head)
and glides to center stage. WALTER *paces, arriving at the house. He*
knocks. The house opens. Vacuum sounds fade. WALTER *kneels and*
shows Briefcase, beginning another sale. . . . Blackout.

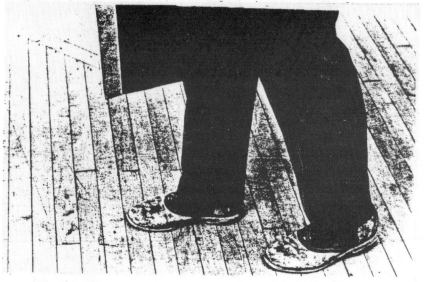

WALTER FACES THE VACUUM

SCIENTIST *(mixed with sound of vacuum sucking):* A vacuum is theoretically space without matter. . . .

HOUSEWIFE: A sucking motion. . . .

SCIENTIST: A perfect vacuum. . . . *(Blackout.)*

WALTER KNOCKS ON DOORS

NARRATOR: Now, he thought that he could understand it all—that there was a fine line between selling and loving. That both were an interchange of communication, and each had the possibility for cheating and hurt. Was the difference between buying and selling the difference in the pay schedule? Was it that, in selling, you were paid for your giving up front, whereas when giving you were paid later? Now he saw it more clearly than he'd ever seen it before: that if everything came to a stop, if there were no buying and selling, then there would be a vacuum.

SALESMAN 1: Nobody's going to buy a product like a vacuum cleaner if it's door-to-door if you don't *present* it. You can't walk up to the door and say, "Hi, Mrs. Jones, I'm Ray Buddovitch with the Kirby Company, and I'm here to sell you a Kirby. How many would you like to buy?" I'll guarantee you, that you could walk till *doomsday,* and you might find somebody that their vacuum *just* broke down who'll say, Hey, I'll buy one. But chances are you'll never sell it. You've got to get in, you've got to show the product, you've got to be enthusiastic—you've got to ask them to buy! "Do you like what I'm showing you, Mrs. Jones? What do you think of that product—isn't that nice? Thank you very much! Can I write it up for you? Let's go to the kitchen table."

Interview with Chris Hardman

Rick Foster interviewed Chris Hardman on September 5, 1983.

FOSTER: *Vacuum* is constructed out of three very different kinds of materials. There is the documentary which provides more than half the sound score; there is the deliberately banal story line which might have been lifted from some old *True Confessions Magazine*; and there is the very sophisticated and rather abstract visual design. Much of the impact of the piece comes from the way these disparate elements play off one another. Tell me first about how you got into using the documentary approach.

HARDMAN: The initial purpose was to gather material from the public and invite them in to see the show that they had in some sense co-authored. That was the initial premise: to find ways to involve the audience in the entire process of making theater. So we decided to do a show about vacuum cleaner salesmen. We chose this because on the one hand it has to do with the home, with cleanliness, with the great American preoccupation with selling, and on the other hand the selling of vacuum cleaners is such a common activity we knew we'd find lots of people who had some kind of story relating to it. It would give us access to a lot of houses.

FOSTER: And of course the very word vacuum gives you a powerful metaphor for emptiness.

HARDMAN: Oh yes. I'm a sucker for that kind of territory. I knew that we would also be asking scientists about vacuums and psychiatrists about vacuums. That we'd be working on the level of metaphor and collecting different impressions of what the word means.

FOSTER: Were you also aware that you were going to get such wonderful material from the professional vacuum cleaner salesmen?

HARDMAN: No. That was the major surprise, that it worked so well. And in retrospect I can see we were incredibly lucky to have decided to do vacuum cleaner salesmen because they are natural performers.

FOSTER: Their story-telling personas—which you were able to tape—are in fact the chief tools of their trade. So you were able to bring that salesmen's reality right into the theater.

HARDMAN: Yeah, and that led me to be very optimistic about using documentary material in other shows. I was going to do the next project using detectives. But unlike storybook detectives, the actual field of private investigation is filled with extremely bland and boring people. I did gather a lot of material from real detectives when I started working on *Artery* but the people were so dull and so worried about the legal implications of what they might tell me that I couldn't use it in anything like the way I could use the salesmen. The salesmen are born storytellers who constantly hone their material.

FOSTER: Yes, it's clear that Ray Buddovitch and Jerry Schuler have told their stories a thousand times. Merely reading the text, which is a transcript, it's perhaps less clear, but when you hear the tape with all the practiced inflections you realize just how masterful these guys are.

HARDMAN: They know exactly how to get their effect. And the salesmen's tapes contrast with the material from, for example, Mrs. Miller, the older housewife, which was also played verbatim. There's none of that skill involved with her, just a sincere telling of how much she likes to vacuum.

FOSTER: How did you get Mrs. Miller?

HARDMAN: She came from the questionnaires. You see, as we were interviewing the professionals in the field we were also sending out thousands of questionnaires to get people's attitudes to vacuum cleaners and to door-to-door salesmen. We especially needed to find some people who had positive attitudes to vacuuming. We did follow-up interviews and that's where we taped Mrs. Miller. And the stuff we got from her was so good it made a whole scene for us. We got it all in one sitting. That was the best example of how the questionnaires led us in a direction we could use for the play.

FOSTER: All right, now I understand how this mixture of public-opinion survey and investigative journalism produced the documentary material on the sound tape. But the story, which is also on the sound tape, seems to be from another world—this seemingly fictional character, Walter, who makes himself into a salesman, and Mary, the lonely housewife with whom he has an affair. Did that also come out of the interviews or was the story something you started with?

HARDMAN: The skeleton of the story came before I did any interviewing. I knew we'd have a novice salesman who would be rejected and then come back as a professional determined to make good his previous defeat. And I knew we'd move into the larger picture of vacuum as empty space and the loneliness of housewives who need the kind of communication that a business deal can provide in this society.

FOSTER: So here you're behaving like a playwright and not like a journalist.

HARDMAN: Right. And then the problem was to bring the pre-determined story together with the documentary material and to have them influence each other and to see if they all could hang together. So we were interested in vacuum cleaner salesmen talking about sexual events in their vacuum-cleaning lives.

FOSTER: That doesn't get into the documentary material which the audience hears.

HARDMAN: No, but we did gather enough material to confirm that the story might well have happened. The really successful salesmen had the attitude that sex with their clients was always possible, but it wasn't what they wanted because it slowed them down and didn't help business. They would intimate things about sexual relations but their story-telling imaginations weren't really activated. The wonderful details we got about selling—the "house with a red-shingled roof," the "sleeping in your own dead flesh," the confusion of Mayfair and Mayflower—these wonderful touches never entered the sexual stories which were vague and blurred.

FOSTER: So we've covered how the documentary and the play-wrighting streams were working together in the creation of the show. The design is a completely separate stream that seems not to be determined by either of the others. Were you tempted to let the documentary invade the visual design?

HARDMAN: Oh yes, that was a big worry. I thought I might have to have slides of real vacuum cleaners and stores and people using the product. But as I thought about that the piece began to feel too much like a real documentary and I wanted to keep the poetic aspect.

FOSTER: So you finally chose to confine the documentary to the sound design.

HARDMAN: Yes. I needed to juxtapose what I called the hot and the cold information. You have the very hot, very alive sound track with real people, with their environmental sounds coming through—they were literally coming from another space than the theater where the audience and the visuals were happening. I felt that if the visuals were equally hot, there would be no juxtaposition, no depth, no textural possibilities. The piece would lack depth. That's why I kept the visuals cool and abstract. I think this made the voices sound like disjointed, fragmentary gods, commenting on the story.

FOSTER: I think that juxtaposition was particularly effective in *Vacuum*. When we talked a couple of years ago you planned to continue working with documentary elements. But that doesn't seem to be the direction your work has taken since. What happened?

HARDMAN: The piece I did right after *Vacuum* was called *High School* and it actually was equally documentary. I recorded a young man who had just graduated from Tamalpais High School in Mill Valley, all of his experiences, and the audience listened to his rap on Sony Walkmen, while following a pre-determined path around the campus of the school. Then there were certain planned events like boys whizzing by on skate boards or the audience received diplomas at the end of the tour.

FOSTER: And here the documentary and the Walkman worked well together.

HARDMAN: Right. But when I started working on *Artery*, as I said before, I tried to gather documentary material on detectives and it was just not giving me anything I could use. Meanwhile, the Walkman was opening up a whole new world of possible relationships between the audience and the theater. By having the hi fi sound score going directly into the audience's head, and having the audience move through a real environment, or sculptured environment, or some combination of the two. . . well, there are huge possibilities. Working those out is what I'll be doing for the foreseeable future.

POSTSCRIPT

Chris Hardman has continued his explorations with Antenna Theater into the theatrical uses of Walkmans, developing a theatrical form of his own which he calls Walkmanology. These explorations have ranged from the highly structured to the almost random. In *Artery*, each individual member of the audience, guided by the taped soundtrack which also contained the entire story of the play, walked alone through a created environment constructed in a maze-like pattern. The text for the play was a mystery and the listener, as the perpetrator of the crime, was the only actor.

In *Amnesia* (1983), performed at the 1984 Olympic Arts Festival in Los Angeles, four separate soundtracks guided a number of audience members simultaneously through four stories within the same room—each listener following a separate path, guided by the taped narration. In this piece each audience member interacted with masked actors during the course of following each story. *Adjusting the Idle*, created by Hardman for the Mark Taper Forum/ Museum of Contemporary Art *Carplays* festival (1984), used some thirty separate tapes to which audience members had access at random. Audience members could simply observe the action, or could participate in it by following the instructions on one of the tapes. As in *Vacuum*, the texts on the tapes were developed through the interview process.

In 1984, Hardman and Antenna Theater also branched out into radio drama with a series of programs aired on Berkeley's Pacifica station, KPFA. Here, too, though in a far more modified fashion, listeners were given instructions to follow. *Russia* (1985), Hardman's most recent work, returns to the format first explored in *Vacuum*, developing a text from audience-elicited interviews.

—Robert Hurwitt

Twenty-Four Hours

INTRODUCTION

Twenty-Four Hours was developed by the Playwrights Lab at
the Back Alley in Los Angeles. The lab began in 1981 when Laura
Zucker and Allan Miller, producers of the theater, invited a dozen
playwrights based in Los Angeles to develop a workshop, hopefully
to create new plays that might ultimately be produced by the Back
Alley. From its original dozen playwrights, the group had grown to
an active 75 members at the time of this production (all of whom
could find seats at sessions as long as at least ten didn't show up),
with a long waiting list. *Twenty-Four Hours* was devised as a
project to unify the group, each playwright asked to write a piece of
approximately five minutes in length with two restrictions: each
play should involve no more than four actors, two men and two
women, maximum, and each should be set at a specific hour of the
day or night.

Ultimately over one hundred plays were written, most being
labbed at the Back Alley prior to production. On a given lab night
playwrights were asked to see and then comment on as many as sixteen new plays. Finally fifty plays were chosen to be submitted—
without the names of their authors—to the seven directors who had
agreed to direct them. The directors read and scored the plays. The
thirty plays that scored highest were then put into rehearsal. Six
were eliminated during the rehearsal process, primarily because of
casting problems rather than script.

Though the plays had been created so that four actors might con-
ceivably play all the roles, the abundance of acting talent in Los
Angeles made this restriction seem foolish. Ultimately sixteen very
gifted actors were chosen for the fifty roles that comprise *Twenty-
Four Hours*. It had also been thought in the beginning that the plays
might all be done in a single evening. However, as several were
longer than five minutes and almost none briefer, it was decided to
play the plays in two evenings—or, ideally, as a matinee and an
evening.

Though mounting twenty-four individual plays at first seemed
like a somewhat Herculean effort (it was labeled a mini-*Nicholas
Nickleby*), production proved to be relatively simple thanks
primarily to a unit set with only basic pieces of furniture that
allowed the plays to flow easily and rapidly. While a bed was essential to the plays in *A.M.*, it was discovered during rehearsals that all
of the plays in *P.M.* could be performed without a bed, allowing for
additional variation in staging. The blackouts between plays were

kept to an absolute minimum with brief musical inserts used to bridge the darkness.

Acting roles were juggled so that performers rarely moved directly from one play to the next. Props were also kept to a minimum, the actors usually bringing on and also carrying off their individual props. Where sinks or other complicated set pieces were needed, they were pantomimed. It was also found that the bed worked better stripped of its coverings, using only the bottom sheet with the actors pantomiming their coverings as needed.

It is, of course, possible to juggle the order in which the plays are presented. However, as time sequence is the game, it is hoped that the order will not be violated. It is also hoped that producing *Twenty-Four Hours* will bring as much excitement to your group as it did to the Playwrights Lab at the Back Alley.

— Oliver Hailey

Twenty-Four Hours: A.M.

Daniel Gregory Brown
Pamela Chais
Michael Leeson
Jeff Levy
David Link
Jerry Mayer
Allan Miller
Christine Rimmer
Susan Silver
Terry Kingsley-Smith
Lee Thomas
Bonnie Zindel
Paul Zindel

Twenty-Four Hours: A.M. was originally presented on September 30, 1982, at the Back Alley Theatre, Van Nuys, California, with the following cast:

Faro Rides Again

WOMAN	Elizabeth Hoffman
MAN	John Anderson

Directed by Dona Cooper

Sleeping Together

JACKSON	Jim Hornbeck
KELLY	Paul Keenan

Directed by Beverly Sanders

Shotgun Willis

WILLIS	John Anderson

Directed by Dona Cooper

Four in the Morning

WOMAN	Joy Garrett
MAN	Jim Hornbeck

Directed by Marcia Rodd

I Want to Hold Your Hand

OLDER MAN	Alan Oppenheimer
YOUNGER MAN	Paul Keenan

Directed by Marcia Rodd

Love Sonnet

ADA	Doris Roberts
LOU	John Anderson

Directed by Will Mackenzie

Joe's Not Home

MARK	Alan Oppenheimer
JUNE	Doris Roberts

Directed by Allan Miller

The Underachiever

JENNY	Joy Garrett
STEVE	Jim Hornbeck

Directed by Will Mackenzie

Sunny Side Up

LORRAINE	Elizabeth Hoffman
HARRY	Alan Oppenheimer

Directed by Barbara Schultz

Pelicans

JAKE   John Anderson
LOTTIE   Elizabeth Hoffman

Directed by Barbara Schultz

Lemons in the Morning

CLAIRE   Doris Roberts
MR. HILLARY   Alan Oppenheimer
BETSY   Margaret O'Keefe

Directed by Allan Miller

Five Minute Romance

HE   Jim Hornbeck
SHE   Joy Garrett

Directed by Allan Miller

Production conceived by Oliver Hailey
Produced by Laura Zucker
Direction supervised by Allan Miller
Set designed by Zoe Wells
Lighting designed by Christopher Milliken
Costumes coordinated by Hilary Sloane
Music composed by Dick De Benidictis
Sound designed by Leonora Schildkraut

Faro Rides Again
Allan Miller

At rise: dark bedroom. Queen-size bed. Door opens. WOMAN *yells out from the bed, still half asleep.*

WOMAN: Huza...whar!!!
MAN: Sssh.
WOMAN: Who is that?
MAN: It's me, go to sleep!
WOMAN: What time is it?
MAN: Eleven o'clock.
WOMAN: Where were you?

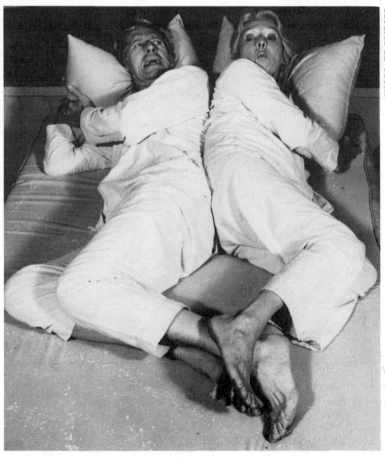

MAN: I went to the bathroom; go to sleep.
WOMAN: Don't bounce the bed.
MAN: Go to sleep.

The WOMAN moves the luminescent dial clock on the bed table.

WOMAN: It's one-thirty. Why did you tell me it was only eleven?
MAN: Ssh, I'm sleeping!
WOMAN: How long were you out there?
MAN: What difference does it make?
WOMAN: My God, your feet are like ice! Get over here. . . . Get over heeere. . . ! Ohh, my God. Rrrrr. . . ! Move your elbow. . . . OoOhh. . . ! What's the matter, I can hear you thinking. . . ? Matt?
MAN: Will you stop?
WOMAN: No, I'm not going to stop. I want to know what you're thinking!
MAN: I'm not thinking, I'm trying to. . .
WOMAN: You are, I know when you are. . .
MAN: GO TO SLEEP!
WOMAN: Now tell me or you'll never get to sleep!
MAN: What is the matter with you?
WOMAN: What is the matter with YOUUU?
MAN: Nothing!
WOMAN: I can't sleep when you're thinking loud!
MAN: I'm thinking about Faro!
WOMAN: What about him?
MAN: He's dead!
WOMAN: He is not. . . ! Matt? Matt, where is Faro?
MAN: On the sofa.
WOMAN: He knows he's not allowed on the sofa.
MAN: Will you go to sleep?
WOMAN: Did you let him on the sofa?
MAN: I didn't have to let him, he climbed up there to die, for God's sake!
WOMAN: When?
MAN: An hour ago.
WOMAN: He did not. . . ! Matt!
MAN: Will you let me sleep?
WOMAN: What were you doing out there all this time?

The WOMAN switches on her lamp. MATT has one of his two pillows over his head. She pulls the pillow off.

MAN: Will you stop?

WOMAN *(hitting him)*: Will I stop? Will I stop?

MAN: Stop it!

WOMAN: Why do you say these things while I'm trying to sleep? God, you're mean. You're stupid and you're mean. . . . Are you all right?

MAN: Yes, I'm all right.

WOMAN: Is Faro all right? Matt. . . ? Where is Faro?

MAN: He's out there.

WOMAN: What did you do with him?

MAN: I left him lying on the sofa.

WOMAN *(hitting him again)*: Noo, you know he's not supposed to go on the sofa!

MAN: It was his last request, for God's sake!

WOMAN: Oh God—the whole sofa's going to stink for a week!

MAN: *(putting the pillow on his head)*: Turn out the light.

WOMAN: How can I sleep now?

MAN: Where are you going?

WOMAN: I'm going to get that dog off the sofa!

MAN: He's not on the sofa, I put him out back!

WOMAN: Where, in the garage?

MAN: I buried him!

WOMAN: Oh, my God, why didn't you call me?

MAN: I knew you'd be upset.

WOMAN: I'm upset anyway!

MAN: I wanted it to be private!

WOMAN: Private?

MAN: God, woman, after thirty-seven years together, I wanted *something to be private*!!!

Suddenly offstage, there is a loud barking and the clatter of a large dog's claws scrambling on a hardwood floor, trying to get up momentum, then the quick flap-flap of a doggie door. The dog's barking continues outside the house.

MAN *(yelling)*: Faro, shut up! Farooo. . . ! Bad dog! Nooo!!!

The dog stops barking. Sound of doggie door flap-flapping, then the quiet tread of the dog's paws on the hardwood floor.

WOMAN: God, I hate you sometimes.

MAN *(calling)*: That's a good boy, Faro. Easy now. . . !

WOMAN: Good Faro! That retarded dog. Your friend!

MAN *(calling)*: Go to your bed, Faro. Go to your bed. . . !

Sound of dog's tread to another room. The WOMAN *gets into the bed and snaps off the light.*

WOMAN: Come on now, get over here. . . . Come on. . .! Rrrr. Why don't you wear socks at night?

MAN: Go to sleep.

The WOMAN *grunts, shivers a little, and there is silence. Fade to black.*

Sleeping Together
David Link

JACKSON *sits on the edge of the bed fully clothed.* KELLY *stands beside the bed putting on his shirt. He is younger than* JACKSON *and very well-built.*

JACKSON: I'm really sorry.

KELLY: It's all right.

JACKSON: No. I mean, I'm really sorry.

KELLY: I said it was all right.

JACKSON: I could have sworn I was homosexual.

KELLY: I'm sure lots of people make that mistake.

JACKSON: Do you think so? It's just that, when I was breaking up with my wife, well, things were really slow there toward the end. But we had this gardener, he was about twenty, blond hair, a nice looking guy. Kind of like you, actually. And I just. . .you know, felt this longing. So I figured that's it, that's the problem. But I guess it isn't.

KELLY: Here's your jacket.

JACKSON: You're mad.

KELLY: No, I'm not mad. I've still got a couple of hours, maybe I can hit the baths.

JACKSON: The baths? You mean public sex?

KELLY: We don't do it on The Phil Donahue Show, no. What's the matter?

JACKSON: It just seems so. . . . Do you do it often?

KELLY: Maybe once a week.

JACKSON: God. I didn't do it with my wife that often. During our good times.

KELLY: Look, it's going to take me a while to get over there. Can I drop you somewhere?

JACKSON: Oh, God. I don't know how to say this, but I was sort of hoping to be able to spend the night here. I kind of burned my bridges behind me back home and I don't have anywhere to go. I don't know anyone I can wake up at two a.m.

KELLY: All right; you can stay here till morning. I probably won't be back till ten or so anyway. If you leave before then, just lock the door.

JACKSON: Here? Alone? God, I don't even know your name.

KELLY: What does that have to do with anything?

JACKSON: We're complete strangers. How did I get into this?

KELLY: My name's Kelly, OK? It's been nice meeting you.

JACKSON: My name's Jackson. Jackson Bridges. Don't go.

KELLY: Why not?

JACKSON: How do you do it? Have sex with strangers?

KELLY: Sometimes I like it that way. That's what you were going to do here tonight.

JACKSON: I know. I was.

KELLY: Why did you want to do it?

JACKSON: I don't know. There's so much pressure on a guy these days. You see gays everywhere, on the news, in TV shows, newspapers, movies, the office, and all they talk about is how fulfilled they are, and I always had this huge gap inside, something that was never satisfied, so I thought, well, maybe that's the answer.

KELLY: Why did you get married?

JACKSON: I was twenty-five and had a good job and people kept asking me when I was going to get married and I got tired of it.

KELLY: I know what you mean.

JACKSON: And my wife was very pretty and very attentive and I think we loved each other. A little. Have you ever been in love?

KELLY: I doubt it. I don't know. There was this guy last year. . . . It didn't work out. We were really good in bed, but that was it. You know?

JACKSON: That's our problem these days; we know so much about sex and we're completely naive about love. Sometimes I don't know if there is such a thing. You're sure it's OK if I stay here?

KELLY: Uh-huh. What time did you say it was?

JACKSON: It's almost a quarter after two.

KELLY: You know, by the time I got out there, it'd be three or so and there wouldn't be much action probably. I think I'll stay here, too. That OK with you?

JACKSON: Sure. I can just sleep here on the floor. God knows I'm sure used to it.

KELLY: Don't be ridiculous. I've got that huge bed. There's plenty of space for both of us. It's much more comfortable. If you want to.

JACKSON: Sure.

KELLY: I think that for one night at least, we should both stop worrying so much and just get some sleep. Come on, let's go to bed.

JACKSON: I'm with you.

KELLY *removes his shirt again, kicks off his shoes, starts to remove his trousers, hesitates, decides for* JACKSON's *sake to keep them on, slides into bed still wearing trousers.* JACKSON *climbs into bed fully clothed except for his shoes. Each turns away from the other, assuming the fetal position, back to back and very much on his own side of the bed.*

KELLY: Goodnight, Jackson.
JACKSON: Goodnight, Kelly.

Lights fade to black.

Four in the Morning
Daniel Gregory Brown

Setting: a bedroom with imaginary bathroom downstage right. A middle-aged MAN *sleeps, snores. His middle-aged* WIFE *cannot sleep. His back is to her, curved fetally. She gets up, pulls on a robe that matches her nightgown, and goes into the bathroom. The sink and its cold water seem to pull her like an oxygen mask would for a woman who can't breathe. The mirror above the sink is the audience, herself. She looks full front into a pool of light.*

WOMAN *(with a laugh)*: It's like one of those dreams where you're dreaming that you're yourself sleeping, and now it's time to wake up, which you do, and you're about to go through tomorrow, that is, the day you had planned for yourself tomorrow. And you think you're awake. You think, this is real. Because everything is very literal. All the edges have clear lines. The colors are right. Nothing seems to be happening out of a logical time sequence. Real. Only, of course, you're still asleep. You have not awokened. Awakened? Awoke. Whatever. I never can get that tense. *(Laughs.)* Well, I get that tense all the time. I meant, time-tense. It is spelled the same way, isn't it? It is a word? Anyway, there I was... Here I am... *(Laughs again.)* It's four in the morning, the end of December. The end of something. It hasn't been an easy night. In the same sense of... it wasn't an easy birth. And she dragged herself to the bathroom, and looked in the mirror, and lo and behold she didn't recognize the person looking back. Has that ever happened to you? It happens to me every once in awhile, but normally I don't let on. Of course, at four in the morning, who's keeping score? The age doesn't seem right, the weight doesn't seem right. Never did. And why did I do my hair *this* color? Oh, God. What am I wearing? I wouldn't buy anything like this. Hookers in Vegas. No, a Mexican *movie* of hookers in Vegas. *(Stares very intently, sighs.)* Actually, it's very expensive, very correct. Just remember your name. Remember your name, and everything else will fall back into place. There are probably a lot of people out there who would not believe that a middle-aged wife is actually having difficulty remembering her name. Unless, of course, she's drunk or has taken too many pills, which you have not. It's Ruth. Of course, it is. Your name is Ruth. You're halfway home, now just get the other half and you'll be fine. It goes with what'siz name on the other side of the bed. The one with tiny hands who could lose a few pounds. He does have small hands. Harry. Come on, you'll get it. This is ridiculous. Harry. No, that's his brother. Sam, Harry. No, Sam's the brother. This is Harry. And you are Mrs. Harry, Mrs. Harry... Castleman! Yeah? Of course, it is. Now wait a minute. Those were White Castle hamburgers for twelve cents, and Castle Carpets for twelve ninety-five a square yard. Of course, it's Castleman. You wouldn't just pull that out of thin air. (*Suddenly crying, almost.*) Actually, sweetheart, I wouldn't go back in there, if *I* were you, unless I were absolutely sure. I mean, who knows? He rolls over, he's Bruno Somebody, and then what do you do? No, you did not leave a Bruno. You left a Harry. Thinning hair, could use a little sun. Sinus problems, bursitis, potbellied... And his eyes... Well, he squints so much, you never could tell what color his eyes were.

She goes back into the bedroom to get back into bed, but stops. She looks at a pair of man's trousers dropped across the back of a chair. She goes to the chair and picks up the pants.

MAN: Are you okay?

WOMAN (*laughs*): You scared me.

MAN: I scared *you*? What are you doing?

WOMAN: What do you mean, what am I doing?

MAN: I mean, what are you doing, going through my pants?

WOMAN: What is this all of a sudden? Secrets?

MAN: Look, Louise, sweetheart...

WOMAN: What did you call me?

MAN: I mean, you've been in the bathroom now for what? Forty-five minutes. I know you can't sleep, you get up to take a pill...

WOMAN: I didn't take a pill.

MAN: But forty-five minutes. What were you doing in there?

WOMAN: I didn't disturb you?

MAN: No...

WOMAN: I didn't turn on the light. Was I talking to myself?

MAN: I don't know. Were you?

WOMAN: No, of course, I wasn't.

MAN: What were you doing?

WOMAN: I thought I felt a pimple.

MAN: At four in the morning?

WOMAN: Sometimes a blind pimple can be very uncomfortable. I didn't want to squeeze it, I couldn't find it...

MAN: Then you should have turned on the light.

WOMAN: I didn't want to disturb you.

MAN: Why are you going through my pockets?

WOMAN: You really want to know?

MAN: Well, since there aren't any matchbooks with waitresses' phone numbers—I mean, what are you doing? You want to see how much cash I carry, what?

WOMAN: I was going to look at your driver's license.

MAN: My what?

WOMAN: Your driver's license.

MAN: My driver's license? What for? You're giving me a ticket?

WOMAN: I couldn't sleep. . .

MAN: I know you couldn't sleep, you never sleep. You think because I'm snoring, I don't know you're wide awake?

WOMAN: But I was dozing, I *think* I was dozing. . . . And I had this dream, only it didn't seem like a dream. And I couldn't remember what our name was. *(She laughs.)*

MAN: So? You're awake now. . .

WOMAN: Am I? *(She laughs.)* Of course, right. Anyway, I just wanted to look at your driver's license to see if it was a dream. I mean, I know it isn't. But I just had this funny feeling that I'd look at your driver's license and it wouldn't be our real name, it would be the name in the dream.

MAN: Louise. . .

WOMAN: You said that before.

MAN: I said what before?

WOMAN *(taking a wallet out of the man's pants)*: Is this your wallet?

MAN: Of course, it's my wallet.

WOMAN: Your wallet's brown.

MAN: So?

WOMAN: This wallet's black.

MAN: There's no light on, it *looks* black.

WOMAN *(pulling the license from the wallet)*: You didn't get one of those fake driver's licenses, did you? For a joke or something? For a sales meeting.

MAN: What are you talking about?

WOMAN: Could you please turn on the light?

MAN: Louise. . .

WOMAN: My name is Ruth.

MAN: Ruth?

WOMAN: And this says your name is Sam Bruno. *(She laughs.)* Who's Sam Bruno?

MAN *(turning on the light)*: Louise, what were you taking in there?

WOMAN: You're not Harry.

MAN: Who's Harry?

WOMAN: You're not Harry Castleman at all. What's going on here?

MAN: Louise. . .

WOMAN: I want someone to please tell me. . . what's. . . going. . . on. . . here!?!?!? I mean, so, okay, life didn't work out. You never really expected it to. And you adjust. You come to grips with who you are, and who this person is you're living with, even though it is not the person you would have picked. Okay, so that's my fantasy and life is reality, but I will not have the cast changed on me in the middle of the night, do you understand? I won't. So whoever you are, or whoever it is you *think* you are, or whoever it is you're trying to *prove* to me you are. . .

MAN: Okay, just calm down.

WOMAN: I will not calm down!

MAN: Louise. . .

WOMAN: Who?

MAN: *Louise!*

WOMAN: Who? *(Very loud)* Who? *(Then softer)* Who? Who? Who? Who? Who?

Blackout.

I Want to Hold Your Hand
Terry Kingsley-Smith

Place: The tourist class of an airplane.

Time: Dawn is just about to break.

At rise: a YOUNGER MAN *sits, holding the hand of an* OLDER MAN *who is asleep. The* OLDER MAN *comes awake, is aghast when he realizes that the* YOUNGER MAN *is holding his hand. He attempts to free his hand, but the* YOUNGER MAN *holds on tightly.*

OLDER MAN: What the hell do you think you're doing?!

YOUNGER MAN: Please, please, I can't let go yet.

OLDER MAN: Let go of my hand!

YOUNGER MAN: It won't be long now. It'll be light soon and then I'll let go. (*Looking at his watch.*) It's already after five. Soon it'll be light. I'm usually all right after six.

OLDER MAN: What are you talking about? Are you some kind of pervert?

YOUNGER MAN: It usually hits me when I wake up between five and six in the morning. I call it my dinosaur hour. I try to get back to sleep, but I can't, and it gets worse until it's daylight. Then I have my coffee and everything's all right again.

OLDER MAN: Then let's get you some coffee.

YOUNGER MAN: I already asked the stewardess while you were asleep. She said they're not serving yet. When she saw that I was holding your hand, she asked if I wanted a blanket. I understand on these red eye flights people do things together underneath their blankets.

OLDER MAN: That's disgusting.

YOUNGER MAN: I think so, too.

OLDER MAN: Then would you let go of my hand!

YOUNGER MAN: You don't want me to stop breathing, do you? That's what would happen if I let go of your hand. You're my life line until six o'clock.

OLDER MAN: What do you mean, stop breathing?

YOUNGER MAN: I get this terrible pressure against my chest. It's the lava coming and I can't breathe. If I let go of you, I think I'll suffocate.

OLDER MAN (*pointing upwards*): Maybe if they drop one of these oxygen masks down.

YOUNGER MAN: They only drop down if we crash. It won't be long now. Come six o'clock, I'll be fine.

OLDER MAN *(glancing at his watch)*: But it is past six. You haven't advanced your watch. You're still on Los Angeles time.

YOUNGER MAN: No matter where I go, I'm always still on Los Angeles time. Maybe that's part of my problem.

OLDER MAN: If you'd just let go of my hand and advance your watch.

YOUNGER MAN: It won't do any good. As far as my body knows, it's still 5:45 a.m. in Los Angeles.

OLDER MAN: What if I have to go to the bathroom?

YOUNGER MAN: Can you hold it till after six?

OLDER MAN: This is ridiculous! I'm ringing for the stewardess. *(And ring for her he does.)*

YOUNGER MAN: It won't be long now. The dinosaurs are starting to pass.

OLDER MAN: What is this nonsense about dinosaurs? What are you talking about?

YOUNGER MAN: Did you ever see the movie, "One Million BC"? I mean, the old one in black and white with Victor Mature and Carole Landis.

OLDER MAN: Not unless it was on an airplane. That's the only time I ever. . . . *(Then firmly)* No.

YOUNGER MAN: I saw it on television when I was very little. I suddenly felt like down deep I was one of those prehistoric people, that there is no God in this world and there's no reason for living except to be buried alive by lava or trampled by a dinosaur. I felt as alone as those people must have felt without television, radio, or anything. And I've been feeling pretty much that way ever since between five and six in the morning before I'm awake enough to get my defenses going.

OLDER MAN: You're very sick.

YOUNGER MAN: I know.

OLDER MAN: When you're home, and this "lava" business happens. . . do you have somebody with you? Isn't there a girl friend or somebody who could. . ?

YOUNGER MAN: There's just my cat, Rocky. He's always asleep at that hour.

OLDER MAN: I wish you'd let go of my hand.

YOUNGER MAN: I can't. Not just yet. When the dinosaur was coming, I looked over at you and you reminded me of my father. The only time I held his hand was when he was dying. I took his hand and, for the first time in his life, I told him that I loved him, but I don't think he heard me because he was in a coma. You remind me of him. I don't think he would have liked my holding his hand like this either, unless he was in a coma.

OLDER MAN: What about your mother? I'm sure she would. . .

YOUNGER MAN: I can't afford to fly anywhere unless it's for a funeral and my family sends me the money.

OLDER MAN: Jesus! You mean your mother. . . ?

YOUNGER MAN *(nodding):* But I'll be all right—at six.

The OLDER MAN *suddenly looks up as a* STEWARDESS *arrives.*

STEWARDESS: You rang?

OLDER MAN: Yes. I. . . *(Then reluctantly, as he looks over at the* YOUNGER MAN*)* We need a blanket.

Blackout.

Love Sonnet
Michael Leeson

Setting: on the stage is a formica kitchen table and four vinyl and chrome kitchen chairs. At stage left is a door. At stage right is another door, identical to the first, but painted a different color.

At rise: the door at stage left opens and a woman ADA *enters. She wears an old housecoat, the hem of which is starting to fall. Around her neck hang eyeglasses. She eats a chicken drumstick. Silently, she reads from a piece of paper held in her other hand. She moves to the table, sits, puts on her glasses—which are now seen to be smudged to the point of translucence—sticks the drumstick in her housecoat pocket, and pulls out a chewed, yellow wood pencil with which she makes a change on the paper.*

ADA: A poem to our son on the occasion of his thirtieth birthday. "'Twas nineteen hundred and fifty-two/When the angels in heaven sent us you." That's nice. I like that. *(She nods and smiles; she likes this.)* "'Twas a blessing then, 'tis a blessing still/Of blessings, dear son, we've had our fill."

*The door at stage right opens and a man (*LOU*) enters. He is slightly older than the woman and is dressed in a neat plaid robe and blue suede slippers. His hair is combed. He looks at her, then at his watch, which he winds by swiveling his wrist—it's a self-winder. He approaches the table, craning his neck to see what she's writing.* ADA *looks up.*

ADA: Top 'o the mornin'. *(He doesn't reply.)* You're up early. *(He doesn't reply.)* Would you like some coffee? *(He looks down at the paper.)*
LOU: What are you doing there . . . altering my will?
ADA: No. I'm not altering your will. How about if I pour you a nice cup of coffee? *(She starts to rise.)*
LOU: Don't do me any favors.

She sits. He sits, touching the pit of his stomach and grimacing.

ADA: What's the matter? Is your hiatal hernia acting up again?
LOU: Maybe. I think it's your coffee that does it to me. I couldn't sleep last night.
ADA: Did you take your medication?
LOU: I put the cotton from the bottle in my ears. It didn't help.
ADA: Was I snoring?

LOU: There was so much racket, I couldn't hear myself think. It came right through your door, across the house, through my door...

ADA: All right. I have to finish this. *(He is silent for a long moment.)*

LOU: I thought I was sleeping in a Greyhound Bus depot. You were putting on the air brakes all night. And snoring! You were snoring from both ends. I never heard such a racket. God almighty! Neighbors were pounding on the walls...

ADA: Well, I'm not making any noise now, so why don't you go back to bed?

LOU: I'm not tired. What are you writing there? A letter to your boyfriend?

ADA: It's a poem for Daniel's birthday.

LOU: Daniel's birthday? When is it?

ADA: Today. I'm going to read it at his party.

LOU: What party?

ADA: Maureen is throwing him a big surprise party. You were sitting right there when she told us about it.

LOU: I never heard about any party. Did you buy him a present, at least?

ADA: I am writing this poem.

LOU: That's his present? What the hell kind of present is a poem?

ADA: It's from my heart.

LOU: We should at least give him something he can exchange.

ADA: This is a special poem. I opened my eyes this morning and I looked at the clock, and it was exactly 6:01 a.m. That's exactly the time thirty years ago that I gave birth to Daniel. You have to admit that's something.

LOU: So twice in thirty years you woke up early. Is that it?

ADA: It's a good thing I know you love me.

LOU: Do I? I would've left you long ago, but I was waiting for the price of gasoline to go back down.

ADA: Do you remember the afternoon Daniel was conceived?

LOU: What the hell kind of question is that?

ADA: We drove with the kids to my sister Bessie's. We had the Hudson, and I remember you tied the back doors shut because you thought Alan might try to open them and shove Sally out. It was the summer they couldn't go into the lake becaue of polio. So Bessie took them to town to see the movies. We were all alone in the house.

LOU: I thought you were getting me coffee.

ADA: I was wearing that yellow bathing suit. You always said I looked like Jane Russell in it.

LOU: *You* always said you looked like Jane Russell.

ADA: We made love in that back bedroom. The window was open and the curtains—beautiful lace curtains—blew in the balmy breeze.

LOU: Are you making this up as you go along?

ADA: We were lying there afterwards, just holding each other. . .

LOU: I can't listen to this.

ADA: When the door opened. And there stood Alan. I remember thinking, "Oh, my God, why isn't he at the movies?" He had this look on that little face. . . . We were both so speechless, then you said, "Get out!" And, of course, he did.

LOU: That never happened.

ADA: Sometimes I wonder. He's never mentioned it. You and I never talked about it. We didn't make love again that summer, so I know it was that afternoon that Daniel was conceived. And when we got back home, you started sleeping in the spare room. It was as if you were ashamed to be in the same bed together. Was that it? Was that why you moved out of our bedroom?

LOU: I don't think it's really any of your business.

ADA: I don't know why I never asked you before. I always meant to. Thirty years goes by so fast, you don't always get around to things.

LOU: You want to know why I moved to my own room? Because you're sloppy. I like a neat room, and you always had your clothes heaped all over the place and you ate that damn chicken (ADA *glances down at her pocket.*) and you'd sleep in those hairnets that'd come off in the middle of the night and collect at the bottom of the bed and it just made me sick. If you want to know, it was your fault, Ada. It was you that ruined our marriage. (ADA *is silent.*) Look at you.

ADA: I never claimed to be the neatest housekeeper. (*She makes a half-hearted move toward the table and blows as if to clear the table of dust.*)

LOU: I can't stand looking at you. If you want to know the truth, I can't stand even being around you.

ADA (*rises*): This started out to be such a lovely day, and now look at it, and it's not even seven o'clock. (*She begins to cry as she crosses to her door. She stops, comes back, and slides the chair under the table; then exits.*)

LOU (*picks up the poem*): You even write sloppy. (*He starts to read aloud.*) "'Twas nineteen hundred and fifty-two/When the angels in heaven sent us you." Jesus. "'Twas a blessing then, 'tis a blessing still/Of blessings, dear son, we've had our fill/Now you have seen thirty years of life, filled with joy and free of strife... *(His reading slows.)* We hope you have love, the best it can be/Like the love that God gave to your father and me..." *(He looks up from the paper.)*

As LOU *lowers the paper, the lights fade out.*

Joe's Not Home
Lee Thomas

At rise: JUNE *is peeling carrots over a kitchen sink.* MARK *enters from the outside, knocks a couple of times on the door jamb.*

MARK *(tense, trying to be warm):* June? Hiya.

JUNE *(the voice is familiar):* Mark? *(Pause.)*

MARK: Joe around?

JUNE: Gone already. To the office. Shouldn't you be...?

MARK: Yeah, I was on my way out... to the office... too.

JUNE: Well, Joe's... uh, gone.

MARK *(sighs nervously):* I was just pulling out of the driveway. And then I just kinda... stopped. It just happened like that. I stopped!

JUNE: Car trouble again?

MARK *(tensing):* I couldn't... just couldn't get out of the driveway.

JUNE: I know Joe would be happy to let you use his automobile club card, but he's gone. I'm sorry.

MARK *(tightly, pensively):* And I finally said to myself, have you got the courage... to get out of this car... go over to the Smith's house... and tell June... tell her... just tell her... that you lo... *(He looks away, swallows hard.)*... lov... ah, lov... love her.

JUNE *(distractedly):* Funny... Ah, Joe's not home.

MARK *(very uncomfortably):* Maybe you didn't hear me. What I just told you, June, is that... *(Quietly)* ...I love you.

JUNE: And I feel really good about that. Living right next door to each other... sometimes it's hard to get along... and now that I know how you feel... right now... I feel good and I know Joe will, too... when he gets home.

MARK: I mean, it's not that I don't love Alice. I still, ah... love Alice.

JUNE: Alice is my best friend.

MARK: And she's been a good wife, too.

JUNE: And I'm sure she'll be glad to drive you to work if your car's not working.

MARK: My car's fine.

JUNE: Then what... did you want to see Joe about?

MARK: I didn't want to see Joe! *(Stops for a brief anxiety attack, then continues.)* I wanted to make sure he wasn't home... so I could say something to you in private.... There's been something eating away at my insides for the past several months! I was sitting in my car and suddenly it hit me... you cannot let another day go by, sweating over those goddamn meaningless ledgers, being the sole support for this behemoth called a family... without having some small and personal... thing of your own... even if it just means expressing a deeply private feeling... which is what I'm trying to do with you!

JUNE: Mmm. I almost cut my finger.

MARK: Does that mean I'm getting through to you or what?!

JUNE: I don't know if you've been drinking, or on drugs...

MARK: I don't drink in the morning. And I don't take drugs!

JUNE: You're a good man, Mark.

MARK (*a groan, to himself*): I love you, June.

JUNE (*avoidingly*): Great.

MARK: That doesn't mean anything to you...?

JUNE (*coolly, trying to break the mood*): I've got to go to the super-market in a little while.

MARK: Is that all you can say?

JUNE (*becoming uncomfortable*): I really don't know what you want from me.

MARK: I'm really putting myself on the line here! I've finally sum-moned up the courage to tell my wife's best friend and my neigh-bor that I love her and all you can say is, "I have to go to the supermarket!"?

JUNE (*becoming annoyed*): What do you want me to say?! Let's leave our kids and get out of town?! How was I supposed to know you were feeling this way? You just barge in the back door one morning, looking for Joe, and tell me you love me!

MARK (*self-disgust*): I'm making a fool out of myself.

JUNE: You're not making a fool out of yourself. But this is a little un-expected.

MARK: You don't remember the kiss at the barbecue?

JUNE: What... barbeque?

MARK: Last Saturday night. My yard? At the end of the evening, we all said goodnight... and there was kiss.

JUNE: I didn't know it was serious. Wasn't it just a friendly kiss?

MARK: There was more warmth than usual, more pressure.

JUNE: I'm sorry.

MARK: No, it was lovely!

JUNE: I don't know what you're looking for, Mark.

MARK: Well, why can't we just be natural, and see what happens?

JUNE (*cooly, speculating*): You want to... have an affair?

MARK: We don't have to just blurt things out like that!

JUNE *(heavily)*: I don't know if I have the energy for anything like that.

MARK *stares at* JUNE.

MARK: Well, if you. . if it's a. . . if you. . . I mean, if it's just a matter of what. . . sleep?!

JUNE: No. . . it's Joe.

MARK: Well, I wouldn't expect you to. . . you wouldn't want to tell Joe!

JUNE *stews for a moment, avoids looking at* MARK.

JUNE: Joe wears me out. I don't know any other way to say it.

MARK: He. . .?

JUNE: It's every night, and every night.

MARK *(more confused)*: He's got you working nights?

JUNE: I'm not sure you understand, Mark.

MARK: No, I'm not sure I do, because everytime I come over here at night, you're lounging around the house!

JUNE: Joe wants to have sex every night! And it's not just every night, but the afternoons on the weekends!

MARK *(indignant)*: What the hell's the matter with him? You've been married for a lot. . . a lot of years!

JUNE: Eight years. . . and he's so hairy. . . and enormous. And he gets that look in his eye. And it's every night, and *every* night!

MARK *(put off)*: That's really disgusting!

JUNE: So I just don't see myself having an affair with you.

MARK: Of course not. You're. . . ah, worn out! *(He tears his eyes away from* JUNE; *begins twisting uncomfortably.)*

JUNE: Are you. . . all right?

MARK: Oh, I. . . ah. . . ah, was just starting to think about my car, and getting a. . . ah, mechanic.

JUNE: I thought there was nothing wrong with your car.

MARK *(tightly)*: Well, there is. . . a kind of clunk.

JUNE: Joe. . . would know what to do.

MARK *(painfully)*: But he's not here! And I just don't know if I should drive it with that sound coming from under the hood!

JUNE: You want me to drive you to work?

MARK *(annoyed)*: No, Alice can do that!

JUNE: I'm sorry, Mark. I really am.

MARK: What's there to be sorry about?! There's nothing to be sorry about! *(Lowly, hurt)*: It's funny how some things. . . just get spoiled.

Slow fade to black.

The Underachiever
Jerry Mayer

Fade up on a master bedroom. STEVE, *in a jogging suit, is running in place on one of those mini-trampolines, while he stares at a television set. We don't see the screen.* JENNY, *in bed, opens her eyes and sits up, noticing him.*

JENNY: What are you doing?

STEVE: I'm working.

JENNY: Do you have to watch that "brain sucking box" even while you're exercising? *(He stops running.)*

STEVE: This "brain sucking box" is how I earn my, and *your*, living. I turned the sound down.

JENNY: What could be on this early?

STEVE: It's a cassette of that pilot that's in the running against mine.

JENNY: Oh? Is it as good as yours?

STEVE: It's a piece of shit.

JENNY: You didn't answer my question.

STEVE *(reacts, controlling his anger)*: I deserved that. I gave you the perfect straight line.

JENNY *(looks at the television screen)*: What's the pilot about?

STEVE: A talking panda. And those shmucks at NBC are considering it for prime time. It's a goddam kids' show.

JENNY: Honey, be honest. Yours is too.

STEVE: Mine's about an orphaned teenage girl facing the problems of adolescence. That does *not* make it a kids' show.

JENNY: What about her other problem? Being a witch?

STEVE: That was sarcasm, wasn't it?

JENNY: Would *I* be sarcastic about something that puts food in my mouth?

STEVE: For your information, they tested "Teen Witch" last night, at the Preview House. We got more laughs than "The Magoo."

JENNY: "The Magoo?"

STEVE: The cartoon, "The Nearsighted Mr. Magoo." They use it to test the audience. If they laugh at that, they're normal. *We* were *funnier.*

JENNY: That's going to be your total accomplishment in life, being funnier than "The Magoo?"

STEVE: Why do I have to be Jewish? Why can't I just hit you, like a gentile would? Would it kill you to give me some support?

JENNY: Do you want support, or do you want the truth? If you insist on doing television, why can't you at least work on a decent show, like "Masterpiece Theatre?"

STEVE: Here it comes, the Woody Allen Speech.

JENNY: Yes, the Woody Allen Speech. Why do you always have to sell yourself short?

STEVE: A good salesman knows his merchandise. I am not Woody Allen.

JENNY: Woody Allen wasn't Woody Allen until one day he heard that voice that said, "You are better than television."

STEVE: Woody Allen hears voices. All I hear is you.

JENNY: Steve, can't you at least get started on that play we used to talk about?

STEVE: You mean *you* used to talk about.

JENNY: Well pardon *me* for giving you a little nudge, because I know you have a wonderful play inside you.

STEVE: You've been peeking at my X-rays again?

JENNY: I remember the way you used to talk about writing. You wanted to make some statement. You wanted to rise above mediocrity.

STEVE *(getting irritated)*: I was *wrong*. I've made peace with mediocrity. I'm very good at being mediocre. I excell at it. Call me a hack if you will, and you *have*, but being mediocre can be as comforting as the check in a Mexican restaurant.

JENNY: Steve, can't you hear yourself? Even when you talk about being mediocre, you *soar*. There'a wonderful Carl Sandburg eloquence about you. You're "Everyman." Put that quality on paper.

STEVE: I'm not "Everyman," I'm "Any Slob." And I'm not putting anything on paper. I tried that, remember? Six months of spec writing for a lousy one act play that my agent refused to show anyone.

JENNY: Well I thought it showed promise. It was early Brecht.

STEVE: You say Brecht. He said dreck. Jenny, I'm a good journeyman joke writer, not a playwright. I've got no big statement to make. My life is a Chevrolet.

JENNY: "My life is a Chevrolet." Woody Allen would *kill* for a line like that. Write it down.

STEVE: I already did. I used it on a "Brady Bunch."

JENNY *(total frustration)*: How *could* you?!

STEVE *(with building anger)*: Jenny, I know you're going to hate me for saying this, but I'm happy with my life. I'm happy with my writing. I know it's shit, but it *works*. I'm even happy with *you*. You're the one *un*mediocre thing that ever happened to me.

JENNY *(softening)*: Really? You've never said that before.

STEVE *(sharply)*: You've never pissed me off this much before!

JENNY: It was worth it.

STEVE: I don't want to spend every day suffering, comparing my writing to Woody Allen and Neil Simon, while they compare theirs to Moliere and Chekhov. Can you get that straight?

JENNY: Yes, Darling.

STEVE: So don't *bug* me, okay?

JENNY: Okay.

STEVE: Just forget about the goddam play!

JENNY: It's forgotten, sweetheart.

STEVE: *Good! (Steve starts running on the trampoline again. Jenny moves to him.)*

JENNY: Steve?

STEVE: Yeah?

JENNY: Kiss me. *(He stops running, stands on the trampoline.)*

STEVE: I didn't brush yet.

JENNY: Who cares?

She has stepped onto the trampoline. They kiss. The kiss lingers, as we fade to black.

Sunny Side Up
Pamela Chais

At rise: HARRY *and* LORRAINE FARBER *sit in the kitchen of their Tarzana home, having breakfast. He's fifty, feisty, jumpy, volatile. She's fifty, a twenty-eight-year victim of being married to someone feisty, jumpy, volatile. They are both in their bathrobes.*

LORRAINE: Annie wants to know if she can drop the kids off this morning. She has to go to the doctor. She has this weird lump on her arm that won't go away and. . .

HARRY: What time is it?

LORRAINE *(checks a wall clock)*: Nine. . . exactly.

HARRY: That means it's noon back there. Right? Nobody in New York goes out to lunch until maybe twelve-thirty-one. Right? You'd leave by noon if you're having lunch across town. Maybe he's having lunch across town. No, he's in his goddamn office right now. I know it.

LORRAINE: Maybe he hasn't had time to read it yet.

HARRY: He said he'd read it last night. He swore he was taking it home with him and reading it last night.

LORRAINE: Is it all right if Annie leaves the kids here?

HARRY *(incredulous)*: I'm talking to you about. . . Jesus, Lorraine, you have the attention span of a cocker spaniel. Has anyone ever told you that? I mean, have they?

LORRAINE *(quietly)*: Not since the last time you were waiting for your agent to call you.

HARRY: My *agent*? Gene is not just my agent. He's been my closest personal friend for twenty. . . no, what am I talking about?. . . twenty-three years.

LORRAINE: May your daughter with the suspicious lump on her arm leave her children here around eleven?

HARRY: When he got his divorce from that pinhead, I was the one he turned to. I was the one who actually saw him cry. What time is it?

LORRAINE: Nine-o-two.

HARRY: It's a damn good play. I mean, even if he never calls, I know that. You know those things. *(He jumps up, crosses the kitchen.)*

LORRAINE: What are you looking for?

HARRY: To see if the phone's off the hook. You do that a lot now. Are you aware of that?

LORRAINE: Must be hardening of the arteries to my brain. (HARRY *returns glumly, sits down.)* Did I leave it off the hook again?

HARRY: Dirty son-of-a-bitch. Would it break his ass to call before lunch just once in his life?

LORRAINE: What about Annie? Is it all right if she brings the kids over while they do a *biopsy* on her arm?

HARRY: The man deals with writers every day of his life. Doesn't he know how destructive this is, how. . .

LORRAINE: Harry. Go to your typewriter. Start another play, an epic poem. . .

HARRY *(earnestly, looking for trouble)*: Lorraine, there's something I've been meaning to talk to you about. Those brown liver spots on your hands. Have you always had them?

LORRAINE *(helpfully)*: No, no, actually, they began to appear about the same time you began losing your hair.

HARRY: Well, they're running amuck! *(The phone rings.* HARRY *leaps up, catches it on the second ring, his voice jovial.)* Hello? Hello? Gene, guy, is that you? *(Clenched teeth)* Ace Carpet Cleaning? And you're going to be in my neighborhood today. . . . Well, guess who else is going to be in my neighborhood today. . . *(Savagely) Me*, shithead! Waiting for the goddamn phone to ring! *(He smashes the phone down, returns to the table.)* What time is it?

LORRAINE: Three past nine.

HARRY: There are restaurants all the way cross town from his office. The Brittany, places like that. He'd have to have left half an hour ago. . . wanted to finish reading the play, but didn't have time. . . . Maybe he tried to call and the lines were jammed up. It happens all the time.

LORRAINE: You have to stop this, Harry.

HARRY: Would it hurt him? Just one lousy phone call. . . even to tell me he hadn't read it yet. Doesn't he know I'm sitting here fucking paralyzed?

LORRAINE: Go shave, Harry. Take a nice hot shower.

HARRY *(suddenly very "up")*: You know what else it could be? Maybe after he read the play last night, he got so excited he shot it over to, oh, say a Morty Gottleib or Alex Cohen, and he wants to surprise me with a quick offer. Like he'll call today and say, "Guess what, pal, your play's been optioned. . . just like that." What do you think?

LORRAINE *(unsmilingly humoring)*: Anything's possible.

HARRY: He hates it. He hates and despises every word of it. The play is shit. It's shit. You've read it. You can admit that. You're my wife. You can tell me. *(LORRAINE stares impassively; too smart to fall for that number.)* Then let me tell *you* something about the typing! After all these years, you'd think you'd have picked up something about spacing and margins, to say nothing of three quarts of Liquid Paper on every page. And the binding... that mottled, bile-yellow binding. How many stationers did you have to go to to find something that hideous? You can tell me.

LORRAINE: I covered the whole west valley, Harry. It wasn't easy.

HARRY: If he doesn't call in half an hour, he won't call for the next two hours. I can just write the next two hours out of my life while his fat ass hangs off both sides of some art deco chair while he dribbles nouvelle cuisine down his lapels.

LORRAINE: Call him. *Now.*

HARRY: You're right. You're right. Why the hell shouldn't I? We're friends. It's not like I'm just a client. I mean, I love the guy like a brother. He cried on my sofa, for Christ's sake! (HARRY *crosses to the phone, returns to the kitchen table, sits down, direct dials, mutters to himself.)* He's read it and he's going to duck my call. He's going to have his secretary say he just stepped down the hall, then in eight, nine days I'll get a manila envelope in the mail...postage due, most likely... *(Brightly, into phone)* Gene Lordigan, please... Harry Farber calling.... Yes, I'll wait... *(Savagely to himself)* ...while you two cook up some charitable lie to dust me with... *(He listens, his eyes registering growing shock)* Are you serious? I can't believe it. He was mugged and shot on his way home last night? That's just so.... I can't believe it... on his way home... God, we're like brothers... *(Despite himself, a smile creeps across his face. He covers receiver, whispers, thrilled, to* LORRAINE) He never got home. He hasn't read it yet. *(Emotionally, into phone)* Intensive care! God, that's so terrible. Look, I want to be able to do something... anything. I could jump on a plane and fly there, if you thought it would do any good... *(Aside, to* LORRAINE, *ecstatically)* Never read it. Not a word. *(Earnestly into phone)* Look, it's just a thought, but I know when you're lying in bed, strapped to all that life support equipment, time can hang so damn heavy, I thought... listen, it's just an idea... but maybe someone could track down my new play and have it brought to his bedside.

LORRAINE *suddenly rises to her feet and lunges at* HARRY *with a large bread knife.* HARRY *reacts violently.*

HARRY: Lorraine! Are you out of your mind? *(The knife penetrates his chest; he gasps into the phone.)* Listen, it's in a decorator yellow binding... a two-character one set play...

Both HARRY *and the curtain fall quickly.*

Pelicans
Christine Rimmer

At rise: JAKE *and* LOTTIE *on a park bench next to an overflowing garbage can.* LOTTIE *is holding a Bible.*

JAKE: Can we read the letter now, Lottie? *(Pause.* LOTTIE *hands her Bible to* JAKE.) Lottie, you promised.

LOTTIE: Close your eyes.

JAKE: You said we could read it when we got to the park. You'd think they'd hose off these benches once in a while.

LOTTIE: Close your eyes.

JAKE: Lottie. . . nobody looks for signs in the Bible anymore.

LOTTIE: As long as I'm still doing it, somebody does.

JAKE: We don't need a sign yet. We don't even know what she has to say.

LOTTIE: I should know my own daughter. I want to be ready.

JAKE: Lottie. . .

LOTTIE: Close your eyes. Okay now. . . just let it fall open. . . . Good. Read it to me.

JAKE: Can I open my eyes?

LOTTIE: Jake. This could be very important.

JAKE: All right. All right.

LOTTIE: The first words you see. Go ahead.

JAKE *(reading)*: "I resemble a pelican of the wilderness. I have become like an owl of the waste places. I lie awake. I have become like. . ."

LOTTIE: That's enough. The waste places. . . that could definitely be Los Angeles. And I haven't been getting much sleep lately.

JAKE: We got the mail when the post office opened at eight-thirty. We couldn't read it there because the clerk had a swastika tattoed on his arm. That was a bad sign. We had coffee at Winchell's at nine. We couldn't read it there because the cream curdled when you poured it in your cup.

LOTTIE: But why a pelican?

JAKE: No, we had to come all the way over here to MacArthur Park. . .

LOTTIE: Why an owl?

JAKE: It's eleven now. I've waited long enough to find out how they are up home.

LOTTIE: Pelicans like fish, don't they?

JAKE: I can't wait any longer, Lottie.

LOTTIE: You always hated fish.

JAKE: I'm going to read it now.

LOTTIE: But me. I don't mind it. So, I could be the pelican. What are you doing?

JAKE: What I should have done two and a half hours ago.

LOTTIE: I'm not ready.

JAKE: I'll read it to myself. *(Pause. She peers over his shoulder at the letter.)* Here.

LOTTIE: You know I can't see things close-up.

JAKE: If you put on your glasses. . .

LOTTIE: No, no. I like things fuzzy. Makes a softness. Lately, I can use all the softness I can get. You'd better read it out loud. Well. Go ahead.

JAKE *(reading)*: "Dear Mom and Dad. Of course I have no way to be sure that this will reach you. . ."

LOTTIE: Still harping we should give them an address.

JAKE: "But we cannot allow ourselves to give up hope that you will see the pain you cause those who love you most and return to us."

LOTTIE: Who do you think she means by "us"?

JAKE: She did come to see us the first Sunday of every month up there to the Glorious Golden Years Retirement Environment.

LOTTIE: Glorious Golden Years. Don't we know. Places like that are a crime against nature. Sitting around with a bunch of old people, waiting to die. . .

JAKE: She thought she was doing the best for us.

LOTTIE: Go on.

JAKE: "Of course, you have a right to live your lives as you please. . ."

LOTTIE: That's big of her.

JAKE: "But we can't help but be concerned for you, at your ages, traipsing around the streets of Los Angeles. If, indeed, that's where you are now. . ."

LOTTIE: Oh, Jake. Our own daughter. She refuses to admit how it was for us.

JAKE: You give Carlotta some credit now, Lottie. She did see the light about that detective Jasper hired to bring us back.

LOTTIE: Not until I threatened to write a letter to the Union Bulletin.

JAKE: Put yourself in her shoes, Lottie. She's got a reputation to uphold.

LOTTIE: Don't we know. What if it came out her folks would rather take their chances on the streets of LA than stay where she put them? How would she face all her do-gooder society friends then? Keep reading.

JAKE: "At the mercy of the criminal element and the unsatisfactory sanitary facilities..."

LOTTIE: Stop.

JAKE: Now, Lottie...

LOTTIE: You just read it to yourself and tell me the parts you think I have to know.

JAKE: Well, now... she says if we don't want to go back to the Glorious Golden Years, she and Jasper would be willing to buy us a condo right there in Walla Walla.

LOTTIE: A condo. Don't we know. The kind with the poor little marigolds lined up like soldiers by the front walk, all in even rows.

JAKE: Marilee is going to have a baby.

LOTTIE: Well. That's nice.

JAKE: In September. She and Floyd are going to be studying Lamaze.

LOTTIE: That's real nice.

JAKE: Our first great-grandchild.

LOTTIE: "Lo, children are a heritage of the Lord and the fruit of the womb is his reward." Psalm One-twenty-seven, verse three.

JAKE: Uncle Herbert passed on.

LOTTIE: Oh.... Well, we knew that was coming. Uncle Herbert was no spring chicken.

JAKE: Peaceful. In his sleep. After spending the day laying fertilizer into his squash beds.

LOTTIE: He did love that garden.

JAKE: Ah, Lottie... sure would like to...

LOTTIE: Jason Barnaby Butz, we cannot even consider such a thought. Remember the Glorious Golden Years. Think of the marigolds all in even rows.

JAKE: I want to see my great-grandchild.

LOTTIE: She's just trying to lure us to Walla Walla so she can lock us away in that condo.

JAKE: We got away before.

LOTTIE: They didn't expect us to break out then. They'll be ready for us this time.

JAKE: You'll think of something. Ah, Lottie... our first great-grandchild.

LOTTIE: That would be something... to put it over on them all again. To see that little baby and get away before.... Oh, Lord. Forgive me, Lord. Pride. Pride cometh before the fall.

JAKE: Now, Lottie...

PHOTO: ED KRIEGER

LOTTIE: We'll wait for the Word.

JAKE: We have six months.

LOTTIE: We'll watch the signs and we'll do what the Lord wills. "Like a pelican in the wilderness, like an owl of the waste places..."

JAKE: You think you can come up with a sign in six months?

LOTTIE: Close your eyes.

JAKE: Lottie...

LOTTIE: Go on. Do it. *(He closes his eyes; she leans her head on his shoulder.)*

JAKE: Well?

LOTTIE: Shh.

JAKE: Ah, Lottie. I dream of home. . .

LOTTIE: I know, Jake. I know.

Blackout.

Lemons in the Morning
Bonnie and Paul Zindel

At rise: BETSY *and her mother,* CLAIRE, *enter from an audition. They both look defeated. We see the shadow of* MR. HILLARY *leaning over his work. He puts his pencil down as* CLAIRE *tries hard to cover her depression.*

CLAIRE: I need something to drink. I'm so dehydrated. What about you, Betsy? (BETSY *stalks into her room without a reply.* CLAIRE *opens the refrigerator and pulls out some lemons.*) It's a good thing I didn't use all the lemons up in the tuna salad yesterday.

MR. HILLARY: I guess you didn't get it, Betsy.

CLAIRE (*bringing the lemons over to the counter and pulling out the juice squeezer—she lets out an audible sigh*): Ohhhh.

BETSY (*offstage*) No, Dad.

MR. HILLARY: Well, don't worry about it. At least it's over, kid. Maybe you'll get a good sleep tonight.

CLAIRE (*now squeezing the lemons into a glass*): Damn politics, it's all damn politics. I tell you, Jack, she was terrific. Our little girl couldn't have been better. Right, Betsy? She danced, she twirled, she was almost dancing off the ground, that's how good she was. By rights, she should have gotten the part. (*Sound of shoes thrown against a closet wall offstage.*) But someone is slapping someone else with a favor. You know this one friend asks another friend. . . . You rub my back and I'll rub yours and boom, you get the job. (BETSY *reappears, pulling on a sweater.*) Talent isn't the issue here, that's pretty clear to me.

BETSY: I don't think that was it, Mom.

CLAIRE: Isn't anything pure around here? Has the world gone mad? A simple "Lassie" audition. . . . I'm telling you, that runt that won must be playing cards with the producer.

MR. HILLARY: Who won?

CLAIRE: A homely midget.

BETSY: Rose Urbell. The producer called her out of class.

CLAIRE: Where's the sugar? (BETSY *slams the sugar bowl on the table.*) Oh, here it is. (*She puts some into the lemonade.*) A midget dancing to "Rhapsody in Blue"!

MR. HILLARY: She must be good if she won.

CLAIRE: I'm telling you, Jack, it's fixed. You used to watch the "$64,000 Question" and not believe it was rigged, either. I couldn't pull you away from the television. But I'm telling you,

the midget's mother must be washing someone's hands because she doesn't even look fifteen. She's skinny! And she came out with too much fringe! Imagine, fringe! There was nothing sweet about her. I just don't know.

BETSY: I think she was better than me, Mom.

CLAIRE: How can you say that? You weren't sitting out there watching like I was. A dancing dwarf with fringe popping up and down. She looked like she was trying out for the Rockettes. Not for "Lassie."

BETSY: Well, I don't think it was fixed. I just wish I had won for you.

CLAIRE *(continuing to make the lemonade)*: For me? What about for you?

MR. HILLARY: I told you not to build her hopes up.

CLAIRE: If we didn't have hope, we'd be dead!

MR. HILLARY: All she got out of it is another disappointment.

CLAIRE: She got experience! That's what she got—experience! She was number *two*. She came close to *winning*! And they'll remember the girl who did "Slaughter on Tenth Avenue." The next time they might say, "Hey, what about that girl?"

MR. HILLARY: The next time. It's always the next time.

CLAIRE: She could have been six or seven, but she wasn't! She was number *two*! *(She finds a spoon in the drawer and starts mixing the lemonade.)* And maybe it was a blessing in disguise. *(She takes out three glasses.)* Maybe she would have gotten tied up when there would be something wonderful just waiting for her around the corner. Maybe the dog would have bitten her. Who knows? Fate works in strange ways.

BETSY *(her eyes lighting up, as she gets animated)*: Dad, I didn't tell you the good part.

MR. HILLARY: Tell me the good part, honey.

BETSY: I got to meet Lassie. She was beautiful, just like we saw her in "Lassie, Come Home" on television. I know this wasn't the real, real Lassie, but it was the Lassie of today. When I petted her, she was so silky like someone sat and brushed her for hours. That takes a lot of work. Her eyes, Daddy, were dark brown and she looked right into my eyes, as if she knew me. And we were relating to each other. Imagine that. Lassie and me, and she liked me. Oh, I know she did.

CLAIRE: She was a friendly dog, all right. Out of the ordinary, I'd say that. This dog was a real dog, nothing faggy about him.

BETSY: Want to hear the best part? You want to know what he did?

MR. HILLARY: What?

BETSY: I reached down to pet his stomach and then he sat and kissed me right here. *(She points to her cheek.)* On my cheek. That was the best part of the whole day. We liked each other.

CLAIRE *(pouring the lemonade into glasses)*: I'm telling you, she related to that dog best. Boy, they really missed the boat on this one.

BETSY: Mother!

CLAIRE: No one could have worked better with Lassie than Betsy. . .

BETSY: Mom, don't spoil it. . .

CLAIRE: She's got something, our girl. We've got a star here. . .

BETSY: I'm not a star. I don't want. . .

CLAIRE: A star. A real star!

BETSY *(blowing up)*: I DIDN'T WIN, MOM. I DIDN'T WIN! WHY WON'T YOU ACCEPT IT? I LOST. I LOST! I FEEL TERRIBLE ABOUT IT! I DO! I HATE AUDITIONS! I HATE THE WAY IT MAKES ME FEEL! SOMEONE ALWAYS JUDGING ME. SOMEONE ALWAYS BETTER! I HATE LOS-ING! I HATE LOSING FOR YOU! *(She bursts into tears.)*

CLAIRE *is near shock.* MR. HILLARY *hides in his ledger, relieved* BETSY's *finally stood up, but not knowing how to help* CLAIRE *at this moment.*

CLAIRE *(barely audible, trying to grasp the new status)*: You didn't lose, honey. What'd you lose? *(Weak laugh, still finding words desperately hard.)* A job? *(Now her way of apologizing to her husband.)* Dad makes enough money for us. Don't you, Jack?

MR. HILLARY: Yep.

CLAIRE: See, you don't have to get a job. . .

MR. HILLARY *(hidden delight at this recognition)*: That's right. Don't try to knock me out of my job. I take care of my girls.

CLAIRE *(fighting a profound sense of loss, struggling still to realize* BETSY *is not going to be her "Star")*: Cheer up, Betsy. Cheer up. You had a special day. I mean, Lassie liked you. Of all the girls there! He picked you. You both shared something special together. . . *(She realizes she's actually talking about something she and* BETSY *once shared, which they must share no more. Now* CLAIRE *bursts into tears.* MR. HILLARY *finally has to look up from his ledger at the sight of* CLAIRE *and* BETSY *both bawling their heads off. It should be delightfully amusing, filled with relief.* CLAIRE *now pulls herself together, gaining strength and acceptance that* BETSY's *her own girl.)* You had a very lovely moment with Lassie. . . . You have a special way of reaching out to dogs. . . and people. . . . People and dogs respond to your warmth. . . that's your strength. That's it! You care about people and you're not afraid to show it. . . ! I don't know what's the matter with me. I forgot that prizes come in all different shapes and sizes and some of them even bark!

MR. HILLARY *(tasting the lemonade)*: Too much sugar.

CLAIRE: My ass, too much sugar.

BETSY: Mom, imagine how excited you would have been if I had won. . .

CLAIRE: Forget it! I'm past the "Lassie" audition! I'm even past the dwarf! That's gone, Betsy. We're moving on. All of us! Jack! Jack, close your books. Close the month of February! It'll be there tomorrow. Believe me, it has a habit of not going away! *(*JACK *laughs, gives her a kiss.)* You know, Betsy, we came home a couple of lemons today, but we sure as hell made it into lemonade! Right, my darlings? So we win, after all! WE REALLY WIN! NOW DRINK! AND DRINK! AND DRINK. . . ! (Victorious laughter. . .)

Blackout.

The Five-Minute Romance
Susan Silver

The suggested staging is a very simple stylized approach. No props, no sets. Each actor stands in a pool of light which goes immediately to black after each vignette. Each moment should have a different rhythm (almost as though a different musical piece plays in the background to set each tone). When they are on the phone, they should stand at an angle facing away from each other to denote a less personal contact. In the two pieces where they actually make love, the lights should be out... and we only hear them.

At rise: two very attractive people notice each other. SHE, *early thirties;* HE *, a bit older. They are very taken with each other at first sight.*

HE *(eyeing her, finally)*: Hi.
SHE: Hi.
HE: How're you doing?
SHE: Fine.
HE: Mind if I sit down?
SHE *(shrugs, then)*: Just move in?
HE: Yeah.

> *Quick blackout. Lights up. They stand as if talking on the phone, some days later.*

HE: What are you doing tonight?
SHE: I'm busy.
HE: Tomorrow night?
SHE: I'm busy, too... sorry. I really am busy.
HE: No problem. I'm a patient guy.

> *Quick blackout. Lights up. They are at her door at the end of the first evening.*

HE: It was your smile. If you hadn't smiled, I probably wouldn't have come over to you.
SHE: Really? You want to know something funny? I always seem to be... I don't know, intimidating or something... so I was "practicing." I said, "He's cute.... I'll smile and see what happens." *(Then)* Just promise me one thing... that no matter what, we'll be friends... okay? *(Instead of answering her... a long, passionate kiss that makes her knees buckle.)* Oh, my God... I...

HE: You know what? I better go.
SHE: What? Aren't you coming in?
HE: Call you tomorrow.,

> HE *leaves and SHE can't believe it.* SHE *keeps waiting for him to come back, but* HE *doesn't. Blackout.*

They have just made wild, passionate love, all draining love—in darkness.

SHE: That was the best. . . the best.
HE: You are something! I knew it. . . but whoa. . .!
SHE: It's scary, isn't it? I mean. . . I feel I know you so well.

> *Blackout. Lights up. They speak as if on the phone.*

SHE: I'm sorry.
HE: You make another date for Saturday night? I can't believe it! What's wrong with you?
SHE: Well, we're going out tonight. . . and Sunday. I mean, it's not like we're in high school. . . . Why is Saturday night so special? *(Then)* Maybe I was feeling a little. . . pressured. . . . I don't know. You're so intense.

> *Blackout. Lights up.* HE *comes to the door.* SHE *opens it quickly.*

HE: Miss me?
SHE: Yes, you shit! Where have you been?
HE: Well, you were so "busy." Missed me, huh? I *knew* you would.

> *Quick blackout.*

HE: Why are you getting so upset? I mean, I just said, "Why would someone as terrific as you want me?" I mean, you could have anyone. . .
SHE: I hate it when you put yourself down.
HE: Maybe I need you to build me up.

> *Blackout. Then, as if after sex.*

SHE: Oh, it just keeps getting better and better. Nobody ever made me feel the way you do.
HE: I can feel every inch of you responding. . . I envy you. Women are lucky. . . they can just go on and on. . .

> *Blackout. Lights up.* HE *is headed for the door, angry.*

HE: And take your goddamn letters! Quit writing me letters. Quit lecturing me. You're not perfect, either, you know.

SHE: I never said I was! But at least I'm trying to work on myself. Trying to figure out *why* I do what I do. Why I fuck things up.

HE: That's your problem. You listen to your shrink and your friends. . . . You listen to everyone but yourself.

SHE: And you don't listen to anyone! That's why you're forty years old and unable to sustain a relationship. This is going to keep going around and around forever! Go back to her and leave me alone!

HE: I'll go back to her! *She* love me! She'd do anything for me. She thinks I'm the kindest man she's ever known. Don't call me and don't write me any more damn letters!

Blackout. Lights up. They are on the phone.

HE *(nervous laugh)*: So what do you say? You want a roommate?

SHE: I'm scared.

HE: I'm scared, too. But you say you love me.

SHE: I do.

HE: I don't believe you.

SHE: Stop it.

HE: I think you're just lonely and you're almost forty and you want to play house.

Blackout. Lights up. HE *comes in.* SHE *waits like a little girl, expectantly.*

SHE: Welcome home. Like the decorations?

HE *(nervous, guilty)*: Yeah. I . . . uh. . . . I guess I should have brought wine or flowers or something. I knew I should have, but . . .

SHE *(hurt)*: It's okay. I called you about five times this morning. Where were you? You said you'd be here by noon and it's almost four.

HE: Look, it wasn't easy. I mean, I dated the girl eight months. It was a very difficult thing to do. To hurt another human being. I mean, you wouldn't want me to do that to you! You should be happy I'm not that kind of guy.

SHE: I don't want to talk about her anymore. You promised me it was over.

HE: I'm here, aren't I?

Blackout. Lights up. SHE *paces. His back is to her.*

SHE: I'm walking on eggs in my own house! Nothing pleases you. "There are no Q-tips?" My God! I'm sorry the accommodations aren't suiting!

HE: I told you to give me a few days to adjust. Just lay back. I know I'm not giving you enough, but. . . just don't push! *(Then)* Oh, God. . . what am I doing here?

SHE *(a long moment, then swallows and)*: Well, as long as you've brought it up. . . . I was going to wait until the weekend.

Blackout. Lights up. They are on the phone.

SHE *(tired of it all)*: Please stop calling me! I don't want to talk about it anymore. Just pay me back the money and leave me alone.

HE: How can I pay you back. . . you know I don't have any money. Jesus. . . why can't you just look at it like you did something nice for someone. You saved someone from drowning. Besides, you threw *me* out!

SHE: What? You're crazy! I never saw anyone pack so fast in my life.

HE: All I asked was, "What am I doing here?" And boom! I figured I better get out before I found my things piled on the driveway.

SHE *(mechanically)*: There was no joy. You acted like you were going to the gas chamber. If it's not great in the beginning, when is it ever going to be?

HE: Maybe we rushed into it. Maybe she meant more to me than I thought. Hey, you were relieved. I saw it on your face.

SHE *(drained)*: You wanted me to throw you out! You did everything you could to make me. I don't want to talk about it anymore. Just pay me back.

HE: Well maybe I can pay a little at a time. There's such a long line ahead of you.

Blackout. Lights up. They are kissing.

SHE: Please, don't. No. . . come on. No fair.

HE: I've been dreaming about you. Have you been thinking about me? Wild, horny sexy dreams. . . . I need you.

SHE: Don't. Come on. Just take your mail and go. Come on.

HE: Just let me touch you. Come on. You know you want to. Why can't we just be "fucking friends?" Huh? come on. (HE *nuzzles her neck and* SHE *weakens.*)

SHE: Okay. Let's go in the bedroom.

HE: No. you're right. What kind of guy am I? I'm living with her and I'm here with you. I can't. I mean, the girl's feeding me, for God's sakes.

SHE: You call me every day. You beg me to see me. I finally say yes and you're just playing games! You're sick! Get out of here!

HE: Why are you getting so upset? What's wrong with you?

Blackout. Lights up. They are on the phone.

HE: Hi.

SHE: Who is this?

HE: It's me!

SHE: Oh, I didn't recognize your voice.

HE: So. . . how are you? You in love or anything?

SHE: Why? What do you care?

HE: Aw, come on. I'm jealous. All my friends tell me I made the worst mistake of my life with you.

SHE *(finally)*: No, I'm not in love.

HE: Remember the first time we went out. . . you said, "Let's always be friends?" Why can't we just be friends? *(Then softly)* You didn't love me anyway, did you?

SHE *(softly)*: Yes. I *did*.

Blackout.

Twenty-Four Hours: P.M.

Sam Bobrick

Dana Cooper

Oliver Hailey

Beth Henley

Rick Lenz

Michael Lewis

Jack Matcha

Jim McGinn

Ann Raymond

Marcia Rodd

Fredi Towbin

Twenty-Four Hours: P.M. was first presented on October 1, 1982, at the Back Alley Theatre, Van Nuys, California, with the following cast:

The Termination

OWENS	Sandy Kenyon
YOUNG	Phillip R. Allen

Directed by Marcia Rodd

An Eastern Fable

MAN	Sandy Kenyon
WIFE	Mary McCusker
DOCTOR	Phillip R. Allen

Directed by Dona Cooper

Lifeline

WOMAN	Rosanna Huffman
WAITER	Peter Van Norden
PA	Val Bettin

Directed by Marcia Rodd

Aerobics

MAYBIN	Rosanna Huffman
HARRY	Sandy Kenyon
CISSIE	Jackie Cassell
TOM	Phillip R. Allen
LEADER	Mary McCusker

Directed by Beverly Sanders

Sunrise on Earth

OLD MAN	Val Bettin

Directed by Dona Cooper

About Time

HER	Maxine Stuart
HIM	Sandy Kenyon

Directed by Barbara Schultz

Rules of the House

JOSEPHINE	Mary McCusker
FLOYD	Peter Van Norden
MABEL	Maxine Stuart

Directed by Barbara Schultz

Conversation 2001

MAN   Phillip R. Allen
WOMAN   Rosanna Huffman

Directed by Beverly Sanders

So Long, Mr. Broadway

MAN   Phillip R. Allen

Directed by Dona Cooper

Opening Night

YOUNG MAN   Sandy Kenyon
SECOND MAN   Phillip R. Allen

Directed by Dona Cooper

Love in a Pub

LINDA   Jackie Cassel
ED   Sandy Kenyon

Directed by Michael Lessac

Hymn in the Attic

MISS MAYBELLE   Maxine Stuart
GEORGIA RAY   Mary McCusker
STEVIE   Peter Van Norden

Directed by Barbara Schultz

Production conceived by Oliver Hailey
Produced by Laura Zucker
Direction supervised by Allan Miller
Set designed by Zoe Wells
Lighting designed by Christopher Milliken
Costumes coordinated by Hilary Sloan
Music composed by Dick De Benidictis
Sound designed by Leonora Schildkraut

The Termination
Jim McGinn

Setting: a conference room.
At rise: WENDALL YOUNG, *early forties, forces* CHARLES OWENS, 55, *through a door. Both are dressed in business suits.* YOUNG *covers the older man's mouth with his hand and propels him to center stage, slamming the door behind them.* OWENS *is angry;* YOUNG *tries to pacify him.*

OWENS: Stop it! Let me go!

YOUNG: Calm down, Mr. Owens. Just cool it! *(He releases* OWENS, *who shouts at the door, shaking his fist.)*

OWENS: Cool it? Thrown out on my ass after thirty-two years and you want me to cool it? Out of my way! (OWENS *bolts for the door. Once again* YOUNG *grabs him and pushes him to center stage.)*

YOUNG: Don't, Mr. Owens! It's the wrong approach. *Please* don't! *(OWENS shakes his fist again, but avoids wrestling with the younger, strronger man.)*

OWENS *(shouts)*: Ingrates! Thirty-two years and this is what I get! *(YOUNG offers* OWENS *a chair, but* OWENS *waves it off.)*

YOUNG: Now just sit down and get it all out. All the emotions. Go ahead. But do it in here. *(Confidentially)* Just you and me.

OWENS: Just you and me? Hell, I don't even know who you are!

YOUNG: Oh, I'm so sorry. I grabbed you when you tried to choke Mr. Kinchlow and we never had a chance to introduce ourselves. *(He extends his hand for shaking, smiling charmingly.)* Hi, I'm Wendall Young, your Outplacement Counselor. (OWENS *disdains the proferred hand and concentrates on the door.* YOUNG *blocks him off.)*

YOUNG: Good! You're showing emotion! Let it out! (OWENS *raises his fists and starts stalking* YOUNG, *who backs up trying to avoid a physical confrontation.*)

OWENS: Out! Ya hear me?

YOUNG: *(backing up)*: This is wonderful. You're off to a very good start. Stalk me, if you want, even swing a fist or two. Believe me, I've seen it all. . . . The important thing is, do it *in here*, not out there. I reserved this conference room just for the two of us. And I scheduled your termination for lunchtime so everybody else would be gone.

OWENS: You did *what?* *(He throws a fist at* YOUNG , *narrowly missing him.)*

YOUNG: That's it. Get all the anger out. Feel better, do you? *(*OWENS *swings again, almost tagging* YOUNG *on the chin.* YOUNG *laughs nervously.)* Oops! That one was close! (OWENS *charges into* YOUNG *with his fists flailing.* YOUNG *subdues him with a bearhug and plants him in a chair.* YOUNG *is losing his professional cool.)* Let's move on to Phase Two, Mr. Owens. Just sit there and cry.

OWENS: Thirty-two years. *(Shouts off.)* Bastards!

YOUNG: Like some water? *(*OWENS *rises and heads for the door.)*

OWENS: No. A drink. A good, stiff one! *(Once again,* YOUNG *grabs* OWENS *and plants him back in the chair. More brutally.)*

YOUNG: Wrong! Wrong! *Wrong!* The worst thing you can do is go downstairs and tie one on. The absolute worst! (OWENS *realizes that* YOUNG *isn't going to release him until he wants to.)*

OWENS: What the hell *is* this? Am I in jail? Who gave you the right to tell *me* what to do? I don't even *know* you!

YOUNG: Let's just stay seated here and start at the beginning. Calmly. Okay? Good. Now. . . (OWENS *partially relaxes in his chair.* YOUNG *leans against the table—or the back of another chair. Bu[t] he keeps himself between* OWENS *and the door.)* My name [is] Wendall Young. I'm with the firm of Fuchs, Cuthrell and Co[m]pany. . . (*He pulls a calling card from his wallet and hands it [to]* OWENS, *who half listens to him and reads the card. Earnestl[y]* We specialize in the outplacement of terminated executives.

OWENS: What?

YOUNG: When firms let someone go, we help them. It's the com[pas]sionate way.

OWENS: How much help did they need to boot me out?

YOUNG: Oh, you'd be surprised! We suggested who should [go] where, what time of day, how to say it, everything.

OWENS: Well, in my opinion, Kinchlow screwed it up.

YOUNG *(agrees)*: Yes, I've heard better. Frankly, I think he [ ] for you.

OWENS: Bastard. Been laying for me for ten years.

YOUNG: And now the *real* work starts. Don't say *anything* to anybody. You'll need references from everybody on this floor. Even Kinchlow.

OWENS: Jesus!

YOUNG: Go straight home. No drinks, no barroom conversations. In fact, I'll escort you to the train. (OWENS *is relaxed now. He sighs, thinking about his immediate future.*)

OWENS: Martha. How do I tell her?

YOUNG: Mrs. Owens?

OWENS: Yes. What do you say after thirty-two years? (YOUNG *pulls a pamphlet out of his suit pocket.*)

YOUNG: This pamphlet covers it. Basically, you tell her the truth with just a touch of optimism. (OWENS *looks doubtfully at the pamphlet.* YOUNG *starts selling him.*) You know what lies before you, Mr. Owens? A *world* of opportunities! By the time you finish our psychological tests, you'll know *exactly* where you stand, where you should be.

OWENS: I should be here. Two offices down.

YOUNG: Nonsense! That's yesterday. When's the last time you really *enjoyed* working here? Felt challenged by it? Looked forward to it?

OWENS: Well, '61 was sort of fun. And, in '74, we had that convention in New Orleans.

YOUNG: See? Drudgery! That's why you were terminated. *You* wanted out. The Real You. You pushed Kinchlow until he had no choice. *You* fired *you!* (OWENS *thinks about it, but isn't convinc*... We start tomorrow, nine a.m. sharp in my office. We'll help ...nd a job that is better than anything you've ever imagined! ... your lucky day, Mr. Owens, you're starting a whole new

...*etly*): Bullshit. (*He stares at the pamphlet. His shoulders* ...*s crying, too embarrassed to look up.*) Thirty-two ... ...*e.* Just like that. . . Gone!

...UNG *sits next to* OWENS *and places a supportive arm* ...*Silently,* YOUNG *encourages the older man to cry* ...*best not to join him. When* YOUNG *finally speaks,* ...*is gone.*

...u something. . . I *know* we will. ...*out at the audience. Tears stream down his* ...*ile*): Hey, Martha! Good news! I've been

An Eastern Fable
Sam Bobrick

Time: the present. Evening.

Place: a New York apartment on the East Side.

At rise: a MAN *sits comatose in a chair, draped in a blanket. His* WIFE *paces nervously.*

WIFE: Don't worry, darling. He said he'd come and I have every reason to believe he will. Just try not to worry. I'll do that for both of us. *(Doorbell rings.)* That's him. I'm sure that's him. *(She goes to door.)* Please, please, let it be him. *(She opens the door. There is a man with a medical bag, the* DOCTOR.*)* Oh, Doctor. Thank you for coming. Please come in.

DOCTOR: You're very lucky I live in the building. I find house calls extremely depressing.

WIFE *(leading the* DOCTOR *to her husband's bed)*: See, darling, the doctor did come. Everything's going to be all right now. Oh, Doctor, I just hope and pray you're not too late.

DOCTOR: It's that serious, is it?

WIFE *(coming apart)*: Oh, Doctor...

DOCTOR: Yes?

WIFE: Doctor... *(She starts to cry.)*

DOCTOR: Yes?

WIFE: I think my husband is... is...

DOCTOR: Yes? Yes? Out with it.

WIFE: I think my husband is shallow.

DOCTOR *(a beat)*: He's what?

WIFE: Shallow, Doctor. I don't think there's any question about it.

DOCTOR: Oh, my God. Shallow! A shallow man living in New York. I've always feared such a thing.

WIFE: It happened so suddenly.

DOCTOR *(feeling* MAN's *pulse)*: I must know everything. Let's hope this is not the start of an epidemic.

WIFE: It was right before dinner. We were having a Campari on the rocks. I love their ads. They're so delightfully subtle.... And as usual we were having a normal profound discussion, you know, the merits of good and evil, the meaning of everything, the pleasures of sushi...

DOCTOR: Fine, fine topics.

WIFE: When... when right in the middle of this worldly inter-

change he looked up at me and said he'd like to live in Los
Angeles.

DOCTOR: Oh, my God.

WIFE: Naturally, I ingored it at first.

DOCTOR: Very wise.

WIFE: I continued on our esoteric course, the future of contemporary Norwegian literature, Pablo Picasso, legend or louse, and
why I preferred the veal marsala at Romeo Salta's over the clams
at Patsy's.

DOCTOR: And his reaction?

WIFE: He said he'd like to live in a place where you can swim and
have a sun tan all year round.

DOCTOR: What about ideas? Did you tell him there were no ideas
out west? That no one talked Nietzsche or Stendahl or Schopenhauer?

WIFE: I love Schopenhauer. Couldn't you just die from his pessi-
mism?

DOCTOR: What true New Yorker can't? When he said the world was
a piece of shit, you felt like you were right there.

WIFE: Oh, Doctor, you just gave me an intellectual chill.

DOCTOR: Thank you. *(He feels the* MAN's *forehead.)*

WIFE: I then tried to get him with Dickens. I talked about the in-
evitable bi-sexuality of Oliver Twist.

DOCTOR: I love that kind of repartee.

DOCTOR: He just said he would like to see Disneyland as soon as he
could. I felt so betrayed.

DOCTOR: You poor thing.

WIFE: I became desperate. I started to grab at straws. Crime,
theater, Barbara Walters, an intellectual look at jug wine, the
cheese cake at Maxwell's Plumb. He treated them all as if they
didn't exist.

DOCTOR: To think we breathe the same air.

WIFE: He said he would just like to own a new Cadillac Eldorado
and know that nothing in the world was his fault.

DOCTOR: The poor bastard. The poor shallow bastard. *(He listens
to the* MAN's *heart with his stethoscope.)*

WIFE: What do you think, Doctor? I'm filled with grief and tor-
ment. Can he be saved?

DOCTOR: My honest opinion?

WIFE: Yes, if it will help. *(The* DOCTOR *puts away his stethoscope.)*

DOCTOR: I'm afraid, without the capacity for honest Big Apple
chitchat, he's as good as dead. The important thing now is you.
Why don't you come up to my place for a drink? We can put on a

little Bartok and discuss the restaurants where Woody Allen likes
to eat.

WIFE: Perhaps I should. It would be so good to have depth and
meaning in my life again. It's been almost four hours.

DOCTOR: Of course. And bring along a toothbrush just in case we
decide to discourse all night long.

WIFE: Yes. Yes, I will. *(Runs to* DOCTOR's *arms.)* Oh, Doctor, Doctor. . . . Hold me. Once it was him and me forever and now five
minutes later it's you and me for tonight. That's what I like about
this city—the pace.

They kiss. Blackout.

Lifeline
Ann Raymond

The Scene: the empty, dimly-lit dining room of a small Melrose Avenue Italian Restaurant.

The time: the after-lunch, pre-cocktail, pre-dinner hour—approximately 4:00 p.m.

At the rise: a green-and-white ascotted, darkly Italian WAITER *flicks a cloth across the table. He pushes in the chairs—after dusting the seats. Hearing a noise, he turns to behold this bizarre sight: an ancient, decrepit semblance of a human male is being pulled into the dining room by way of a rope tied securely around his waist. Pulling him along and behind as a child would a treasured wagon is a middle-aged, buttoned-up, mannish* WOMAN. *She wears a business suit, shirt, and tie.*

WOMAN *(calling to the* WAITER*)*: Hold that table! It's still ten minutes before the kitchen closes for lunch! *(Turning to face the old man.)* Pa—will you hurry?! C'mon—you're wasting time!

Not only can the old fellow not hurry—he can barely navigate. But, holding onto the rope, he struggles and shuffles one foot painfully ahead of the other and does, indeed, make it to the table.

WAITER *(standing his ground)*: I'm sorry, Madam. The dining room is closed for luncheon. We begin dinner service at 5:30. Perhaps you'd like to wait in the bar?

WOMAN *(formidable)*: Oh it is not! I checked at the door. We've still got ten minutes. You try pulling your father half way across town! Bring the menus and a carafe of your house wine. White! I'll get him settled.

The WAITER *checks his watch. Then, obviously upset, he exits. Pulling out a chair, the* WOMAN *helps the old man get settled in. She ties the red-and-white checked napkin around his neck, infant style. Then she pulls out the other chair, sits primly, and carefully unfolds her own napkin, placing it carefully over her knees.*

WOMAN: Comfy, Pa? This is nice, isn't it? Quiet. *(His head is bent—looking into his chest.)*

PA: I'm not wasting time. Time is wasting me.

WOMAN *(absently)*: OK, Pa.

PA: I don't like Italian food!

WOMAN: Oh you do too! We came here for your birthday last year and you loved it!

PA *(head unmoved)*: Who said I loved it?

WOMAN: Pa—I'm not going to fight with you. Haven't you noticed that yet? No fights. I didn't argue about the walker. You don't want to use your walker—fine! You wanted to be pulled on your rope—fine! "OK," I said. "Fine." Whatever you says goes, Pa. This is your birthday. No fights! *(She is fighting for control.)* PULL YOUR HEAD UP, PA!!

PA *(head still bent as in prayer)*: My head is up.

WOMAN: Whatever you say, Pa. Fine. Your head is up. If you think you're going to get me into a dispute over the angle of your head —you're wrong! No fights today. No fights.

PA: Good! *(He places both hands beside his face and painfully, carefully, adjusts his head upward.)* Better, Milly? Is this better?

MILLY *(with compassion)*: Isn't it better for you? Can't you see things more clearly with your head up like that?

PA: Maybe I like the view from my own chest.

MILLY: Whatever you say, Pa. *(The WAITER returns with two menus, two glasses, and a carafe of white wine. MILLY grabs both menus as the WAITER waits, pencil poised.)* Well—we're going to need another carafe of this! *(Pause.)* We'll have the mine-strone—and he'll live with it. Then, we'll have the spaghetti and meat balls—and I'll live with it. For dessert—we both like the spumone. *(Very bossy)* And be sure to have the chef put one of those little candles in my father's! Because this is his birthday. *(WAITER exits. MILLY pours the wine into both glasses—measuring carefully. Then, tenderly, she places one glass in PA's hand. Raising her glass)* To your health, Pa.

PA *(staring at MILLY)*: HA!

MILLY: And a very happy birthday, Pa! Many, many more.

PA *(still staring)*: HAH!! *(They drink: MILLY, eagerly; the old man, gratefully—rolling the liquid around on his tongue, taking for-ever to swallow. Then he does, finally—noisily.)* Did I tell you I saw a dead sparrow the other day? Just lying on the ground at the home. Little feet pointed straight to heaven, like little tiny tri-angles. He was just lying there on his back—peaceful. Wasn't any reason for him to be dead. I picked him up and looked at him all over. Cat didn't get him or anything and...

MILLY *(interrupting)*: You've already told me that story!

PA: Well, it isn't going to hurt you to hear it again, is it? There wasn't a mark on him. Hadn't been shot or clawed or anything. I always thought you had to kill a sparrow. Hit him with a broom or something. First time I ever learned that a sparrow could die of natural causes. *(Pause.)* Too bad your mother isn't here. She would have buried that sparrow. Said a few words over him and put a little flower. . .

MILLY *(interrupting angrily)*: Mother was very good at burying things! *(Pause. Drinks.)* Pa—why won't you use your walker like the other people at the home? Why this rope thing? Why do you want to be pulled?

PA: Because I'm tired of being pushed.

MILLY: Pa. . . .

PA: I'm not crippled! I'm just lame, is all. *I need a little pull.* Lame is not the same as crippled!!

MILLY: OK, Pa. No fights! OK? Let's just have our lovely little birthday luncheon and. . .

PA: *(interrupting quickly)*: You never liked your mother, did you Milly? Well, I did. I loved that woman. Most beautiful woman I ever saw. Small-breasted but beautiful. I had a dream about her again last night. *(Pause—drinks.)* She came to me clear as daybreak. And her breasts were bare and big—like melons. She told me a doctor in heaven had given her a silicone job. *(Pause—drinks.)* Damned nice job.

MILLY: She always wanted a son instead of me.

PA: Better she didn't live to know that in you she'd get both!

MILLY *(staring meaningfully at PA, points her finger in his face)*: DON'T START!!

PA: Well, it isn't right. It isn't natural. Two woman together. . .

MILLY *(near tears)*: Pa—do you mind? We're celebrating your birthday here, dammit! *(They stare at each other.)*

PA: You could have been a normal woman and given me grandchildren. Did you know that in China they put the little round fat grandchildren in the same bed with the old men? Do you know why they do that, Milly? Because there's nothing in this world that will warm the old bones of the human body like the warmth of a little grandchild. Nothing.

MILLY: I gave you a perfectly good electric blanket. Try using it! We are not Chinese! *(Drinks.)* And I did not choose to be what I am you know. I inherited my sexual preference.

PA: What the hell does that mean?

MILLY: I've been looking for a woman to love me all my life! And I've finally found that in Isabelle. You should be glad for me and open your heart to her. Because. . . because. . . *(She stops—*

grown quiet now.)

PA: Sometimes it seems my goddam brain is busting open with white hot questions and I'm a son-of-a-bitch if I can find one green answer. *(Softly)* Lucky sparrow.

MILLY: What did you say, Pa?

PA *(firm)*: I said lucky sparrow. Lucky goddam free creature! What the hell does he know about endings? You think that dead feathered thing with his little triangles pointed to heaven knew his little sparrows would never beget other little sparrows? You think he knew it was all over? Death is not the end, Milly. Leaving nothing behind. That's the end. Nothing. Nothing. Goddammed nothing. *(Drinks wine—composed.)*

MILLY: Lucky—lucky sparrow.

Blackout.

Aerobics
Jack Matcha

*At the rise, we are in a gym where an aerobics dancing session is
starting. The music is already on. It goes down to background level
as the characters deliver their interior monologues.*

LEADER'S VOICE *(offstage)*: All right, everybody take your places for
the aerobic dancing. *(As she goes on, four people enter dressed in
gym costumes and begin to go through the exercises to the lively
music. All are in their late twenties or early thirties.* MAYBIN *is
very athletic looking and does the motions with greater zest than
anyone. Her husband,* HARRY, *fights to conceal his weariness.*
TOM *looks like a football player in good condition.* CISSIE, *the
youngest in the group, moves into the dance slowly, then picks
up as she goes along. The characters never stop moving, whether
they are speaking or silent.)* Keep in time to the music, please.
Try not to lose the rhythm and follow me closely... One...
two... three... four.... Get closer together, Maybin and
Harry. Okay, five... six... seven... eight.

MAYBIN: Get closer together, Maybin and Harry. That's the only
way it's going to happen... if the leader orders it. I wish I could
take her home with me so she could order us to share the same

bed. He looks at that model more than he does me. I don't know what's happened to Harry, but bringing him here isn't helping. I thought if he came here and did the exercises it might put him back in shape... and, incidentally, remind him of my shape.... Forget it.... He doesn't know I'm alive....

HARRY: Look at them jumping up and down with all this aerobics crap, like it's the most important thing in their lives. That's all they ever think about... aerobics, tennis, jogging.... If anybody caught them reading a book, they'd drop dead.

CISSIE: He's good looking.... Wonder what he thinks of me? Probably thinking, "She's gorgeous. Great pair of legs." So, why doesn't he ask me for a date? He's been staring at me all week.

TOM: She's gorgeous. What a great pair of legs. But out of my league.... She looks expensive and she's too attractive.... Where could I take her? Shakey's Pizza? She probably eats at La Scala or Ma Maison, where you're lucky if you get an omelette for ten bucks.

MAYBIN: He used to be the most passionate lover. Now he acts like I'm his grandmother. He hasn't touched me in weeks.... I wonder if he's impotent.

HARRY: Why do I keep letting her drag me here every night? If she sent me through a car wash, I couldn't think of a worse way to end the day.

CISSIE: I'll give him till the end of the week. If he doesn't ask me out by then, I'm switching to Jane Fonda's workouts.... Trouble with that is, it's mostly women.

TOM: I'm tempted to ask her.... If only she didn't give off that Polo Lounge look.... I'd be willing to go as high as Two Guys from Italy.... I have a half-price coupon for them. Forget it... she'd die laughing.

MAYBIN: In the beginning, he was as crazy as I was about sports.... He loved to play tennis, go jogging, hiking.... We'd do it every weekend...

HARRY: It wasn't so bad when we crammed all this shit into a weekend... but this kind of schedule would kill a horse!

CISSIE: It's the same old problem. He figures, I'm a model.... I go out with film producers, movie stars, that kind of thing... so I'm out of his reach. Well, just try me, dammit.

MAYBIN: Impotent-shimpotent... he's got another woman.... It's obvious. I do everything I can to arouse him. What else can I try? I shop at Frederick's of Hollywood.... I wear the sexiest perfume on the market... and he still looks at me as if I'm Howard Cossell.

TOM: Maybe she would come. What's so bad about Two Guys from Italy? Christ, if she can't sit down and have a bowl of spaghetti with me... who needs her?

CISSIE: How do I let him know that I don't expect anything fancy? That I'd be happy to go anywhere with him?

MAYBIN: He's having an affair with someone and she wears him out.... Everytime I suggest sex, he goes into a crouch like the hunchback of Notre Dame. "Oh, my back, my aching back."

TOM: The hell with it... I'll ask her as soon as the session's over. The worst she'll probably do is say she hates Italian food... in which case I'll suggest Pedro's Hacienda... great Mexican food. In fact, I'll try that first.... Mexican food is kind of classless, especially when you wash it down with strawberry Margaritas...

HARRY: I just can't go on this way.... I may look like I'm thirty-eight, but I'm fifty-three, damn it, and I don't know how much longer I can do this every night, ten hours a day at the office, and still have sex with her twice a week.

MAYBIN: Maybe it's me.... Maybe if I took a couple of weeks off and went to one of those fat farms, I'd be able to look like that model. (TOM *and* CISSIE *are now exchanging affectionate glances as they continue exercising.*)

HARRY: She's going to have to accept reality... face the fact that she's living with a man who is not ten, but twenty-five years older than she is.... Who dyes his hair and spends a Chinese fortune on drugs and masseurs to keep up his image of flaming youth... who's lied to her about his age ever since they've been married for fear of losing her, and who just cannot keep up with her and her physical fitness. Maybe she'll walk out on me when I tell her. Who knows? One thing I do know... I just can't go on living with a time bomb.

LEADER *(offstage)*: Okay, everybody... let's do thirty-two push-ups!

HARRY's *face freezes in panic at this announcement. The others begin the pushups. He is on the verge of collapse. Blackout.*

Sunrise on Earth
Michael Lewis

Lights up on an OLD MAN. *He seems to be looking down from a height.*

OLD MAN: Well. Nearly sunrise on the earth. There she lies—my mother-to-be—in the final throes of labor. *(He watches for a beat, then)* It's so peaceful up here, floating bodiless above her. Why must I go back to all that sweat and effort? I left the world as an old man, broken, useless. I shall re-enter the world as an infant, also useless. Why bother? *(He turns to leave, then stops.)* What was that? Did she cry out to me? No? *(Watches her for a moment.)* She's having a bad time of it—I must be her first. *(Trying to convince himself)* Oh, I suppose it won't be so bad, really—being alive again. I *have* been dead a long time. *(Nobly)* Being alive! To think, to reason, to act! To read breakfast cereal packages, to trim hedges, to scratch an insect bite. To wonder: *why?* To wake at dawn and taste the dew; to feel the air in whispers; to walk through a meadow and hear nothing but the patter and splash of my dreams! To have everything to live for! To have nothing to live for! *(Drops the noble mien.)* I do hope I don't make a botch of it this time around, making the same mistakes. The bad choices I made... *(Pause.)* will make again, piling about my feet and rustling as I walk. The doors closing behind me... *(A protest)* Why should I go back...wear a body; become subject to the weather of the world; the politics and the bad jokes of the world; the blazing sunlight of the world—where it's too bright to see anything but the world. I'd hide there, in the light, like I did last time. *(Shakes fist.)* I *won't do it! I can't do it!* *(Thinks.)* But I *will* be young again, for a time—for what that's worth. It will be nice...to feel that. *(He watches her again.)* And I'm sure she'll be fine with me—she looks terribly sincere. *(Sighs, suddenly very tired.)* The prospect is so-o exhausting. To start a-all the way from scratch again: nursing, crawling, walking, talking, learning, getting into trouble, bouncing checks, rush hour, relatives, retirement, oblivion. If only something would *change*...*(An idea occurs to him, exciting his interest.)* But then there is that—"twinge." That sense of life; that awareness of being aware. It happens rarely, but inevitably, sometime—maybe only once. Yet when it does, no matter where you are or what you're doing, whether lying in a pool of mud or extracting cube roots... you know you're *alive*. You know it completely, thoroughly. And though it only lasts less than an instant—this twinge—there's no greater feeling—not even in heaven. *(Pause.)* I want to feel that twinge again. *(Resolute)* Very well. I may be a fool, but I'll give it another go. I'll give it another go—for the *twinge! (Pause. Eyes light.)* There it is: sunrise on the earth. Time to *be!*

There is strength and hope on his face as the lights black out.)

About Time
Oliver Hailey

At rise: a middle-aged couple sit rocking on a front porch. They rock in silence for a beat.

HER: What'd he say?

HIM: When?

HER: When he fired you, of course.

HIM: What time is it?

HER: How'd he put it? Just.... "You're fired"?

HIM: What time is it, dammit!?

HER: How would I know?

HIM: What's that on your arm?

HER: The watch you gave me last Christmas.

HIM: Well—can't you look at that and tell me what time it is?

HER: You've got to be kidding. This thing stopped three weeks after you gave it to me.

HIM: And you're still wearing it? You're such a sentimentalist.

HER: Not really. The clasp is stuck.... I can't get it off. *(Beat.)* Come on, tell me what he said.

HIM: Here—let me see what I can do with it. *(He wrestles with it— to no avail.)* Well, shit. Have you tried soaking it?

HER: Soaking it? It's not a ring, it doesn't slip off over a knuckle—it has to slip off over an entire fist. *(She demonstrates by making a fist.)*

HIM: Well, you can't go around wearing a watch that doesn't work for the rest of your life.

HER: That thought has crossed my mind, too. *(Beat.)* It's not as if you liked the lousy job anyway! Thank God for that. You loathed it for twenty-nine years. And you were never very good at it, either. So the joke's on them! Ha, ha, ha!

HIM: I was so proud when I gave you that watch.

HER: Were you really? *(She glances down at the watch.)* I've certainly grown to hate it.

HIM: It seemed like such a good idea... a calendar watch.

HER: Yeah? I've had watches that lost time before, but a calendar watch... in the first three days, it lost a year and a half.

HIM: I've never known a quartz to behave that poorly.

HER: What makes you think it's a quartz?

HIM: Because it says so right on the face.

HER: Does it?

HIM: Yeah. Look.

HER: You look!

HIM *(he does—and spells it out)*: Q-U-E-R-T-Z.

HER: Which spells Quertz. And should've been your tip-off.

HIM *(staring in disbelief at the face of the wristwatch)*: Quertz? Quertz?

HER *(pointing to the face of the watch herself now)*: Yes—Quertz of Taiwan. Apparently, it's a brand name.

HIM: Those goddamn Taiwanians!

HER: Taiwanese. *(Beat.) Please* tell me what he said. After you called, I tried to imagine it. All afternoon, I kept putting myself in his place. As if I were asking you for a divorce after twenty-nine years. But I just couldn't do it. I just wouldn't know how to put it. How'd *he* put it? I'd really *love* to know.

HIM: Damn, I wish I knew what time it was. I hate to get up and go in the house.

HER: Wouldn't do you any good anyway. I unplugged the electric clock.

HIM: When?

HER: Right after you called to say you'd been fired.

HIM: Why?

HER: I thought I'd save a few pennies.

HIM: How much does it cost to run an electric clock?

HER: A few pennies. We'd better start saving them.

HIM: I don't think that's it at all. I don't think—bottom line—you don't give a damn what time it is! And you never have!

HER: Not true. I used to love knowing what time it was. Even our wedding night, I kept looking at the clock. Surely you remember.

HIM: Yeah, I kept wondering what you were timing.

HER: Just life. *(Beat.)* Was he at least gracious about it? Did he take you to lunch?

HIM: My God, what time is it?! I may have to go next door to ask.

HER: Oh, you'd love asking *her* what time it is, wouldn't you? But do you honestly think she'd give you the time of day?

HIM: I don't want her to give it to me—just to tell it to me.

HER: And once you find out what time it is, what'll you do then?

HIM: What I always do once I know. Calm down. Get a grip on myself. And then get on with it.

HER: On with *what*?

HIM *(a roar)*: That depends on what time it *is*, dammit! I'm so confused, I don't even know if it's a.m. or p.m.

HER: You remind me of my Quertz.

HIM: Why are you so mean about the time?

HER: Why is it called Greenwich mean time? I suppose because time brings out the worst in people. I had an old maid aunt who used to swoon just at the mention of it. She said time had passed her by. That it just wasn't on her side. She had plenty of it on her hands, but none on her side.

HIM: Dammit, don't mock it. Time may have lost its meaning for you, but not for me, by God. Wherever there's a clock ticking, I'm there, too. Whenever one strikes, my heart beats a little faster. I don't ask if the bell tolls for me, I just count the number of *times* it tolls.

HER: What in hell did he say?! You work twenty-nine years for a man, you're never tardy, you're always on time. What did he say, dammit?! How in hell did he end it?

HIM *(a long pause—then finally)*: He said he was sorry... he knew how much I'd looked forward to my thirty-year retirement watch.

HER: And what did you say to him?

HIM: I did a strange thing... I just suddenly blurted it out.... I couldn't help myself...

HER: What? What?

HIM: I asked him what time it was.

HER: And...

HIM *(near tears)*: He wouldn't tell me. He said I had to get used to not knowing—to not caring. I just don't know if I can do that.

HER *(taking his hand)*: Sure you can. I'll help. We'll do it together.
HIM: Do what together?
HER: Kill time.

> *And she begins to rock again—determinedly. A beat and then he,
> too, begins to rock—with equal determination. Slow fade.*

Rules of the House
Dona Cooper

Setting: FLOYD *and* JOSEPHINE WATKINS, *a married couple in their early thirties, living in a small Southern town, are getting ready for evening church services.* JOSEPHINE *is dressed in a prim navy blue and white linen suit, with matching white accessories.* FLOYD *wears a seersucker suit and is reading the paper.* MABEL, JOSEPHINE'*s mother, is upstairs somewhere.*

JOSEPHINE *(calling upstairs)*: It's almost seven o'clock, Mama. It's time to go to church. *(To* FLOYD, *after a pause)* Is Mama ready to go?

FLOYD: Don't know.

JOSEPHINE *(to* FLOYD*)*: Honey, get your head out of that paper and put on your new tie. *(Calling upstairs again.)* Mama! *(To* FLOYD, *after a pause.)* Where's Mama? Do you know where Mama is?

FLOYD: Bathroom, most likely.

JOSEPHINE: Mama? *(Louder)* Mama! *(A pause.)* Mama, can you hear me? Can you hear me, Mama!? *(To* FLOYD*)* Floyd, can Mama hear me?

FLOYD: Couldn't say.

JOSEPHINE: You know, Floyd, I really wish you'd speak in complete sentences, I really do.

FLOYD: I don't know if your mama can hear you. I know I can.

JOSEPHINE *(in full voice)*: Mama! Can you hear me?

MABEL *(bellowing from offstage, where she remains for the rest of the play)*: Yes, I can hear you. Now leave me alone.

JOSEPHINE: It's almost seven o'clock, Mama. It's Sunday; it's time to praise the Lord our God.

MABEL: I'm not going. I've decided to take a bubble bath instead.

JOSEPHINE: Now, Mama, there's no time for fooling. Floyd's putting on his new tie and I have on my good pantyhose, so let's get moving.

MABEL: I told you, I'm not going.

FLOYD *(to* JOSEPHINE*)*: Now, honey, maybe your mother's tired after her bridge game this afternoon.

JOSEPHINE *(calling upstairs)*: Mama, you know the rules of this house. Ever since you moved in with us, you've been going to church every Sunday . . .

MABEL: I know, and I've tried to be a good sport about it. Every Sunday, I've sat and listened to that preacherman squawk, but tonight I just can't take it. I'm going to take a bubble bath instead.

JOSEPHINE: Mama!

MABEL: Quiet, dear, Mama has a hangover.

JOSEPHINE: I don't believe you, Mama. I don't believe you for one minute.

MABEL: About my bath? Well, I'm taking my clothes off right now; you can come watch if you want to.

JOSEPHINE *(in a building frenzy)*: But you can't take your clothes off; it's almost seven o'clock.

MABEL: Well, I'm doing it. Yep. Here I am, in all my naked splendor.

JOSEPHINE: Floyd, honey, do something. Make her stop.

MABEL: It's too late. My foot's in the water. Now both feet. Now my astabula. . . *(Enjoying the warmth)* Ah. . . *(Slight pause.)* Floyd, honey, I hope I'm not embarrassing you.

JOSEPHINE *(flailing her hand in front of* FLOYD's *face)*: Floyd, take my hand. Take my hand, Floyd, honey. I need your support. Mama's getting weird again.

FLOYD: She's not getting weird, she's just not going to church.

JOSEPHINE *(more insistent)*: Have you got my hand, Floyd? Have you got my hand?

MABEL: Take her goddamn hand, Floyd. Maybe then we can get a little peace around here and I can enjoy my bath.

JOSEPHINE *(weak with dramatic despair)*: But Mama, it's almost seven o'clock. It's Sunday. It's time to praise the Lord our God.

FLOYD *(to* JOSEPHINE*)*: Honey, why don't we just let your mother enjoy her bath?

JOSEPHINE *(to* FLOYD, *in a flair of indignation)*: And I'm supposed to tell the Lord our God she's not coming? Am I really supposed to tell the Lord our God that?

FLOYD: Lord our God. Lord our God. Can't you just call the son-of-a-bitch "Jesus"?

JOSEPHINE: Floyd, don't mess with me.

MABEL: I don't suppose while we're having this discussion, anyone could bring me a beer?

JOSEPHINE *(still going strong)*: My own Mama, done gone to hell!!!

MABEL: Floyd, do you think you could get her out of here now?

FLOYD: Maybe we should be going. It's almost seven o'clock.

JOSEPHINE *(to* FLOYD*)*: I know what time it is! I'm the one who's been telling you!

FLOYD *(with a hint of firmness)*: I really think we better get going. . .

JOSEPHINE *(digging her heels in)*: I'm not going anywhere till Mama gets out of that tub.

MABEL *(getting ready for a showdown)*: You really want me to get out of this tub?

JOSEPHINE: Yep!

MABEL: You really want me to get out of this nice warm tub?

JOSEPHINE: Yep!

MABEL: You really want me to get the hell out of this tub?

JOSEPHINE: Yep!

FLOYD: Absolutely not!

MABEL *(there is a sudden surprised silence before she speaks with genuine relief)*: Thank the Lord our God.

FLOYD *(now taking charge)*: Josephine, you pick up your purse; we're going to the car. Mabel, you can stay in that tub till you turn to prune, for all I care. But I want to get to church and get it over with so I can watch the fight with the boys. *(To* JOSEPHINE*)* Are you ready?

JOSEPHINE *(with surprising meekness—clearly attracted by* FLOYD's *sudden show of strength)*: Yes, sir. *(She picks up her purse and moves to the door; then yells)* Good night, Mama! I'll pray for you!

JOSEPHINE *and* FLOYD *exit. Blackout.*

Conversation 2001
Marcia Rodd

At rise: three men and three women of various shapes and ages, dressed in party clothes, weave in and about each other. They all hold champagne glasses; the women carry identical purses; the men carry identical shoulder bags. The MAN *and* WOMAN *spot each other and move together. (Note: the* MAN *and* WOMAN *can be any age from 30 to 45. The presence of the other couples is optional.) The light focuses in on the two of them. The others pair off in the shadows and, in pantomime, echo the action of the two principles.*

MAN: Hello.
WOMAN: Hello. *(They eye each other for a beat.)*
MAN: OK?
WOMAN: OK.

> *They move to sit. He reaches in his bag as she starts to open her purse. They stop. She nods for him to go first and closes her purse. He draws out a pocket computer. He presses a button and speaks quietly into it.*

MAN: Cocktail party, October third, two thousand one, 8:37 p.m. *(He presses a few more buttons, waits a beat and begins. Note: as he and the other couples proceed, there is a musical background of pings as info is being fed into the computers.)* I.D. number?
WOMAN: 447-23-7803.
MAN: Age?
WOMAN *(after a beat)*: Between thirty-five and forty-five.
MAN *(looks at her a beat)*: College graduate?
WOMAN: Yes... almost.
MAN: Heterosexual?
WOMAN: Yes.
MAN: Religion?
WOMAN: Yes. *(The* MAN *looks at her.)* I mean, no.... I mean, not really. Presbyterian as a child...a couple months as a Buddhist... and then, I don't know, I just got busy and sort of lost interest... *(She winds down.)*
MAN *(a beat)*: Do you like children?
WOMAN: I have two from my first marriage.
MAN: I repeat the question.
WOMAN: What question?
MAN: Do you like children?

WOMAN: Oh. Not especially.

MAN *(almost inaudibly)*: Good.

WOMAN: What?

MAN: How many times have you been married?

WOMAN *(surprised)*: Once!

MAN: Divorced?

WOMAN: Once!!

MAN: Then why did you just say "my *first* marriage"?

WOMAN: Did I say that?

MAN *(retrieving computer info)*: "Two children from my first marriage."

WOMAN: Oh, yes. I did, didn't I? I don't know why I said that. I guess it's kind of a figure of speech. Isn't that odd? What *should* one say? "Two children from my *only* marriage"? "From my *ex-*marriage"? Sometimes language is so inadequate, don't you think?

MAN: Are you interested in a second marriage?

WOMAN *(a beat)*: Oh. I see why you picked up on that "first" business. . . . Christ, I dunno, I'd settle for a decent affair.

MAN: Do you like sex?

WOMAN: Yes.

MAN: How often?

WOMAN: That depends.

MAN: On what?

WOMAN: The conditions.

MAN: What conditions?

WOMAN: The man, the time, the place, my health, his health, my mood, his mood, the strength of the attraction, the size of the bed, the lighting, the temperature, my weight, and what's on cable.

MAN: Do you like to read?

WOMAN: What??

WOMAN: *Do you like to read?*

WOMAN: What an odd question. I mean, no one's asked me that in *ages*. Actually, yes.

MAN: What?

WOMAN: Yes, I do.

MAN: No. *What?*

WOMAN: What *what?*

MAN: *What do you like to read!!??*

WOMAN: Oh. *(Slightly embarrassed)* Well, my favorites are old Time magazines. You remember them? They used to be published every week, with a lot of stuff on, you know, current events, and people in the news, and. . .

MAN: My god, yes! When I was a kid, I used to send the covers off to be autographed. I'd wait for the mail every day—to see if any came back signed.

WOMAN: And did they?

MAN: Yeah, quite a few. *(A little sadly)* I don't know whatever happened to my collection.

WOMAN: What a shame.

MAN: Yeah. *(Suddenly catching himself)* Oh, my god, I'm sorry, I'm sorry. Where was I? *(Refers to computer.)* Oh, yes. Do you like to travel?

WOMAN: Yes.

MAN: Interplanetary?

WOMAN: When I can afford it.

MAN: Current passport?

WOMAN: Yes.

MAN: Credit?

WOMAN: Good.

MAN: Therapy?

WOMAN: Tuesdays.

MAN: Allergies.

WOMAN: Seasonal. *(The dialogue from here to the end of his questions gets faster and faster.)*

MAN: Color?

WOMAN: Green.

MAN: Food?

WOMAN: Pasta.

MAN: Sport?

WOMAN: Soccer.

MAN: Season?

WOMAN: Summer.

MAN: Black.

WOMAN: White.

MAN: Cold.

WOMAN: Hot.

MAN: Soft.

WOMAN: Hard.

MAN: Loud.

WOMAN: Soft.

MAN: Jack.

WOMAN: Jill.

MAN: Fast.

WOMAN: Slow.

MAN: Light.
WOMAN: Dark.
MAN: Stop.
WOMAN: Go.

> *Long pause during which a flurry of pings indicate information being tabulated. Then total silence. They are both a little exhausted. Finally...*

MAN: Well, I think that just about does it.
WOMAN: If you're sure... *(She reaches in her purse and draws out an identical pocket computer. Her actions are echoed by the couples in shadows. Repeating the MAN's earlier actions, she speaks softly into her computer.)* Cocktail party, October third, two thousand one, 8:42 p.m. *(The melodic pings start up again as she presses buttons on the computer.)* I.D. number?
MAN: 553-26-2731.
WOMAN: Age?
MAN *(after a beat)*: Over forty.
WOMAN *(she smiles at his answer)*: College graduate? *(At least half the MAN's attention is still on his computer which is totalling up the input.)*
MAN: Masters, actually. Business administration.
WOMAN: Religion?
MAN: Brought up Episcopalean. Now, more or less agnostic.
WOMAN: Do you like chi...
MAN *(interrupting her)*: Wait a minute. *(Checks his computer, then looks at her.)* I'm sorry. It's no good.
WOMAN: What?
MAN *(showing her his computer)*: See. It's "no." I'm, uh... I'm sorry.

> *He exits. She sits there, surprised and saddened. Slow blackout.*

So Long, Mr. Broadway
Rick Lenz

At rise: lights come up on a MAN *in his early forties. He speaks to the audience in a very comfortable, story-telling fashion.*

MAN: It was only 9:30 in the evening, but the show was over and the curtain came down early. "So Long, Mr. Broadway"—let me explain that. My friend, Walter, was acting a small role in his first New York play about twenty years ago. One night, after his show let out, I met him at the theater and we went uptown to a party given by another friend and his fiancee, whose name was Nerissa. Nerissa was a bright girl with a barbed acerbic wit. Walter was a little full of himself, there's no question, what with being a big-time actor now. And Nerissa didn't miss a beat. All evening, in front of a lot of people, she used Walter for target practice. She started in calling him Mr. Broadway. She and a small handful of others delighted in her contempt. We were still young twenties. *(Smiles.)* I remember the first enterprise Walter and I were involved in was a summer stock company. It was the idea of a girl who'd been a few years behind me in high school, an aspiring actress named Wendy Fezzler. She'd found a vacant barn near our home town—Pontiac, Michigan. Wendy'd been an average pretty fifteen-year-old little cheerleader, the last I'd seen her. When Walter and I went to Pontiac in April to do a fund raiser, Wendy met us at the airport. The three of us were going to read some marvelous scenes from various plays to get together some money for productions costs... Wendy had grown. She was six-foot-one, with arms like a steel worker. One of the roles she was going to read for the fund raiser was Puck in "A Midsummer Night's Dream." *(Gestures.)* She was pretty, though. Big, but pretty. In fact, we both had a crush on her. Anyway, we had a lot of work to do before our big night—painting, brush clearing, cleaning away the evidence of the livestock that had played there before us. Adding to the whole thing, Walter had a cold, Wendy was having trouble picturing herself as Puck, and worst of all, for me, I'd been too busy to learn my lines. Then, the night before the performance, it rained and we discovered the barn had a hole in the roof. The next morning, instead of rehearsing, I went up top to do the roofing. Wendy was up there, too—tacking up a banner over the main entrance. I had a mouthful of flat-head nails.... I'd really developed a rhythm. *(Demonstrates.)* Well, I

got to going a little fast... *(Glum)* You know that kind of web-
bed part between your forefinger and your thumb? *(Nods.)*
Yeah. Right through it. I thought... oh, hell. The audience is
coming in seven hours, and here I am, unrehearsed and nailed to
the roof. So, I hollered to Wendy: "Wendy, would you come help
me?" And Wendy ambled over and said, "What's the trouble?"
Then she looked down to where I was attached to the roof, and
her eyes just rolled back, she fainted, and rolled off the edge of
the roof. *(Beat.)* And I thought, oh, gosh... and I took the hammer and... *(Makes the sound effect.)* pulled out the nail. Wendy'd broken her arm in two places. She was lucky at that....
When we got back from the hospital, I was all right. They just
bandaged me up and I was fine. But they had doped Wendy up
for the pain, so I knew I was going to have to do a two-person
show that night. But that's not what happened. *(Pause.)* Walter
did the show alone.... This is embarrassing.... But I knew it
would be just he and I that night, and I wouldn't be able to fake
it, which was what I'd had in mind, so I went down to the little
tin house where the firewood was kept—making sure a couple
people knew that's what I was doing, and I picked up some dirt
and smeared it on my face. Then I picked up a rock and very
gently I tapped myself on the forehead, but it didn't raise a
bump. So I covered my mouth, closed my eyes as tight as I could,
and I let myself have it.... I woke up as I was being carried to
the car. I pretended I was still unconscious. I heard Walter's
voice: "Here. He's my *best* friend. *I'll* carry him." *(Beat.)* I am
deeply saddened when I think that I'm allowed to vote.... I
confessed it all to him a week later. He told me he'd never had
more fun in his life than doing that one-man show that night...
Nerissa, who dubbed Walter "Mr. Broadway," crosses my mind
again now—not in anger, because I'm past having any feelings
about most people I haven't seen for twenty years—and yet, I
wonder if there would be any pleasure at all in dropping a note to
her—wherever she is—and say: "Dear Nerissa: It was only 9:30
in the evening, but the show was over and the curtain came
down early... and Mr. Broadway died tonight."

Blackout.

Opening Night
Sam Bobrick

Time: the present. Evening.

Place: Sardi's, New York City.

At rise: a YOUNG MAN *in his early thirties is in the middle of his meal. As he calmly sips his wine, he is approached by a* SECOND MAN *in his forties who stands over the table and stares at him for a beat.*

SECOND MAN: It's done. (*The* YOUNG MAN *looks at him, smiles, wipes his mouth with his napkin, removes an envelope from his jacket pocket, and hands it to the* SECOND MAN *who opens the envelope, removes several bills, and counts them.*) There's six thousand here. I'm only due five.

YOUNG MAN: That's okay. I think I'll be able to afford it now.

SECOND MAN: Thanks. You're a real sport. Can I sit down for minute? I'm a little shaken.

YOUNG MAN: Of course.

SECOND MAN: I'm usually pretty matter-of-fact about these things, but this time I felt a little bit funny. I've never killed a drama critic before.

YOUNG MAN: How about a drink?

SECOND MAN: No, no thanks. I'll be okay. Look, I gotta ask you something that's been bothering me. Why did you want him taken care of that way? I mean, I've killed guys with guns, with knives, even with my bare hands, but I've never poisoned anyone in the ear before.

YOUNG MAN: I'd like to think of it as poetic justice.

SECOND MAN: Yeah, I thought it seemed a bit arty. How many plays of yours did you say he panned?

YOUNG MAN: Four.

SECOND MAN: Boy, that's a lot. How many did you write?

YOUNG MAN: Four.

SECOND MAN: He was really very set in his ways, wasn't he?

YOUNG MAN: Tonight would have been my fifth, but I wasn't giving that bastard another chance.

SECOND MAN: No, I don't blame you. Not with that average.

YOUNG MAN: The son-of-a-bitch deserved to die. Anyone who doesn't understand comedy deserves to die.

SECOND MAN: You might have something there.

YOUNG MAN: What the hell did he expect from me? We can't all be Shakespeare.

SECOND MAN (*nodding*): That's not what's gonna save the country.

YOUNG MAN: Exactly. Well, I'm not sorry for what I did. He never laughed. Four plays and the bastard never laughed.

SECOND MAN: No kidding.

YOUNG MAN: Well, you watched him most of the night, right?

SECOND MAN: Yeah, sure, right.

YOUNG MAN: Well?

SECOND MAN: He was laughing.

YOUNG MAN (*stunned*): What?

SECOND MAN: Yeah. He seemd to be laughing pretty good.

YOUNG MAN: He. . . . He was?

SECOND MAN: In fact, he was hysterical most of the evening.

YOUNG MAN: You sure you got the right man? You did kill the critic from the New York Times?

SECOND MAN: Yeah. Sixth row. F-12, aisle seat.

YOUNG MAN: And he was laughing?

SECOND MAN: At times, a little too loud, I thought.

YOUNG MAN: You sure you went to the right theater?

SECOND MAN: Hey, I don't make mistakes about these things. I don't know about you, but I'm a professional.

YOUNG MAN: I'm sorry, but he was laughing? At my lines?

SECOND MAN: He fell off his seat twice.

YOUNG MAN: This is Thursday night, isn't it? I hope you didn't kill him during one of Doc Simon's openings.

SECOND MAN: No, I killed him during your play. Act III, Scene 14, just the way you said.

YOUNG MAN: Little guy with glasses and bad skin?

SECOND MAN: And laughing his ass off.

YOUNG MAN: I can't believe this. I finally write a play the son-of-a-bitch likes and this moron kills him. (*To* SECOND MAN): You know something? You know crap about the theater.

SECOND MAN (*indicates* YOUNG MAN's *food*): You gonna finish this?

YOUNG MAN: Who can eat now? I blew a New York Times rave. All right, the hell with it. I won't get a rave, but I won't get a rap. That was the whole idea anyway. I know without a rap from the Times, the audiences will love the play.

SECOND MAN (*eating* YOUNG MAN's *food*): I wouldn't bet on it.

YOUNG MAN: They weren't laughing?

SECOND MAN: They weren't there.

YOUNG MAN: They weren't there?

SECOND MAN: Not after the first act. No one was there. Just me and him.

YOUNG MAN: It's a nightmare. I'm living through a nightmare.

SECOND MAN: Hey, listen, far be it from me to tell you how to write a play, but I just don't think a comedy about the crucifixion is funny.

YOUNG MAN: You don't?

SECOND MAN: Hey, are you religious?

YOUNG MAN: No.

SECOND MAN: Well, I'm religious. And charging twenty-eight bucks for one character and no sets. . . . You tell me who's the criminal at this table. . . !

YOUNG MAN (*burying his head in his arms and starting to cry*): He was laughing this time.

SECOND MAN: Maybe you ought to try writing for the movies. They really stink.

The lights dim to black.

Love in a Pub
Fredi Towbin

Place: a bar in New York City.

At rise: ED *sits with his back to the audience. He never speaks.*
LINDA *enters, sits next to him. It's 11 p.m. tonight.*

LINDA *(to* ED): The aborigines are really very nice people once you
get to know them. Did you know that Evonne Goolagong
Cawley was born in the jungle and lived on coconuts until she
was twelve? I mean, Billie Jean King was already wearing
rhinestone eyeglasses. (ED *moves away.)* I'll buy you a drink. (ED
sits back down.) This is my first time here. It's like a meat rack.
You come often? I'm here because tomorrow is my friend Alan's
thirtieth birthday. Men get funny when they turn thirty. I think
it has something to do with hormones. I've gone out with eight,
twenty-nine-year-old men, and within weeks of turning thirty,
five proposed. One was queer as a three-dollar bill. Didn't matter. If they're unmarried at thirty, they want to be married. If
they're married, they want to be unmarried. I mean, five out of
eight are damn good odds. Good as Secretariat. If I keep up at
this rate, by the time I'm ready for Social Security, I'll have been
proposed to by one hundred and six twenty-nine-year-old men.
That's assuming that, when I'm sixty-five, I still find twenty-
nine-year-old men attractive. *(Pause.)* Bet you've turned thirty.
And are separated. Divorced! I can tell by the way you sit.
Something about your knees... the distance between them. Single men sit like this. *(She demonstrates: legs spread apart.)* You
sit like this. *(She demonstrates: knees close together.)* As if you
were hiding something. Have any kids? Boy? Girl! Bet you
wanted a second child but your wife didn't want to ruin her
figure. I hate wives. That's why I have to break up with Alan. I
mean, he's not married or anything. But I know he's going to ask
me. I've even met his parents. They live in Flushing. Very appropriate. What do you do? Don't tell me! Self-employed? Do you
work between 34th and 59th Streets? Between Fifth and Eighth
Avenues? Advertising!... You run a falafel stand? Museum of
Modern Art bookstore?... Am I close?... Give me a hint! Are
these your work clothes?... Panhandler! Construction
worker?... No, they never get divorced.... Do you live in
Brooklyn? Queens? Bronx? Tuscaloosa?... You live in Manhattan... the Big Apple. You think I'm pretty? I mean, I've never

done this before. But there's something about you I like. You're interesting. Your place or mine? Oh, don't worry. I don't live with Alan. I mean, privacy's very important in a relationship. Come on, you know you want to. We have so much to talk about...

ED *takes her by the hand, silently leads her out of the bar. Blackout.*

Hymn in the Attic
Beth Henley

Characters: MISS MAYBELLE, 53, STEVIE's *aunt;* GEORGIA RAY, 27,
STEVIE's *friend;* STEVIE, 27, *a retarded man.*

Setting: the entire action of the play takes place in MISS MAYBELLE's
attic in her home in Canton, Mississippi.

Time: late at night in the summer.

*At rise: the attic door opens and a ray of light spills into the black
room.*

MAYBELLE (*offstage*): He's up in here.

> MISS MAYBELLE *and* GEORGIA RAY *enter, holding each other's
> hands. They start feeling their way across the dark room.* MISS
> MAYBELLE, 53, *is a round, little woman with curly white hair, a
> sweet face, and confused eyes.* GEORGIA RAY, 27, *is thin and
> pretty in a sad, lost way. She carries a brown grocery sack.*

GEORGIA RAY: In the closet?

MAYBELLE: Uh-huh.

GEORGIA RAY: Seems he's stopped his crying.

MAYBELLE: He liked to scare me to death with it. Oh, please,
Georgia, you just hold on t'my hand till we get on the light.

GEORGIA RAY: Hang on, Miss Maybelle. I'm about t'reach it. (*She
turns on the light.*) There.

MAYBELLE: Mercy, I hate it up here. All this old stuff. There's
Papa's broken domino case sitting over there filthy dirty. Any of
this junk you want, you just take.

GEORGIA RAY: Thank you, Miss Maybelle, maybe I will.

> GEORGIA RAY *starts clearing some space on an old sideboard.
> Throughout the following, she takes a jug of grape juice, a loaf of
> white bread, a silver goblet, a silver plate, and a candle out of the
> brown sack.*

MAYBELLE: Anything at all. You're a love to come over here at
twelve o'clock at night. It upsets me t'go out fetching people in
the dark. But he got t'hollering so.

GEORGIA RAY: I'm happy to come. Stevie and me have been friends
for a long time.

MAYBELLE: Well, you're the only one who can help t'make him behave anymore. Ever since he got himself stuck in the tub, I knew

he'd gotten way too big for me t'have t'handle. It just scares me so bad, thinking on what's gonna become of Stevie and what's gonna become of me. It all gets my heart t'beating wild and my hands get all wet and start perspiring.

GEORGIA RAY: Here now, Miss Maybelle, calm down. We'll get him to come out. You'll be down asleep in bed soon.

MAYBELLE: I'm sorry going on like this. What with the misery you've just seen. They say time heals all wounds, but I just can't believe you're ever gonna get over losing that sweet baby of yours.

GEORGIA RAY (*as she starts pouring the grape juice into the goblet*): I don't believe I ever will.

MAYBELLE: And that no 'count husband of yours acting the way he did. Why, you barely had that child buried in the ground and him running off to Houston or wherever it was—some western state. (GEORGIA RAY *anxiously turns away from* MAYBELLE *and goes to the closet to talk with* STEVIE.)

MAYBELLE: Stevie? Honey, it's me, Georgia. Your friend, Georgia Ray. What's going on in there? Are you asleep? (*A loud groan is heard. Then gasping sobs.*) Stevie? Wanna talk? Huh! Want me to sing to you? Are you all right? Stevie? (*The groans and sobs continue, as boxes and furniture crash around inside the closet.*) He sounds bad upset.

MAYBELLE: Well, I told you he wouldn't come out when I brought up his Snow White statue for him and told him he could hold it. I even tried t'lure him out with a big cherry lollipop from Burney's Drugs and chicken fried steak for supper. I tried everything I knew.

GEORGIA RAY: Well, how long has he been in there? (GEORGIA RAY *opens the loaf of bread and, using the top of the juice bottle as a cookie cutter, starts cutting out round bread wafers and putting them on the silver plate.*)

MAYBELLE: Since this afternoon when those Booker kids stole his pet frog off him.

GEORGIA RAY: Roger.

MAYBELLE: It was Roger they took. See, Stevie was standing out on South Grand Street, pretending to direct traffic like regular with his frog stuck up under his foreman's helmet. Anyway, from what I understand from Mary May Parker, those Booker kids come up and told Stevie they'd spray him five times in the face with their water gun if he'd let 'em hold his frog. Well, Stevie agreed and those kids took his frog and threw it right upside that big pine tree in Mary May's yard and then ran off laughing and hollering. Poor Stevie found his frog, but it had gotten plum dead.

GEORGIA RAY: That's terrible.

MAYBELLE: I'd like t'break every one of those kids' necks. I really would love to twist their heads right straight off and throw 'em in a snake pit. Just wait till they get up in your English class then you just flunk 'em.

GEORGIA RAY: Believe me, if I wasn't leaving the teaching profession, I'd do it for sure.

MAYBELLE: What? You're not leaving off teaching, are you? Why, you're the best looking teacher Canton's got.

GEORGIA RAY: Well, my luck's been running so bad. I've gotta do something, Maybelle. Try someplace new. I don't eat or sleep regularly, and my insides start t'feeling like broken glass. *(She lights a candle.)*

MAYBELLE: You could be right. After all, I never found a decent man to marry in Canton though I looked for twenty years. They were all losers of one sort or another. I might even be lonely, if it wasn't for Stevie. That Stevie. He's just a card the way he does.

GEORGIA RAY: Well, I hope this will get him out. I know he always cherished going to the Communion service.

MAYBELLE: It was kind of you to t'take him the times you did.

GEORGIA RAY *(going to the closet door)*: Stevie? This is Georgia again and I have a very special gift for you. Can you hear me? *(A groan comes from behind the closet door.)* You get to go to Communion right here in your home, just like you did it in Grace Episcopal Church. You remember, Stevie, how you got to sing, and kneel down and accept the wine and the holy wafer; and there were all the beautiful burning candles. Remember? *(A grunt comes from the closet.)* So come on out or you're gonna miss everything. Your Aunt Maybelle is all ready for the service. We're both waiting for you. *(Pause.)* All right then, Stevie, we'll have to go on and begin it all without you. *(After a moment)* Will everyone please kneel. (MAYBELLE *kneels.* GEORGIA RAY *picks up the plate of wafers. She makes the sign of the cross.)* The body of our Lord Jesus Christ which was given for the . . .

The closet door swings open. STEVIE, *27, a tall mentally retarded man with a beatific aura, walks slowly out of the closet and watches the ceremony with sad amazement.*

GEORGIA RAY *(placing the wafer in* MAYBELLE*'s hand)*: . . . take this in remembrance of Him. (STEVIE *abruptly kneels.* GEORGIA RAY *moves to give him his Communion.)* The body of our Lord Jesus

Christ which was given for thee. Take this in remembrance of Him. *(She picks up the goblet of grape juice and gives Communion first to* MAYBELLE.*)* The blood of our Lord Jesus Christ which was shed for thee, drink this in remembrance of Him. *(She moves over to* STEVIE.*)* The blood of our Lord Jesus Christ which was shed for thee. Drink this in remembrance of Him. *(She pulls back and speaks to both people as she makes the sign of the cross.)* In the name of the Father and of the Son and of the Holy Ghost. Amen.

STEVIE *and* MAYBELLE: Amen.

GEORGIA RAY: We will now sing the glorious hymn, "Hallelujah!" Will everyone please join in.

They all sing the first verse of Hallelujah!

Christ our Lord is risen today
    Hallelujah
Sons of men and angels sing
    Hallelujah
Raise your joys and triumphs high
    Hallelujah
Sing ye heavens and earth reply
    Hallelujah

The lights fade to blackout.

ORDER FORM

SINGLE ISSUES

West Coast Plays 1 _____ copies at $ 5.00 $_____
West Coast Plays 7 _____ copies at $ 6.00 $_____
West Coast Plays 8 _____ copies at $ 6.00 $_____
West Coast Plays 10 _____ copies at $ 6.00 $_____
West Coast Plays 11/12 _____ copies at $ 9.95 $_____
West Coast Plays 13/14 _____ copies at $12.50 $_____
West Coast Plays 15/16 _____ copies at $12.50 $_____
West Coast Plays 17/18 _____ copies at $12.50 $_____

THE COMPLETE SET

West Coast Plays 1-18 _____ copies at $90.00 $_____
note: volumes 2-7 and 9 are available only in the complete set.

Subtotal $_____
Calif. orders add 6½% tax $_____
Foreign orders add 15% $_____

SUBSCRIPTIONS

One Year (4 volumes, 2 double issues) $25.00
West Coast Plays subscription _____ at $25.00 $_____
Total $_____

STANDING ORDERS ARE AVAILABLE TO LIBRARIES AND THEATERS AND ARE BILLED AT CURRENT COVER PRICE.

Please make check or money order payable in U.S. currency to California Theatre Council.

NAME _____

ORGANIZATION _____

ADDRESS _____

CITY _____ STATE _____ COUNTRY _____ ZIP _____